# CONTENTS

# From the Editor

On 6 January, attendees at the 2011 MLA convention in Los Angeles will have a chance to participate in dozens of sessions grouped under the rubric "The Academy in Hard Times." Sadly, we've all been involuntary participants in that general theme over the past several years, as we've seen working conditions deteriorate, job opportunities diminish, and pressures of all kinds increase. As someone with both an optimistic nature and a pragmatic bent, I find these times especially challenging: my instincts tell me to focus on the positive aspects of our profession and to orient action toward solutions that can improve conditions for all sectors of the academic workforce, but my experience tells me that it will take a lot more than attitude and direction to pull through the difficulties that envelop us. *Profession 2010* reflects the hard times in which we find ourselves, and it offers ideas for a brighter future.

Catherine Porter's Presidential Forum at the 2009 annual convention stimulated much new thinking on the theory and tasks of the vital enterprise of translation. Her introduction to some of the papers that emerged from the forum and related sessions argues that an intellectually demanding concept of translation should inform university studies. Even if you do not know more than one language well—or perhaps especially if you do not—the outstanding essays that Porter has gathered will show how translation, in its capacity to present itself as both opaque and transparent, is an integral part of what we literary and language scholars study.

The Committee on Disability Issues in the Profession serves many functions. Its members advise the MLA staff on accessibility at the annual convention, and they organize panels on topics related to disability studies. They also bring to the attention of MLA members scholarship on disability as it relates to the modern languages. As part of this project, the committee proposed a discussion for *Profession* that would engage the terms used when speaking about disability. As Petra Kuppers explains in her introduction, "language changes just as our cultures do." Until disabilities are liberated from stigmatizing forces, Michael Bérubé argues, we need to be conscious of terminology and figure out which arguments about language might make a difference. Margaret Price explores the term *neuroatypical* for its potential to instigate an "activist stance and a rebellion against the biomedical-industrial complex" linked to the American psychiatric model of mental illness. The terminology used to describe deafness is the subject of Kristen Harmon's essay. Harmon notes that what is at stake "is the prerogative for describing and claiming which language and social grouping is most important for a particular deaf individual." To oppose the expression *hearing loss*, some scholars propose *Deaf gain*. All these essays make it clear that the language of disability can be empowering and that we should rethink our terms of engagement so that language is not reduced to binaries of gain-loss or ability-disability.

None of us can afford to disregard the economic conditions in the academic world, even if we don't have direct budgetary responsibilities in our jobs. Linda Ray Pratt helps us understand the financial landscape of higher education in her essay: she reviews the big picture (what happened on Wall Street, the decline in university endowments, etc.) and assesses what it means for private and public institutions. She is absolutely correct when she notes that the "most vulnerable academic areas will be programs that have few majors or few credit hours in the core curriculum." Finally, Pratt urges faculty members to look for the opportunities that times of fiscal difficulty inevitably present and to find ways to keep what we need most and go after what we want most.

In "Literary History and the Curriculum: How, What, and Why," Jennifer Summit engages with the MLA *Report to the Teagle Foundation* on matters related to teaching literary history. She uses the curriculum at Stanford University as a case study to discuss the decline of generalists and the rise of specialists along with a tasting-menu approach to literary coverage. The imaginative reconceptualization of teaching literary history that Summit describes should encourage others who wish to tackle curricular reform.

Marjorie Garber puts Shakespeare "in slow motion" by asking what it means to close read his works in the twenty-first century. She develops a theory of reading in this mode and shares its pedagogical implications, which she derived from teaching several Shakespeare in Slow Motion courses. By analyzing slow motion as it relates to visual media, Garber infuses her literary teaching with a revelatory potential for "consternation, contradiction, resistance, and surprise."

What does it mean to know English as a language? Tara Williams argues that the History of the English Language course, a staple (if not a relic) of the English curriculum, has a place in today's English department. She notes that the course has changed over time and offers benefits that would otherwise be lacking in the curriculum. Williams writes convincingly of the content and methodological approaches that can appeal to twenty-first-century students and that can help them become more competent analysts of a spectrum of texts and discourses.

In "Valuing Digital Scholarship: Exploring the Changing Realities of Intellectual Work," James P. Purdy and Joyce R. Walker discuss the narrow binary (digital vs. print scholarship) that informs current attitudes toward digital work and that affects how it is valued. They present the components of a framework for understanding the value of various kinds of scholarly work: design and delivery, recentness and relevance, and authorship and accessibility. This thoughtful essay leads us to see how "we might begin to ask about the relations among ideas and publication venues, design and delivery of content, and reader interactions and the dissemination of scholarly ideas."

Sidonie Smith writes about new ways to envision undergraduate education in "The English Major as Social Action." She argues that "every course, and at all stages of the curriculum, could be directed to the real work of producing knowledge and incorporating meaningful student research." Smith thinks about digital environments, including social media, in terms of their ability to connect learners and foster new knowledge. She also reminds us that conceptualizing the English major as social action has implications for a whole host of systems, such as hiring, tenure, and mentoring.

Another essay that focuses on the English major, by Lesley Wheeler, discusses how service learning can enhance the goals of capstone courses, incongruous as this idea might seem at first glance. When college students take poetry on the road (to schools, community centers, prisons, or hospice care centers), they learn about the gap between their classroom experience and literature at work in the larger world. They also "become aware that good teaching requires hard labor subsumed into an appearance of effortlessness and play"—a valuable insight that the service-learning opportunity can provide.

If performing service in academic departments and administrations has caused you to feel queasy, then Katie Hogan and Michelle Massé have the diagnosis—and the cure—for what ails you. In "Tips for Service," they offer a clear, simple checklist to help you determine how service is apportioned and valued at your institution. They then help you see how you can serve your own best interests while also doing necessary campus work.

This issue of *Profession* concludes with a forum containing Philip Goldstein's commentary on Gerald Graff's essay "Why How We Read Trumps What We Read," published in the previous issue, and Graff's response. The exchange takes up the debates about how reader-centered approaches to texts operate and what Graff meant when he repudiated the versions of reader-response criticism that argue that "readers create textual meanings without being answerable to any independently existing text."

The members of the *Profession* Advisory Committee—Katherine Arens, Donald E. Hall, Margaret J. Marshall, and Rei Terada—reviewed the submissions we received this year and provided helpful feedback, for which I am grateful. I also thank my colleagues Barbara Chen, Nelly Furman, and David Laurence for their advice and Carol Zuses, managing editor, for her expert work on the journal. For next year's issue, we welcome submissions on any topic, but we'd especially like to include articles that address the changing modes of scholarly and pedagogical communication now that the digital humanities have become a central part of our academic world.

Rosemary G. Feal

# Presidential Forum: The Tasks of Translation in the Global Context

## Introduction

CATHERINE PORTER

Introductions to a collection of papers such as those gathered here from the three sessions of the 2009 Presidential Forum typically present a glossed table of contents that briefly evokes a theme or argument thought to be central to each text and then offers an overview asserting their coherence as an ensemble. I have several reasons for eschewing that practice here. In the main forum session, Brett de Bary's response constructs a framework for the papers she interrogates that deserves to stand on its own. In the session on translation theory, Lawrence Venuti's paper carries out the work of contextualization that seems crucial. In the session on teaching in translation, the opening pages of Sandra Bermann's paper set forth the background against which the other papers' historical and practical sense can be readily perceived. The effect of the entire collection, with its three distinct foci that illustrate the range, power, and pertinence of translation studies as a horizon of inquiry, is not one I would wish to reduce in summary fashion to a single point or position. The texts presented here contribute to a multifaceted argument of a professional order that I hope will spur continued discussion among teachers and scholars about the tasks of translation in the global context. By way of introduction, I propose to focus on the implications of these tasks in the academy and sketch out briefly what I see as the principal issues at stake.

The author is professor emerita of French at the State University of New York, College at Cortland, and a past president of the Modern Language Association.

The context in which I selected translation as the theme for the 2009 Presidential Forum and chose "English Is Not Enough" as the title of the presidential address was a reflection on the value of multilingualism. The impetus for this reflection came in part from the 2009 MLA *Report to the Teagle Foundation on the Undergraduate Major in Language and Literature*, which asserts that "[m]ultilingualism and multiculturalism have become a necessity for most world citizens" and that "all students who major in our departments should know English and at least one foreign language" (10). This report articulates a comprehensive rationale for an expanded commitment to foreign language study at the postsecondary level. The crux of the argument is worth repeating:

> Our political and social lives are not "English only" domestically or internationally. The value of fluency in multiple languages cannot be overstated in the twenty-first century, when the emergent conditions of life bring more of us more often into circumstances that, on the one hand, ask us to travel through the complex terrain of a globalized economy and, on the other, bring far-flung local parochialisms to our doors through the vastly expanded reach of new communications technologies. Students who study languages other than English are achieving not merely formal communication but also sophistication with the nuances of culture—both in the sense of culture as art, music, and poetics and the broader sense of culture as a way of life. The translator, international lawyer, or banker who successfully conducts business in a language other than his or her native tongue shows linguistic capacity and cultural understanding, something a university education in languages is uniquely capable of instilling. (10–11)

In this text produced by an MLA task force, the allusion to the translator alongside the international lawyer or banker in a real-world situation beckons toward a dynamics of translinguistic and transcultural exchange or transfer in which translation is an operative competency, an ability to transcend linguistic and cultural differences by working out dense and complex equivalencies. Understood as a sophisticated competency or practice, as a modus vivendi for the global citizen, translation is not, then, a simple, linear operation that consists in taking messages emitted in one language and reproducing them in another; it is rather a multidimensional site or field of cross-lingual correspondences on which diverse social and intellectual tasks are performed and in which translations—acts and texts—into and out of innumerable languages are in play. Many of us have lost sight of the era, still with us into the 1950s, when learning a given foreign language was commonly understood to consist in learning to decode propositions in that language and render them in English. We now take for granted the axiom that locates the foreign language student's serious encounter with problems of translation at a relatively advanced level of proficiency, where the thicket of cross-linguistic comparison and the search for elusive semantic equivalences make the intellectual work—which involves controlling elaborate contexts in each of two languages—an immensely complicated, nuanced process. Apprehended in its intricacy and density, translation is an artful inquiry that mobilizes multiple faculties and draws on a copious store of accumulated knowledge.

It is this latter, intellectually demanding concept of translation that underlies the recent emergence, in United States colleges and universities, of courses and programs in translation studies. We can hardly fail to wonder whether the more advanced development of translation studies in Europe and South America does not stem from the multilingual environments that prevail in their academic milieus and distance their faculty members and students from the monolingualism that dominates in the United States. In the multilingual setting characteristic of countries in which children begin acquiring foreign languages early, perception of the need for translations and the understanding of their social and scholarly functions derive not from a sense of linguistic inadequacy vis-à-vis nonnative languages but rather from an awareness of the innumerable languages that even the most accomplished polyglots will not manage to master and thus an awareness of the dependency on translations that anyone who navigates in our global and digital world experiences on a daily basis, knowingly or not.

Given this reality, one of my goals for the 2009 MLA convention was to bring to the attention of our membership the prospects for translation studies in North American higher education. The three Presidential Forum sessions sought specifically to establish key horizons on which students and faculty members in departments of language and literature are behooved to engage with the study and practice of translation. Let me conclude, then, by invoking succinctly the judgment toward which I believe the openings onto translation studies forged by the participants in the 2009 forum should take us.

While it has been primarily in the field of comparative literature that the new subdiscipline of translation studies has begun to take shape in American universities over the last two or three decades, at present many English departments are considering new ways of teaching in and about translation, and many modern language departments, weighing the recommendations of an MLA report on foreign language programs, are factoring its observation of a "great unmet demand for educated translators and interpreters" into their discussions about broadening both the undergraduate major and graduate programs (MLA Ad Hoc Committee

243). If these possibilities are before us, it is surely in large part because the questions put to us by the theory, practice, and use of translation bear on history, society, and culture in a global context. Indeed, in an important, increasingly visible respect, the domain of translation in the academy has come to coincide with that of cultural studies. The issue for the profession is the status translation and translators should have in the light of this development. The field of translation studies, by opening up an exploration of the process of translation, of the role it plays in scholarly life and in real-world settings, and of the insights into language and literature that it can achieve, is confronting the humanities establishment with questions that have not always been welcomed: Is translation itself, at least in some cases, a research practice? To what extent should it be understood as a legitimate form of scholarship?

The argument I have sought to advance, in tandem with an apology for multilingualism, is that the academy's traditional notion of translation—a dismissive view that accords it little or no credit in discussions of hiring, promotion, and tenure—should give way to a far more capacious understanding that treats translation as complex, high-level intellectual work. The task of the translator is often fully commensurable with that of the scholar, as fields like classics, Assyriology, and Semitic studies have long recognized. The serious pursuit of translation, which has much in common with scholarly activities like textual editing, is already understood to be predicated on the kind of preparation provided by doctoral programs and to yield a product subject to peer review. The papers collected here provide us with a probing invitation to reflect on the lineaments of potential new undergraduate and graduate programs in translation studies and, in the light of the disciplinary structure that such a degree implies, to articulate far more subtle parameters for situating the work of translation. The professional credit to which translators performing this task are entitled needs to be recalibrated through a serious comparison with the values ascribed to other forms of scholarship and in relation to the function of translation in the world at large.

## WORKS CITED

MLA Ad Hoc Committee on Foreign Languages. "Foreign Languages and Higher Education: New Structures for a Changed World." *Profession* (2007): 234–45. Print.

Porter, Catherine. "English Is Not Enough." 2009 Presidential Address. MLA, 18 Feb. 2010. Web. 8 July 2010.

*Report to the Teagle Foundation on the Undergraduate Major in Language and Literature.* MLA, Feb. 2009. Web. 23 June 2010.

# Translation "on the Line"

## TOM CONLEY

In his pioneering work on the history and power of writing, Henri-Jean Martin notes that at its origin writing is pictographic and that in Meso-potamia, deployed "something like a grid for the comprehension of the world," it consisted in an "interplay between image and word of its ideo-grams" (14–15). Its original attributes resemble what Walter Benjamin wrote about the effects of poetry, which he called "spontaneous, primary, graphic," in contrast to the lesser order of translation, which is "deriva-tive, ultimate, ideational" (76). Writing is taken to be material, spatial, and immediate. It follows that poetry, like Freudian *Bilderschriften*, is found where its very images are cut into the shape and contour of its lines. Through antithesis Benjamin infers that translators who are worth their salt bring the graphic qualities of the original into the shape and move-ment of the derivative idiom, which, like a tangent, touches the arc of the original (80). His phrasing suggests that the graphic immediacy of a good translation produces events correlative to those marking the original.

Much like that of the poet and philosopher, the task of the translator entails creating events through the work of language seen and read in its material shape. When Gilles Deleuze inquires into their nature, he observes that they can be marked by a nexus of sensations in which per-ception of space is enabled, much as in the interplay of images and words, through the aural and visual components of language. Inventive writing moves along a syllogistic axis, but now and again it flickers and shifts, or

*The author is Abbott Lawrence Lowell Professor of Romance Languages and Literatures and of Visual and Environmental Studies at Harvard University. A version of this paper was presented at the 2009 MLA convention in Philadelphia.*

even turns itself into images in which the abstraction of formal argument, language following a trajectory of reason, suddenly turns on itself or even explodes and scintillates without stopping. Such may be the effect of the event taking place in the manner and matter of writing. Translators, it often appears, seek to craft events much like those of the original. When they do—such is the argument of the paragraphs that follow—they attend to intermediate areas, between images and words, in which the turns and twists of the line or trait of the original become an object of translation. For any translator of poetry, the commanding task is to bring life to the trait, trace, or line of the words.

The line and the event of translation are illustrated by some of the obstacles this translator encountered in preparing an English edition of Deleuze's *Le pli: Leibniz et le baroque* (in French, 1988; in English, 1993). An opaque and seemingly hermetic study of aesthetic philosophy, *Le pli* was born of a philosopher's highly personal idiolect. Riddled with enigmas, it appeared driven by the medieval tradition of commentary in which a dialogue, scripted along the margins of the text, had the qualities of a free indirect discourse. Commentary became the rival of the writing to which it was appended. In *Le pli*, in which close reading of Gottfried Wilhelm Leibniz is adjoined to some broader reflections on the baroque, so melded are text and commentary that in many areas Deleuze is distinguished from Leibniz with difficulty.[1] Not long after publication of *Le pli*, it seemed uncanny that an essay fused with Leibniz would precede the clear and limpid work, responding to the question of its title, *Qu'est-ce que la philosophie?*, that only three years later Deleuze coauthored with Félix Guattari. Even today, for many in the cottage industry of Deleuze studies, *Le pli* continues to resist.

For the translator, the claims that Leibniz is the philosopher of the baroque par excellence, that we live in a baroque age, and that as a result Leibniz is the bedrock of the philosophy of our time are easier to convey than the manner by which the sustaining arguments are fashioned. How could Deleuze's style or way of translating Leibniz into a language of his own, what Deleuze frequently called a *manière de penser* ("manner of thinking"), be turned into English? From the beginning of the book, the choppy rhythm of short sentences, set forward and piled one over the other—lacking an introduction, a teaser, or outline of its aims—causes readers to wonder where they are going, to ask if the author is in the midst of an itinerary of meditation with neither beginning nor end. *Le pli* begins thus:

> Le Baroque ne renvoie pas à une essence, mais plutôt à une fonction opé-
> ratoire, à un trait. Il ne cesse de faire des plis. Il n'invente pas la chose: il y
> a tous les plis venus d'Orient, les plis grecs, romains, romans, gothiques,

classiques. . . . Mais il courbe et recourbe les plis, les pousse à l'infini, pli
sur pli, pli selon pli. Le trait du Baroque, c'est le pli qui va à l'infini.   (9)

The Baroque does not refer to an essence, but rather to an operative
function, to a line. It endlessly makes folds. It doesn't invent the thing:
there are all the folds coming from the Orient, Greek folds, Roman
folds, Romanesque folds, Gothic, Classical folds. . . . But it bends and
twists folds, it pushes them to infinity, fold upon fold, fold after fold.
The Baroque line is the fold that goes to infinity.          (*Fold* 3)

How to deal with the manner both of the thinking and of the writing? A
first clue is found in the *trait* or "line." Endowed with a life and history
of its own, the line replaces an essence or end of philosophy. It identifies
thinking as a process coextensive with writing and drawing. At the outset
we witness a tsunami of lines. Nine times the book's title is furrowed
in the first five sentences, literally *pli sur pli*. Their form is discerned in
epochs classified according to an inherited history of art. The gist of the
sentences as they go, as it were, *phrase sur phrase*, indicates the presence
of an archaeology. Greek folds give way to Roman folds, Roman folds to
Romanesque folds, which open onto gothic and then classical folds. Or
do they? It is we who imagine a linear chronology when our eyes scan the
words from left to right. Greece gives way to Rome and Rome to the Romanesque before the Romanesque stands at the threshold of the gothic.
Implied is a model based on a "life of forms of art," yet no conjunctive
signs indicate that one age yields to the next in an ordered progression.
They are all together, set in a parataxis that makes each at once different
from and coextensive with the others. The sentence moves ahead, aiming
at infinity, but as it goes, like the line it describes, it moves across various
strata of time within a containing form, which the translator is obliged
to take to be each of the sentences and their accumulated sum as one is
added to the next.[2]

Hindsight (or perhaps a second, third, or fourth reading of the incipit
in view of the book as a whole and the repetition and variation of its form
in other books) indicates that another "operative function" integral to
the art of writing—taken here to be a mode of translation—is at work. A
reader of classical orientation might associate this function with quadrature. Following the idiolect of Joachim Du Bellay, who was one of the
great bilingual writers and masters of Latin and French and exploited
translation for the sake of rethinking the art of imitation, the poet must
respect the quadrature or caesura of the written line. The pause that falls
at the end of the fourth beat in a decasyllable, Du Bellay argues polemi-
cally, must be congruent with the syntax (102).[3] The spatial implication

of the term, much like the concurrent sense of *orthography*, which refers both to the disposition of letters and the arrangement of the facade of a building, appears in what elsewhere he calls the art of spacing in translation. In Du Bellay's *Deffence*, the term *quadrature* includes geometrical, architectural, and musical inflections: as a delimited area equal to the surface of a circle it frames; as the relation of a straight to a curved line at the basis of the construction of letters, in accord with contemporary manuals of typography; and as what in French is called *carrure*, what might be the equally aural, musical, and visual cadence of a line of verse.

That sense of quadrature informs the line that runs through the political and aesthetic registers in Deleuze's writing. In the third sentence of *Le pli*, "il y a tous les plis venus d'Orient, les plis grecs, romains, romans, gothiques, classiques . . . ," the baroque line is bracketed or elided in an ellipsis that suspends the end of the historical sketch: gothic, classical, and . . . baroque. The baroque line goes without seeing or saying; it is imperceptible and forgotten when read in an aural register, but when it is seen in a literal sense, in suspension, as a line of writing, it belongs to one of four layers of a landscape familiar to historians of art. Two of Deleuze's works of reference, Heinrich Wölfflin's *Principles of Art History* and Wilhelm Wörringer's *Form in Gothic*, inform the observation. Wölfflin's *Renaissance and Baroque* is cited (two pages further on) below Deleuze's own crosssectional drawing of the baroque house to explain its components. The German art historian notes that the lower floor extends horizontally, the pediment is pushed down, and steps at the doorway are set forward in a curved manner. Matter is treated in masses or aggregations, sharp angles are rounded off, and the right angle becomes looped; rounded acanthus replaces its dashed or jagged counterpart, porous travertine is chiseled to produce spongy, cavernous shapes in which "the constitution of a swirling form is nourished by new turbulence and ends only in the fashion of the mane of a horse or of the foam of a wave" (*Fold* 7). Matter tends to overflow into space and to become fluid at the same time that quantities of water are themselves divided into masses.

Wörringer builds his concept of *Einfühlung* or "empathy," which elsewhere guides much of Deleuze's work on sensation and perception, on the idea of the open-ended or gothic line. It is a line that neither closes itself into a square nor follows the perpendicular development of a meander pattern. At once an organic and inorganic force, it moves ahead ceaselessly, it coils on itself, it turns and curves about, it arches in the direction of infinity by doubling back and over. An emblem of empathy, the moving line is synonymous with the emotion it carries. Identifying Wörringer's gothic line with its baroque sequel, Deleuze uses the line to be what "becomes," to embody what in much of his writing, using an infinitive substantive, he calls *le devenir*.[4]

Elsewhere in *Le pli*, Wörringer's line ramifies so as to cross into other fields of reference or strata of Deleuze's reflections. Invoking Henri Michaux's *La vie dans les plis* ("Life in the Folds"), Deleuze alludes to the poet's work on enclosed spaces (such as in the poem "Mes propriétés") and to Stéphane Mallarmé's fan-verse ("L'éventail de Madame Mallarmé" ["Madame Mallarmé's Fan"] and *Hérodiade*) in order to turn the line as fold into an event that forever (and intransitively) becomes itself: "Le pli est sans doute la notion la plus importante de Mallarmé, non seulement la notion, mais plutôt l'opération, l'acte opératoire qui en fait un grand poète baroque. *Hérodiade* est déjà le poème du pli" (43; "The fold may well be Mallarmé's most important notion, but especially the operation, the operative act that makes him a great baroque poet" [*Fold* 27]). The *acte opératoire* allows the poet to draw lines of verse through different idioms. Michaux's and Mallarmé's poems are ever-translating lines, so much so that they cause their reader's gloss to become the line of the poem cited, thus turning Deleuze into the double of his authors in what might be called a free indirect translation:

> Le pli du monde, c'est l'éventail ou "l'unanime pli." Et tantôt l'éventail ouvert fait descendre et monter tous les grains de matière, cendres et brouillards à travers lesquels on aperçoit le visible comme par les trous d'un voile, suivant les replis qui laissent voir la pierre dans l'échancrure de leurs inflexions, "pli selon pli" révélant la ville, mais aussi bien en révèle l'absence ou le retrait, conglomérat de poussières, collectivités creuses, armées et assemblées hallucinatoires. À la limite, il appartient au côté sensible de l'éventail, il appartient au sensible lui-même de susciter la poussière à travers laquelle on le voit, et qui en dénonce l'inanité. Mais tantôt aussi, de l'autre côté de l'éventail maintenant fermé ("le sceptre de rivages roses... ce blanc vol fermé que tu poses..."), le pli ne va plus vers une pulvérisation, il se dépasse ou trouve sa finalité dans une inclusion, "tassement en épaisseur, offrant le minuscule tombeau, certes, de l'âme." Le pli est inséparable du vent. *Ventilé par l'éventail*, le pli n'est plus celui de la matière à travers lequel on voit, mais celui de l'âme dans laquelle on lit, "plis jaunes de la pensée," le Livre ou la monade aux multiples feuillets.                    (43; emphasis added)

The fold of the world is the fan or "unanimous fold." At times the open fan makes all particles of matter, ashes, and fog rise and fall. We glimpse the visible through the mist as if through the mesh of a veil, following the creases that allow us to see stone in the opening of their inflections, "fold after fold," revealing the city. The fan reveals absence of withdrawal, a conglomeration of dust, hollow collectivities, armies and hallucinating assemblies. Ultimately the fold pertains to the sensitive side of the fan, to sensitivity itself, stirring up the dust through which it is visible, and exposing its own inanity. And at others, from the other side of the fan that is now closed ("the scepter of pink shorelines . . . this closed white flight you are setting down") the fold no longer moves toward pulverization, it exceeds itself or finds its finality in an inclusion, "thick layerings, offering the tiny tomb, surely, of the soul." The fold is inseparable from wind. *Ventilated by the fan*, the fold is no longer made of matter through which we see, but of the soul in which we read "yellow folds of thought," the Book or monad with its many folios.         (28)

The line of writing in these sentences moves toward a fold-event, a sudden and heightened awareness of sensation itself, but a sensation that is elegantly revealed in the words and spacings describing and framing the "operative act" of creation. For Deleuze, sentience is acute where the fan ventilates the atmosphere enough to stir up wind, *vent*, whose movement becomes an event calling attention to the form and force of the writing. It is what later, in the chapter titled "Qu'est-ce qu'un événement?" ("What Is an Event?"), he calls a "nexus of prehensions" in which vibrations or the movement of folds are felt (102). A simultaneous subjectivation and objectivation of phenomena takes place. The philosopher translates that experience into the gist and rhythm, what the translator might call the quadrature, of his words. The line of writing describing the event is both seen (in the world at large) and read (in the soul, the "yellow folds of thought"). The event is translated into the sight and sound of an "éventail," felt in atmospheric turbulence, in wind and the swirl of molecules.

At these and other points in *Le pli*, the shape of the words makes manifest a style or *manière de penser* that becomes the equal of the baroque line that Deleuze draws across a vast sweep of time and space. The sentences seem born of a *Kunstwollen* ("will to art") in the way they move ahead, in what the author calls a line of flight, but at the same time in aggregate they fashion clusters ordered at once by grammatical caesuras and their own visual and musical rhythms.

They are also diagrams in the sense that their political and aesthetic dimensions are meshed. To see how, it suffices to plot the style of *Le pli* onto one of the decisive sentences of Deleuze's *Foucault* (1986) in which the operative function of the line of writing translates itself into the shape of the words and their spacings. At the end of "Un nouveau cartographe" ("A New Cartographer"), originally an essay on *Surveiller et punir* (*Discipline and Punish*), first published in *Critique* in 1985 and then adapted to fit the commemorative study of the following year, Deleuze returns to the logic of the line to identify the politics that inspire the abrupt ending of Foucault's history of the penitentiary. The author sets a "history of forms," an archive that resembles an enclosed sum of knowledge, indeed much like the prison itself, at the threshold of a diagram, a "devenir des forces" that "doubles" it.[5] The archive is an inherited map of knowledge, perhaps a virtual library, in which utopian designs can be drawn and plotted. Forces, Deleuze notes in citing Michel Foucault, "appear in 'every relation from one point to another'" (*Foucault* 51; my trans.), such that a diagram becomes a map or a layering of maps from which new points can be connected by lines of flight, lines that Foucault calls the struggles of a given moment. By virtue of struggle the points, relatively free or unlinked (*déliés*), become sites of "creativity, mutation, resistance" when they are fashioned into diagrams. All of a sudden, in the final flourish to the chapter, anticipating his work on Leibniz, Deleuze invokes Herman Melville and Michaux (and, implicitly, Boulez) to draw a line through his reflection:

> Car chacun témoigne de la façon dont se tord *la ligne du dehors* dont parlait Melville, sans début ni fin, ligne océanique qui passe par tous les points de résistance, et qui roule, entrechoque les diagrammes, toujours en fonction du plus récent. Quelle curieuse torsion de la ligne fut 1968, la ligne aux mille aberrations! D'où la triple définition d'écrire; écrire, c'est lutter, résister; écrire, c'est devenir; écrire, c'est cartographier, "je suis un cartographe. . . ." (51)

> Everyone knows how *the line of the outside* of which Melville spoke has neither beginning nor end, an oceanic line that runs through every point of resistance and that rolls, that clashes into diagrams, always in relation to the most recent. What strange torsion born of the line that was 1968, the line with a thousand aberrations. Whence the triple definition of the act of writing: to write is to struggle, to resist; to write is to become; to write is to write cartographically, "I'm a cartographer. . . ." (my trans.)

Melville's oceanic line, which rolls with the waves, suavely turns into Michaux's "ligne aux mille aberrations." No less abruptly than Foucault at the end of *Surveiller et punir*, the sentence melds with the political allusion to 1968, that here is a utopian cipher or cryptogram in which the 8 of the date draws the line of a double torsion or even a Moebius strip, a $\infty$ at the end of the progression 7-8-9—that is, a sign of infinity at the end of a numerical progression. Where the remark is seen, when its way of turning about becomes evident through a sense of quadrature, it becomes a line that conveys political force.

As Deleuze concludes his chapter in 1986, arching back in order to aim forward, recalling 1968 in 1988, so too we can close on the quadrature of the philosopher's reflection. In what would otherwise be Deleuze's close and sustained reading of Leibniz and of Foucault, a reading in which a free indirect subjectivity prevails, we witness him translating himself into his author.

The words with which the critic burrows into Foucault's world are lines of translation. Following the vector of the sentence and its cadence, seeing and reading it in a spatial continuum, the translator doubles the author.

The translator faces the task of translating the writer who himself is translating: Deleuze appears to vanish into Foucault's work in order to reengage the aesthetic and political events of writing. Born of lines drawn between words and images, the event of Deleuze's concluding remark is perceived in how the writing attends to the way its graphic form or line betrays its mode of becoming. Translators of Deleuze must carry this kind of event from one idiom to another. In a broader sense, translators succeed when they call attention to lines that both inform and riddle the work. The art of translation is one in which tracings and spacings are redrawn so as to create writing-events coequal with those given in the original.

## NOTES

1. Deleuze writes of a "free indirect subjectivity," of a doubling in which two idioms are mixed, in a reading of Pier Paolo Pasolini (*Cinéma* 107–09; my trans.).

2. The observation closely follows the biological model of "the life of forms" of art that Henri Focillon proposed in *La vie des formes*, which he had previously applied to romanesque and gothic styles in *L'art d'Occident*.

3. François Rigolot notes that in his *Quintil horatian*, a critical reading of Du Bellay's treatise, Barthélémy Aneau reveals a misalliance between theory (the *Deffence*) and practice (Du Bellay's *L'olive* of the same year) owing to the polemics in which the work was embroiled (177).

4. Deleuze remarks on German montage: "Wörringer is the first theorist who coined the term 'expressionism' and who defined it in opposition to the *élan vital* in organic representation, referring to the decorative 'gothic or northern' line: a broken line that forms no contour where form and background [*forme et fond*] would be distinguished, but zigzags between things, sometimes drawing them into a depthlessness [*sans-fond*] in which it loses itself, sometimes causing them to twist in a formlessness [*sans-forme*] in which it turns back upon itself in a 'disordered convulsion'" (*Cinéma* 76). He cites a French translation (1941) of Wörringer's *Formprobleme der Gotik* (1912).

5. "L'histoire des formes, archive, est doublée d'un devenir des forces, diagramme" (*Foucault* 51; "the history of forms, an archive, is doubled by a becoming of forces, a diagram" [my trans.]). Deleuze uses the coupling of form and force to distinguish the one from the other. The relation with Jacques Derrida's "Force et signification," a review of Jean Rousset's *Forme et signification* at the outset of *L'écriture et la différence*, could not be clearer.

## WORKS CITED

Benjamin, Walter. *Illuminations*. Trans. Harry Zohn. New York: Schocken, 1968. Print.

Deleuze, Gilles. *Cinéma 1: L'image-mouvement*. Paris: Minuit, 1983. Print.

———. *The Fold: Leibniz and the Baroque*. Trans. Tom Conley. Minneapolis: U of Minnesota P, 1993. Print.

———. *Foucault*. Paris: Minuit, 1986. Print.

———. *Le pli: Leibniz et le baroque*. Paris: Minuit, 1988. Print.

Derrida, Jacques. "Force et signification." *L'écriture et la différence*. Paris: Seuil, 1967. 9–49. Print.

Du Bellay, Joachim. *La deffence et illustration de la langue française*. Ed. Louis Humbert. Paris: Garnier, 1930. Print.

Focillon, Henri. *L'art d'Occident*. 2 vols. Paris: Colin, 1938. Print.

———. *La vie des formes*. Paris: PUF, 1939. Print.

Martin, Henri-Jean. *The History and Power of Writing*. Trans. Lydia G. Cochrane. Chicago: U of Chicago P, 1994. Print.

Rigolot, François. *Poésie et Renaissance*. Paris: Seuil; Collection Points, 2002. Print.

# Living in Translation

## VERENA CONLEY

*Creative betrayal* might be a formula aptly describing the art of translation. In "The Task of the Translator" (1932), the preface to his translation of Charles Baudelaire's *Tableaux parisiens*, Walter Benjamin claims that translators must distort their language in order to render the original faithfully. Writing in the wake of Benjamin and Sigmund Freud, Jacques Derrida and Hélène Cixous both see language not as what translates an originary text but as a verbal swirl about and around the bodies of the speakers. Derrida writes that the metaphor of translation cannot be used as

> the transcription of an original text [that] would separate force and extension, maintaining the simple exteriority of the translated and the translating. This very exteriority, the static and topological bias of the metaphor, would [ensure] the transparency of a neutral translation. . . . Despite the difference of agencies, psychical writing in general is not a displacement of meanings within the limpidity of an immobile, pregiven space and the blank neutrality of discourse.          (*Writing* 213)

More recently, in *Monolingualism of the Other*, he complicates this reflection in stating that he has only one language and that it is not his own. He claims to write doubly, from the idiom of the other and with a drive to introduce new torsions in the dominant tongue.

I inquire into the art of translation by asking two pressing questions for which the title of the Presidential Forum, "The Tasks of Translation

*The author is visiting professor of comparative literature and of Romance languages and literatures at Harvard University. A version of this paper was presented at the 2009 MLA convention in Philadelphia.*

     PROFESSION

in the Global Context," begs response. In a world of increasing movement and displacement, hence of an exponential proliferation of translations, how do we reassess the term *translation*? Correlatively, in a condition of acceleration, and on a planet shrinking under the impact of the sheer speed of the circulation of information, how do the tasks of translation affect theorists and intellectuals who help create new spaces in which we might live in common?

Growing up in Switzerland in the post–World War II era, I suspect that I have internalized some of the problems of translation with which we live today. At an early age, I felt unsettled by linguistic, political, and cultural tensions in a milieu where translation was a matter of everyday life. In the Zurich of my childhood, geography and economy dictated why Swiss German was the dominant idiom. When our family moved to Lausanne in my youth, I witnessed the Swiss French scoffing at German for being devoid of *esprit* (would that they knew of *Geist*) and for being dangerously close to the language of the Nazis. My new coequals found their salvation in France, in the language of good taste and civility. The parochial attitude of those years makes us smile today, long after the barriers of the cold-war years have given way to the global circulation of languages and cultures that, intersecting and interacting multifariously, are the foundation no longer for Towers of Babel but for myriad networks in and between which translations proliferate. Let's say that the title of Sofia Coppola's film of 2003, which claimed that we are "lost in translation," can be turned to affirm that we "live in translation."

Massively and at once willingly and unwillingly people speak and write in languages that are not their own. The same speakers and writers translate their variously inherited cultural sensibilities into other idioms. Samuel Beckett escaped the confines of Ireland to take up residence in Paris, where he wrote in a minimal French prose to avoid living and writing in the shadow of his countryman James Joyce and where he translated his own texts as translation back into English. His situation is sensibly different from that of Derrida, who in his own words wrote as a Franco-Maghrebian in a specific historical configuration, that of a Jewish child growing up under colonial rule and during the world war. France, especially in the halcyon years of *Les lettres nouvelles*, has always translated writers from all over the world for its reading public, but foreign writers living in the country write in French at once to creatively betray the received idiom of the host and to exploit it for the sake of bending and refashioning their own languages and cultures. Under colonialism, the novelists Mouloud Mammeri, Malek Bennabi, and Mouloud Feraoun wrote, as Derrida would have it, in the language of the other. It is rumored that

Albert Camus delayed publishing Kateb Yacine's monumental Algerian novel *Nedjma*, which did not conform to classical French norms, for several years. Kateb called French Algeria *butin de guerre* ("war loot"). Against expectations like those ratified by Albert Memmi, French as a language has not disappeared with decolonization. Rather, its status has changed.

Leading transnational and transcultural lives, many more foreign writers compose in French—that is, already in a kind of translation. Atiq Rahimi, an Afghan writer and filmmaker residing in Paris who received the Goncourt Prize in 2008 for his novel *Singué Sabour: La pierre de patience* (*The Stone of Patience*), and Amara Lakhous in Italy count today among those who adopt French, once a colonial idiom, to turn its dominance against itself. Rahimi, after composing several novels in his native Persian language, has recourse to French, which for him becomes a language of freedom when, from France, he writes about the condition of women in Afghanistan. More resistant because of his Algerian origins, which he still sees tainted by colonialism, Lakhous, an Algerian fluent in Berber, Arabic, French, and now Italian, translates his own writings so as to "mediate between cultures" and to "enrich the *langue d'arrivée*," the language of arrival, with a mixture of words of his own linguistic and symbolic past together with the dialects of other voices (Sforza).

Many writers turn to French for liberation: they exploit traditions inherited from the French Revolution, the imposing heritage of the Enlightenment, to expose repression in their own culture.[1] Moving from country to country while writing in French, Assia Djebar calls attention to a repressive political condition in her native Algeria. French, she avows, provides asylum from Arabic, which, for the speaker of Berber that she is, remains a language imposed by force. French also brings with it a radical tradition, what the philosopher Étienne Balibar calls an "untranslatable *laïcité*" rife with republican and radical echoes (*Droit* 80). The Moroccan Abdellah Taia, growing up poor and speaking Arabic, embarks on translation to realize a desire to speak and write French that comes from the fact that as a child he witnessed the cultural and political elite in Morocco speaking French, a language to which for social and economic reasons he was barred from gaining access. He relates that he taught himself French and wrote a diary in order to master the language and to become the equal of the elite at the university. Now a gay writer residing in Paris, he mobilizes French to translate cultural traits of his childhood for his readers outside Morocco while at the same time addressing Moroccans when he denounces political repression in his own country.

As Benjamin (and later Gilles Deleuze) famously argued, creative translators must distort their own language. Yet those writing through translation also distort the foreign language that is and is not their own. Recalling that not only words but the very function of language differs from one culture to the next, Michel de Certeau wrote that spoken languages

> are fields organized by different social practices in the Maghreb or in France, in Mexico or in the United States; . . . they are thus distinguished not only by variations of norms within homologous systems, but by functionings that are qualitatively foreign to one another. . . . To say that in one society, they participate in the bodily staging of acts of language and, in another, they [ensure] the distribution of the values of speech acts, is tantamount also to perceiving the errors or the innovations of ways of speaking the marks traced in a language and by a practice that originates in a geographic and psychic elsewhere.    (169–70)

What Certeau writes about the spoken word pertains to creative writing. A language is both enriched and distorted through alternative practices coming from elsewhere.

Certeau (twenty-five years ago) and Balibar (today ["Civilization" 776]) have argued that cultural codes such as fashion, music, and food travel and translate easily. Codes pertaining to symbolic networks at the very heart of literature and cultural theory (life and death, sexuality, marriage, gender, justice) do not. They necessitate a cultural translation (see Venuti). When writers write in a language that is doubly not their own, they complicate existing practices and invent new ones. They introduce torsions through error and aberration. Former colonial and now so-called global languages, such as French, English, and Spanish, are no longer simply national. Through various forms of translation, the idioms change. Translations take place less between a major (dominant) and a minor language than among networks of idioms.

Thus new issues of translation arise in a global world. David Damrosch asks to what degree translation should "reflect the foreignness of the original, and how far it should adapt" to what he calls "the host country's literary norms" (75). The distinction between those norms and the writer as translator changes when the opposition between host and foreigner, host and guest (*xenoi* and *hospes*), or citizen and immigrant no longer quite holds (Derrida, *On Cosmopolitanism* 19–20) and when the norms are affected by those already writing in translation. Complications abound when entire populations privately belong to mixed components (somewhat perhaps as I say in my childhood). Hybridity is complicated with many grafts that occur no longer between a dominant language and that of a postcolonial subject but between ever more proliferating (with deference to Deleuze and Guattari) rhizomatic networks of alliances, connections, and negotiations.

Writers are called on to translate in the exercise of their craft, as Lakhous sees it (Sforza); thus they are already acting as mediators; so are theorists, and so is the human polar bear, the soon-to-be-extinct intellectual. Jean-Paul Sartre's universal pronouncements of the 1950s and 1960s, so transparent that they never allowed for the slightest doubt about their meaning, were first complicated when Derrida introduced undecidables and ciphered discourses that brought nightmares to many a zealous American translator. The goal was to show the untranslatability of an idiom that is never pure exteriority but even more to show how, in the philosopher's words, one translates only the untranslatable (Derrida, *Writing* 220).

Several decades later, new issues that arise in a global age compel us to argue that theorists too are increasingly called on to negotiate with others in languages that, like their own, are not their own. According to Bruno Latour and Balibar both, they must mediate in order to create common spaces for dialogue. They do not interpret so much as engage in translation. Translation, even more complicated than it was when Benjamin wrote his preface to Baudelaire, now defines the very practice of critical discourse. Theorists become those who study the invention and art of translation. They also translate themselves into idioms of their choice and yield remainders that define common literary and cultural spaces.

How? Latour argues that we need to construct common spaces in a global mosaic consisting of "different worlds" (22). We live in myriad networks in which we incessantly circulate and through which we derive identities fleetingly and ephemerally. We must negotiate with others by assuming the absence of common denominators. The world has been connected through technology but not unified. What Latour (somewhat hastily) calls the West continues to function as if feedback loops did not exist. Diverse and multipolar, composed of many networks, our habitable world can be held together only through negotiation, mediation, and translation. Latour argues further that rationalists and technocrats should be jettisoned in favor of intellectuals who wear the trappings of diplomats—that is, negotiators who are not simply sublimely neutral arbiters. They have to argue with delicate urgency (Balibar would say with civility) for a common world space. Intellectuals are no longer explicators but mediator-translators who build a cosmopolitics whose defining character, recognizing different worlds, has little to do with a media-driven cosmopolitanism (Latour 43–44).

The mediations in which the translator-intellectual is engaged are not pitched between universals and particulars but rather among competing universals in the matrix of a new kind of universality. Without imposing a vision on their public, intellectuals and theorists speak from their states of residence—but not from their nation-states, as Balibar has shown—to mark their simultaneously transnational, singular, and collective identities. Theorist-intellectuals are citizen-subjects, and, inscribed in geographic, geopolitical, and historical contexts, by definition they are travelers. Migrating among family structures, among professional and political organizations, and from one culture to another, they actively practice what Jacques Rancière calls "dis-identification" from standard, dominant, or normative models of thinking (qtd. in Balibar, *Droit* 74). In adumbrating Deleuze's concept of the nomad, Balibar countenances intellectuals as migrants rooted in the social and political situations in which they circulate. The freewheeling nomad who moves effortlessly over the world could be, he notes, all too readily an affiliate of what he repeatedly calls a "capitalist hyperspace" (71).

Gone are the days when as self-styled leaders public intellectuals believed they could speak in place of or for the masses. The translator subverts an earlier critical function that conferred on the intellectual the mantle of a judge, priest, or censor. Today's newly situated intellectuals, critical and cultural theorists all, are required to accelerate with the world about them. They cannot devise lengthy theories or interpret objects but must be engaged in ongoing negotiations in areas of the world whose future is always uncertain.

I conclude by turning to Balibar once more to show how what is valid for the arts and aesthetics is equally valid for theory. Let us envision the construction of what he calls a new space (*un nouvel espace*) in the age of electronic and economic globalization in which nation-states are no longer leading players. Citizen-subjects who invent their spaces no longer militate against the state but undo visible and invisible borders that surround or enclose them. We who live in translation are witnessing the genesis of a space, be it a state or a region, in a networked world where change is enabled through ongoing migration, translation, and negotiation. Reaffirming the importance of theorists for the twenty-first century, in concert with Balibar, let us note that in a world of acceleration we must plug thought directly into action and continually adapt our critical thinking along both strategic and tactical lines. It is incumbent on writers and theorists alike to address transnational issues where a former universalism has been replaced with myriad, often competing, universalities. To this end, we have to travel mentally and physically in order to translate linguistic, cultural, and social differences. Critics and theorists too are translators and negotiators compelled to institute a cooler climate of civility in an increasingly fragile and precarious world space.

## NOTE ══════════════════════════════════════════════

1. On the repressive heritage, see Certeau, Julia, and Revel.

## WORKS CITED AND CONSULTED ═══════════════════════

Balibar, Étienne. "Civilization and Globalization." *Politics and Poetics.* Ed. Catherine David. Kassel: Kantz, 1997. 774–99. Print. Documenta X.

———. *Droit de cité.* Paris: L'Aube, 1998. Print.

———. *We, the People of Europe? Reflections on Transnational Citizenship.* Trans. James Swenson. Princeton: Princeton UP, 2004. Print.

Benjamin, Walter. "The Task of the Translator." *Illuminations.* Trans. Harry Zohn. New York: Schocken, 1968. 69–82. Print.

Certeau, Michel de. *The Capture of Speech.* Trans. Tom Conley. Minneapolis: U of Minnesota P, 1997. Print.

Certeau, Michel de, Dominique Julia, and Jacques Revel. *Une politique de la langue.* Paris: Gallimard; Bibliothèque des Histoires, 1975. Print.

Damrosch, David. *How to Read World Literature.* Malden: Wiley-Blackwell, 2009. Print.

Deleuze, Gilles. *Essays Critical and Clinical.* Trans. Daniel Smith and Michael A. Greco. Minneapolis: U of Minnesota P, 1997. Print.

Derrida, Jacques. *Monolingualism of the Other.* Trans. Patrick Mensah. Stanford: Stanford UP, 1996. Print.

———. *On Cosmopolitanism and Forgiveness.* Trans. Mark Dooley and Michael Hughes. New York: Routledge, 2001. Print.

———. *Writing and Difference.* Trans. Alan Bass. Chicago: U of Chicago P, 1978. Print.

Latour, Bruno. *War of the Worlds: What about Peace?* Trans. Charlotte Bigg. Ed. John Tresch. Chicago: Prickly Paradigm, 2002. Print.

Rahimi, Atiq. "From Poetic Exile to Poetic Wanderings." Harvard U. 30 Apr. 2010. Address.

Rancière, Jacques. *Disagreement: Politics and Philosophy.* Trans. Julie Rose. Minneapolis: U of Minnesota P, 1999. Print.

Sforza, Tiziana. "Amara Lakhous: Civilisations at Crossroads." Trans. Selina Ravagni-Wishart. *CaféBabel.com.* Babel Intl., 26 Nov. 2006. Web. 23 June 2010.

Venuti, Lawrence. *The Translator's Invisibility: A History of Translation.* New York: Routledge, 1995. Print.

# Translation and the Figure of Border: Toward the Apprehension of Translation as a Social Action

## NAOKI SAKAI

We are urged to acknowledge in knowledge production today the increasing significance of the problematic of bordering. The problematic has to be specifically marked as one not of border but of bordering, because what is at issue is not the old problem of boundary, discrimination, and classification. At the same time that it recognizes the presence of borders, discriminatory regimes, and the paradigms of classification, this problematic sheds light on the processes of drawing a border, of instituting the terms of distinction in discrimination, and of inscribing a continuous space of the social. The analytic of bordering requires us to take into account simultaneously both the presence of border and its drawing or inscription. One might call this focus on bordering the new bordering turn, as it has been most rigorously pursued by Étienne Balibar and by Sandro Mezzadra and Brett Neilson.

At this stage, I do not know whether a focus on bordering has gathered momentum across different disciplines. But the bordering turn must be accompanied theoretically by the translational turn: bordering and translation are both problematics projected by the same theoretical perspective. Just as bordering is not solely about the demarcation of land, translation is not merely about language.

In this essay I pursue a preliminary investigation concerning the discussion of translation beyond the conventional domain of the linguistic. Yet

The author is professor of Asian studies and comparative literature at Cornell University. A version of this paper was presented at the 2009 MLA convention in Philadelphia.

the first issue that must be tackled is how to comprehend language from the viewpoint of translation—that is, how to reverse the conventional comprehension of translation that always presumes the unity of a language.

Translation almost always involves a different language or at least a difference in or of language. But what difference or differentiation is at issue? How does it demand that we broaden our comprehension of translation? From the outset, we have to guard against the static view of translation in which difference is substantialized; we should not yield to the reification of translation that denies translation its potentiality to deterritorialize. Therefore it is important to introduce difference in and of language in such a way that we can comprehend translation not in terms of the communication model of equivalence and exchange but as a form of political labor to create continuity at the elusive point of discontinuity in the social.

It is possible to distinguish the type of translation according to the type of difference in or of language to which translation is a response. To follow Roman Jakobson's famous typology of translation (261), one may refer to a project of overcoming incommensurability as a type of translation—interlingual translation—from one natural language to another. Or one may talk about an act of retelling or interpreting from one style or genre to another in the same language as an instance of translation—intralingual translation. Furthermore, one may cite an act of mapping from one semiotic system to another as a distinctive type of translation—intersemiotic translation. In this typology, however, the unity of a language has to be unproblematically presupposed. Were it not for that supposition, it would be hard to discuss a different language, different from the original language, in an interlingual translation. Neither would it be possible to designate the inside of a language or to refer to a language as the same in an intralingual translation. Thus we are forced to return to the question, What difference?

My inquiry moves from the question of what is different in or of language to another question: What is different from the language? This is to say we must entertain the question of what language is, how the linguistic differs from the extralinguistic, and how the domain of the linguistic is constituted. In the scope of difference in and of language, however, we are still caught in the mode where the unity of a language is assumed. By difference, then, do we still understand that one term in particularity is distinguished from another against the background of the same generality, just as a white horse is different from a black horse among horses in general? Do we have to understand difference necessarily as a specific difference? Can the sort of difference at stake in translation be appropriately discussed in terms of the species and genus of classical logic?

## Many in One

The world accommodates one humanity but a plurality of languages. It is generally upheld that, because of this plurality, we are never able to evade translation. Our conception of translation is almost always premised on a specific way of conceiving the plurality of languages. We often resort to the story of Babel when we consider the unity of humanity but the necessity of translation. But can we assume this unity in plurality trans-historically? That is, can we conceive of discourses in which the thought of language is not captured in the formula of many in one? Are we able to conceive of language in an alternative way?

How do we recognize the identity of each language—that is, justify presuming that languages can be categorized in terms of one and many? Is language a countable, like an apple or orange and unlike water? Is it not possible to think of languages, for example, in terms of those grammars in which the distinction of the singular and the plural is irrelevant? What I am calling into question is the unity of language, a certain positivity of discourse or historical a priori we apply whenever a different language or difference in language is at stake. How do we allow ourselves to tell one language from another, to represent language as a unity?

My answer to this question some twenty years ago (*Voices*) is that the unity of language is like Kant's regulative idea. It organizes knowledge but is not empirically verifiable. The regulative idea does not concern itself with the possibility of experience; it is no more than a rule by which a search in the series of empirical data is prescribed. It guarantees not empirically verifiable truth but, on the contrary, "forbidding [the search for truth] to bring it[self] to a close by treating anything at which it may arrive as absolutely unconditioned" (Kant 450 [A 509; B 537]). Therefore, the regulative idea gives only an *object in idea*; it only means "a *schema* for which no object, not even a hypothetical one, is directly given" (550 [A 670; B 698]; emphasis added). The unity of language cannot be given in experience because it is nothing but a regulative idea, enabling us to comprehend related data about languages "in an indirect manner, in their systematic unity, by means of their relation to this idea" (550). It is not possible to know whether a particular language as a unity exists or not. But by subscribing to the idea of the unity of language, we can organize knowledge about languages in a modern, systematic, scientific manner.

To the extent that the unity of national language ultimately serves as a schema for nationality[1] and offers a sense of national integration, the idea of the unity of language opens up a discourse to discuss not only the naturalized origin of an ethnic community but also the entire imaginary associated with national language and culture. A language may be pure, authentic, hybridized, polluted, or corrupt, yet regardless of a particular assessment about that language, the very possibility of praising, authenticating, complaining about, or deploring it is offered by the unity of that language as a regulative idea. But the institution of the nation-state is, we all know, a relatively recent invention. Thus we are led to suspect that the idea of the unity of language as the schema for ethnic and national communality must also be a recent invention.

How should we understand the formula of many in one, the plurality of languages in one humanity, when the unity of language has to be understood as a regulative idea or schema for an object in idea? For Kant, a regulative idea is explicated with regard to the production of scientific knowledge; it ensures that the empirical inquiry of some scientific discipline will never reach any absolute truth and therefore is endless. Every scientific truth changes as more empirical data are accumulated. Kant also qualifies the regulative idea as a schema—that is, an image, design, outline, or figure not exclusively in the order of idea but also in the order of the sensational.

From the postulate that the unity of national language is a regulative idea, it follows that this unity enables us to organize various empirical data in a systematic manner so that we can continue to seek knowledge about the language. At the same time, it offers not an object in experience but an objective in praxis, toward which we aspire to regulate our uses of language. The principle is not only epistemic but also strategic. Hence it works in double registers: on the one hand, it determines epistemologically what is included or excluded in the database of a language, what is linguistic or extralinguistic, and what is proper to a particular language or not; on the other hand, it indicates and projects what we must seek as our proper language, what we must avoid as heterogeneous to our language and reject as improper in it. The unity of a national language as a schema guides us in what is just or wrong for our language, what is in accord or discord with the propriety of the language.

Of course, *translation* is a term with much broader connotations than the operation of transferring meaning from one national or ethnic language into another, but in this context I am specifically concerned with the delimitation of translation according to the regime of translation by which the idea of the national language is put into practice. I suggest that the representation of translation in terms of this regime of translation serves as a schema of cofiguration: only when translation is represented by the schematism of cofiguration does the putative unity of a national language as a regulative idea ensue. This schema allows us to imagine or represent what goes on in translation, to give to ourselves an image or representation of translation. Once imagined, translation is no longer a movement in potentiality. Its image or representation always contains two figures, which are necessarily accompanied by spatial division in terms of border. Because the unity of a national or ethnic language as a schema is already accompanied by another schema for the unity of a different language, the unity of a language is possible only in the element of many in one.

Translation takes various processes and forms, insofar as it is a political labor to overcome points of incommensurability in the social. It need not be confined to the specific regime of translation; it may well lie outside the modern regime of translation. The modern is marked by the introduction of the schema of cofiguration, without which it is difficult to imagine a nation or ethnicity as a homogeneous sphere. As Antoine Berman taught us about the intellectual history of translation and Romanticism in Germany, the economy of the foreign—that is, how the foreign must be allocated in the production of the domestic language—has played the decisive role in the poietic—and poetic—identification of the national language. Without exception, the formation of a modern national language involves institutionalizations of translation according to the regime of translation.

Most conspicuously manifest in eighteenth-century movements such as Romanticism in Western Europe and *Kokugaku* ("National Studies") in Japan, intellectual and literary maneuvers to invent a national language mythically and poetically were closely associated with a spiritual construction of new identity, in terms of which national sovereignty was later naturalized. As Michael Hardt and Antonio Negri argue, it makes "the *relation* of sovereignty into a *thing* (often by naturalizing it) and thus weed[s] out every residue of social antagonism. The nation is a kind of ideological shortcut that attempts to free the concepts of sovereignty and modernity from the antagonism and crisis that define them" (95). This foundation for the legitimation of national and popular sovereignty was proffered as a natural language specific to the people, which ordinary people spoke in everyday life. This historical development is generally referred to by literary historians as the emergence of the vernacular. The emphasis on ordinary and colloquial languages went with the reconception of translation and the schematism of cofiguration.

In the archipelago off the northeastern shore of the Qing Empire in the eighteenth century, a small number of intellectuals, usually grouped under the heading *kokugakusha* ("National Studies scholars") by present-day historians, began to discuss something like a people. These scholars claimed the significance of their learning only inside the restricted context of Japanese national history. In general education as it was taught in village tutoring schools in the seventeenth and eighteenth centuries (a long time before the introduction of universal national education in the 1870s), the canonical texts were primarily the classics of Confucian and Buddhist traditions. There hardly existed an acknowledged need to distinguish Japanese from Chinese texts or to teach Japanese children Japanese classics. Just as we do not insist on finding the features of national character in the texts of the Qur'an and the Bible or in the textbooks of mathematics and biology today, most people in East Asia did not seek national history in the classics. The trope of lineage was much more decisive in the succession of religious pontificates, poetry schools, and dynastic heirs. Social formations were not organized on the basis of a desire for national or ethnic identity; people lived free from the tenets of nationhood, and accordingly the classics they worshipped stood indifferent to national identification.

The National Studies' insistence on a distinction between the Chinese orientation of the canonical texts of the day and the Japaneseness inherent in a few selected ones was novel and eccentric. Such Japanese texts were the *Kojiki* ("Record of Ancient Matters," an imperial and mythic history compiled by the Japanese court in the eighth century), *Manyôshû* ("Collection of Ten Thousand Leaves," an eighth-century poetic anthology), and *Genji Monogatari* (*The Tale of Genji*, a novelistic narrative privately written in the Japanese court in the eleventh century). The *Kojiki* was a historiographical attempt by the ancient Japanese imperial court to construct the histories of the Yamato dynasties and the imperial lineage. Motoori Norinaga (1730–1801),[2] a leading scholar of the eighteenth century in the National Studies movement, reconstructed this entire work, more than a thousand years after its initial compilation, on the assumption that a Japanese national or ethnic language existed when it was originally transcribed; he thereby translated the *Kojiki* into a self-consciously Japanese text (Sakai, *Voices*, chs. 7 and 8). Motoori insisted on reading the text of the *Kojiki* on the explicitly declared premise that it was written in the Japanese language.

According to Jakobsonian taxonomy, this translation project would be intralingual as well as intersemiotic but never a translation proper, precisely because of Motoori's insistence on the transhistorical existence of the Japanese language. Motoori attempted to institute the discernibility of the intralingual translation from translation proper by translating the *Kojiki* into the forty-four volumes of *Kojiki-den* in essentially phonographic notation. What is the nature of the drastic displacement he brought about in the regimes of interpretation and translation?

Before the massive disruption initiated by the new discourse of the eighteenth century, a formation had existed in which what Jakobson calls translation proper (261) was not an archetype to which all the other types of translation, including intralingual and intersemiotic, were subordinated. How, then, should we assess the significance of Motoori's insistence on the Japanese language? Should we take for granted that the *Tale of Genji*, for instance, was mainly written in Japanese characters of *kana*, unlike many contemporary documents, which were composed in the Chinese logography of *mana* or sometimes in literary Chinese? There could be no clear distinction between intralingual and interlingual translations before the eighteenth century.

In National Studies, as well as in treatises by some Confucian scholars of the *Kogaku* ("Ancient Studies") affiliation, there was not merely an introduction of one more commentary on the ancient text but in fact the creation of a new set of regimes whereby the classic text was read anew, rewritten, and re-created. Therefore it is impossible to understand the works of National Studies simply in terms of Motoori's discovery of the ancient Japanese language, Japanese grammar, phonetics, and syntax, and so on—that is, in those terms believed to have existed before the *Kokugaku* and *Kogaku* scholars' interventions. What Motoori achieved by reading the *Kojiki* was the establishment of the possibility for knowledge of the Japanese language to emerge. In other words, he and others invented the Japanese language as an object in idea of systematic knowledge in the eighteenth century. Previous canonical works clearly lacked a sense of national affiliation compared with his translation of the *Kojiki*. Though some of them were in what were called Japanese notational systems, they were not thought to belong to the tradition of specifically Japanese literature. A few other well-known texts of the eighteenth century can be seen as testimonies to these epistemic changes, but they do not highlight the new possibility as dramatically as Motoori's intralingual and intersemiotic translation. The intellectual and literary maneuvers by the *Kokugakusha* inaugurated the modern prescription of the national imaginary. We cannot fail to recognize the aura of modernity in National Studies precisely because, generally speaking and even beyond the context of Japan's history, the imaginary affiliation with nation and national culture and tradition is modern. To the extent that we take the modern regimes of reading, writing, reciting, translating, and so forth for granted, however, we tend to assume the modus operandi sustained by these regimes to be universally valid. Continuing to project this historically specific modus operandi into the past, we become incapable of imagining the possibilities of regimes other than that of national homolingualism.

## Translation as Continuity in Discontinuity

Returning to the question of the relation between translation and discontinuity, I probe how our commonsensical notion of translation is delimited by the schematism of the world (i.e., our representation of the world according to the schema of cofiguration) and conversely how the modern figure of the world as international (i.e., the world consisting of the basic units of the nations) is prescribed by our representation of translation as a communicative and international transfer of a message between a pair of ethnolinguistic unities.

The measure by which we are able to assess a language as a unity—again, I am talking not about phonetic systems, morphological units, or syntactic rules of a language but about the whole of a language as langue—is given to us only at the locale where the limit of a language is marked, at the border where we come across a nonsense that forces us to do something in order to make sense of it. This occasion of making sense out of nonsense, of doing something socially—acting toward foreigners, soliciting their response, seeking their confirmation, and so forth—is generally called translation, provided that we suspend the conventional distinction between translation and interpretation. The unity of a language is represented always in relation to another unity; it is never given in and of itself but in relation to an other. One can hardly evade dialogic duality when determining the unity of a language; language as a unity almost always conjures up the copresence of another language, precisely because translation is not only a border crossing but also and preliminarily an act of drawing a border, of bordering. Hence I have to introduce the schematism of cofiguration in analyzing how translation is represented.

If the foreign is unambiguously incomprehensible, unknowable, and unfamiliar, it is impossible to talk about translation, because translation simply cannot be done. If, on the other hand, the foreign is comprehensible, knowable, and familiar, it is unnecessary to call for translation. Thus the status of the foreign in translation must always be ambiguous. It is alien, but it is already in transition to something familiar. The foreign is simultaneously incomprehensible and comprehensible, unknowable and knowable, and unfamiliar and familiar. This foundational ambiguity of translation derives from the ambiguity of the positionality generally indexed by the peculiar presence of the translator, who is summoned only when two kinds of audiences are postulated with regard to the source text: one for whom the text is comprehensible, at least to some degree, and the other for whom it is incomprehensible. The translator's work consists in dealing with the difference between them. It is only insofar as comprehensibility is clearly and unambiguously distinct from incomprehensibility that the translator can be discerned from the nontranslator without ambiguity in the conceptual economy of this determination of the foreign and the proper.

It is important to note that the language in this instance is figurative: it need not refer to any natural language of an ethnic or national community such as German or Tagalog, since it is equally possible to have two kinds of audiences when the source text is a heavily technical document or an avant-garde literary piece. *Language* may refer to a set of vocabulary and expressions associated with a professional field or discipline, such as legal language; it may imply the style of graphic inscription or an unusual perceptual setting in which an artwork is installed. One may argue that these are examples of intralingual and intersemiotic translation, respectively. But they can be postulated only when they are in contradistinction to translation proper. The propriety of translation presupposes the unity of a language; it is impossible unless one unity of language is posited as external to another—as if, already, languages were given as countable, like apples. These figurative uses of *translation* illustrate how difficult it is to construe the locale of translation as a linking or bridging of two languages, two spatially marked domains.

Considering the positionality of the translator, we can now approach the problematic of subjectivity. The internal split in the translator, which reflects the split between the translator and the addresser or between the translator and the addressee—and furthermore the actualizing split in the addresser and the addressee[3]—demonstrates the way in which the subject constitutes itself. This internal split in the translator is homologous to the fractured I, the temporality of "I speak," which necessarily introduces an irreparable distance between the speaking I and the I that is signified, between the subject of the enunciation and the subject of the enunciated. Yet in translation the ambiguity in the personality of the translator marks the instability of the we as the subject rather than the I, suggesting a different attitude of address, which I have called "heterolingual address" (*Translation* 1–9) and in which one addresses oneself as a foreigner to another foreigner. Heterolingual address is an event, because translation never takes place in a smooth space; it is an address in discontinuity.

Rejected in homolingual address is the social character of translation, of an act performed at the locale of social transformation where new power relations are produced. Thus the study of translation will provide us with insights into how cartography and the schematism of cofiguration contribute to our critical analysis of social relations, premised not only on nationality and ethnicity but also on the differentialist identification of race or the colonial difference and discriminatory constitution of the West.

## NOTES

1. Here I rely on the classical notion of nationality in British liberalism. According to John Stuart Mill, nationality means that "a portion of mankind are united among themselves by common sympathies which do not exist between them and

any others—which make them co-operate with each other more willingly than with other people, desire to be under the same government, and desire that it should be government by themselves or a portion of themselves exclusively. This feeling of nationality may have been generated by various causes. Sometimes it is the effect of identity of race and descent. Community of language, and community of religion greatly contribute to it. Geographical limits are one of its causes. But the strongest of all is identity of political antecedents; the possession of a national history, and consequent community of recollections; collective pride and humiliation, pleasure and regret, connected with the same incidents in the past" (391).

2. Following the convention of names in China, Korea, and Japan, personal names are written in the order of family name, then given name. Thus Motoori Norinaga means "Norinaga of the Motoori family."

3. The split cannot be limited to translation. As Briankle Chang suggests, the putative unities of addresser and addressee can hardly be sustained, because the addresser is split and multiplies, as is figuratively illustrated by the Plato-Socrates doublet in Derrida's "Envois" (Derrida 1–256). As to communication in general, Chang argues, "Because both delivery and signing are haunted by the same structural threat of the message's nonarrival or *a*destination, the paradox of the signature also invades communication. Communication occurs only insofar as the delivery of the message *may* fail; that is, communication takes place only to the extent that there is a separation between the sender and receiver, and this separation, this distance, this *spacing*, creates the possibility for the message *not* to arrive" (216).

## WORKS CITED

Balibar, Étienne. *Les frontières de la démocratie*. Paris: La Découverte, 1992. Print.

Berman, Antoine. *L'épreuve de l'étranger: Culture et traduction dans l'Allemagne romantique*. Paris: Gallimard, 1984. Print.

Chang, Briankle G. *Deconstructing Communication: Representation, Subject, and Economies of Exchange*. Minneapolis: U of Minnesota P, 1996. Print.

Derrida, Jacques. *The Post Card: From Socrates to Freud and Beyond*. Trans. Alan Bass. Chicago: U of Chicago P, 1987. Print.

Hardt, Michael, and Antonio Negri. *Empire*. Cambridge: Harvard UP, 2000. Print.

Jakobson, Roman. *Selected Writings II*. The Hague: Mouton, 1971. Print.

Kant, Immanuel. *Critique of Pure Reason*. Trans. Norman Kemp Smith. New York: St. Martin's, 1929. Print.

Mezzadra, Sandro, and Brett Neilson. "Border as Method; or, The Multiplication of Labor." Italian as Second Language: Citizenship, Language, and Translation. Rimini. 4 Feb. 2008. Address.

Mill, John Stuart. Utilitarianism, On Liberty, *and* Considerations on Representative Government. 1861. London: Dent, 1972. Print.

Sakai, Naoki. *Translation and Subjectivity*. Pref. Meaghan Morris. Minneapolis: U of Minnesota P, 1997. Print.

———. *Voices of the Past: The Status of Language in Eighteenth-Century Japanese Discourse*. New York: Cornell UP, 1992. Print.

# Translating in a World of Languages

## GAYATRI CHAKRAVORTY SPIVAK

Let us point to Africa before we begin. Because historically it has been treated as a scandal, Africa makes theory visible. In our case, for example, it makes clear, in tranquillity as well as in violence, that a nation is not identical with a language. Let us think also of the itinerary of the ethical in the Buddhist diasporas and the vicissitudes of imperial knowledge in the translation enterprises of the Arabo-Persian empires. These reminders stand as narratives that would annul many of the commonly held presuppositions that support varieties of dominant translation theory. Even attempting such rethinking, we should remember that, whereas much is published on the westward translating arm of the Arabs, little is published on the eastward arm. Let us begin, then, with an appeal for a person with knowledge not only of Arabic, Persian, and Sanskrit but also of Pahlavi.

The best gift of all enlightenments is reasonable doubt. The best guarantee of all worldliness is attention to space and time.

The title of the Presidential Forum invokes Walter Benjamin as well as Paul de Man's Messenger Lecture, a reading of Benjamin. It also invokes Benjamin's book *The Work of Art in the Age of Mechanical Reproduction* (see 251–83)—I deliberately choose the mistranslated title that has passed into common currency to show how much power an English wields. These are great texts caught in a historical moment. Our moment, speaking through us as reasoned spontaneity, produces a difference. Our collective title,

*The author is University Professor at Columbia University. A version of this paper was presented at the 2009 MLA convention in Philadelphia.*

unlike Benjamin's and de Man's, is abstract and plural: the tasks of translation. I can read this already as meeting certain demands of globalization, which deals with the abstract. If it is true that capital translates all objects into abstractions, the appropriate behavior of the organic intellectuals of globalization may be to situate translation as the abstract task of reducing all linguistic performance to equivalents, of establishing the emergence of the languages of the Security Council of the United Nations as general equivalents—in other words, of homogenizing them into a dominant. Yet a context is concrete. And since we are teacher-translators, the context presupposes readers, as we specify in every publisher's marketing proposal. These are Benjamin's well-known words:

> We may define [a bad translation] as the inexact transmission of an inessential content. This will be true whenever a translation undertakes to serve the reader. However, if it were intended for the reader so must the original be. If the original does not exist for the reader's sake, how could the translation be understood on the basis of this premise? Translation is a form. ("Task" 70; trans. modified)

In his comments, de Man explains the dismissal of the reader by literally reading *Aufgabe* as "giving up"—the failure of the translator—and glosses Benjamin in a resolutely Euro-specific deconstructive context, where we can take the risk of saying, "[W]e have no knowledge of the vessel [the original], or no awareness, no access to it, so for all intents and purposes there never has been one" (*Work* 44).

How, then, has the translator's right to determine this form been changed in what we have nonetheless called the global context? Let me quote my current formula: Globalization takes place only in capital and data; everything else is damage control. From my vantage point, to contextualize the global is to step into damage control, and it makes sense for me to unfurl my argument as a development of this gesture. Let me turn the decision we confront into a story. Hegel recoded Christianity as philosophy. Marx put capital in place of the Idea in Hegel. Capital asks for the destruction of the Tower of Babel. The context of this call is not global. It is in the agency of a tribal god. In the global context, the Tower of Babel is our refuge. How and why?

In this forum, we are speaking of translation in the broad purview of the humanities. I don't believe the humanities can be global. I think our task is to supplement the uniformization necessary for globality. We must therefore learn to think of ourselves as the custodians of the world's wealth of languages, not as impresarios of a multicultural circus in English. The task of translation is to translate before translation: languages into equivalence, a different kind of commensurability. This is a suggestion that I have made at greater length in "Rethinking Comparativism."

There is a language we learn first; mixed with the prephenomenal, it stamps the metapsychological circuits of "lingual memory" (Becker 12). Each language of study may be activated in this special way in order to make an effort to produce a simulacrum through the reflexivity of language as habit. Here we translate not the content but the very moves of languaging. This is a form of translation before translation. Naoki Sakai asks us to think of language not as one but as many. The thinking of languaging before language makes this possible. Reproductive heteronormativity, the emergence into birth as death from the uterine world (Melanie Klein) as the theater of the staging of each language, makes Sakai's Kant possible as well.[1]

This is not to make an opposition between the natural spontaneity of the emergence of "my languaged place" and the artificial effort of learning foreign languages. Rather it is to emphasize the metapsychological and telecommunicative nature of the subject's being encountered by the languaging of place.[2] If we entertain the spontaneous-artificial opposition, we will end up valuing our own place over all others and thus defeat the ethical comparativist impulse. Embracing another place as my creolized space, as in migration, may be a legitimation by reversal. If the making and unmaking of an ethical subject—a knowing, feeling, judging subject—are to begin, it does not matter whether the language instrumental in this is recognizably hybrid or not. If, on the other hand, we recall the helplessness of subjects before history—our own history and that of the languaged place—in their acquisition of their first dwelling in language, we just may sense the challenge of producing a simulacrum, always recalling that this language too, depending on the subject's history, can inscribe lingual memory. In other words, I am calling for a sense of equivalence among languages rather than a comparison of historico-civilizational content. Étienne Balibar has suggested that equivalence blurs differences, whereas equality requires them ("Entretien"). Precisely because civil war may be the allegoric name for an extreme form of untranslatability, we need such blurring. The Tower of Babel, the condition of (im)possibility of translation, is thus a refuge in thinking the apparent global contemporaneity of languages before their historical inequality.

Listening to a version of this argument, my colleague Suva Chakravarty Dasgupta, of Jadavpur University, made me think of the value form in its expanded format. Indeed, Marx was productively counterintuitive in suggesting that value is already implicit in use and in deepening the

value form unconfined to the economic. If in languaging we are equivalent, as it were, and we want to disciplinarize this equivalency and keep it
upstream from verbal translation, we understand Marx's insistence that
the value form is contentless and his choice of foreign language learning
as an example of revolutionary practice (375).

The task of translation in the global context should be thought in this
frame, where the learning of languages is the first imperative—the production of translation an activism—and not simply a giving in to the demand for convenience in a country where multiculturalism goes hand in
hand with monolingualism. Our obligation to translate should be recognized as, at the deepest level, determined by "the idea of the *untranslatable* as not something that one cannot translate but something one never
stops (not) translating," a persistent epistemological preparation rather
than merely a response to a global market understood as a call to equitable pluralism.[3]

Globalization demands from us an epistemological change. Claims for
an epistemic change are often quickly made on the grounds of immediate
information command. An epistemic change is in fact diagnosed only be-
latedly, *nachträglich*. We cannot look around that corner; it is in the future
anterior, something that will have happened. We can, however, be responsible for epistemological change as tertiary and posttertiary teachers.
As such, we might tell heritage students; multicultural students; military,
diplomatic, human rights, and business students that you do not learn
culture as content, you learn language as practice. We learn to think a
tremendously diverse shared history, literally an inventory without traces,
where a trained imagination may be our only practical refuge. Some years
ago, Jack D. Forbes described something like such an imagination in his
account of the racial heterogeneity of the greater Caribbean:

> [t]hree hundred to four hundred years of intermixture of a very com-
> plex sort, [and] varying amounts of African and American ancestry de-
> rived at different intervals and from extremely diverse sources—as from
> American nations as different as Narragansett or Pequot and the Carib
> or Arawak, or from African nations as diverse as the Mandinka, Yoruba,
> and Malagasy.                                                   (270–71)

"For the perceptive reader," I then commented, "Forbes's book at once
opens the horizons of Foucault's work, shows the immense, indeed perhaps insuperable complexity of the task once we let go of 'pure' European outlines, and encourages a new generation of scholars to acquire the
daunting skills for robust cultural history" ("Race" 53). Today, ideologi-
cally held by a simulacrum of contemporaneity in the global, the call is

to rethink the historical as such as always contemporary and to train for a mind-set that will be equal to the task. It is precisely in this contemporaneity that we have to train ourselves to imagine the equivalence of all languages. Jacques Derrida has a lovely passage, which I often quote, on the need for learning to translate today: "It remains to be known, so as to save the honor of reason, how to *translate*. For example, the word *reasonable*. And how to pay one's respects to, how to . . . greet . . . beyond its latinity, and in more than one language, the fragile difference between the *rational* and the *reasonable*" (*Rogues* 159).

You see here not an abdication of translation but, once again, a recognition of it as an active practice: the idea of the untranslatable as not something that one cannot translate but something one never stops (not) translating.

The unending negotiation with the untranslatable will today be judged an impractical project. But in our professional organization, we should at least talk about the philosophy of our task instead of simply accepting that, caught up in the current corporatization of the university and in the financial crisis, we will never be able to perform the task that translation must carry on in the mode of pursuing what is persistently around the corner, in order to supplement the uniformization of the global.[4] Immense structural changes will of course be needed in order to think the equivalence of languages. The lack of parity that currently exists between established and less-taught languages goes against the very spirit of an enlightened globalization of the curriculum. This lack of parity is matched by that between teachers of language and teachers of literature at all United States universities and probably at universities everywhere. I continue to think of the MLA as a force of change rather than compromise. I have been a member since 1964, and in those early times we believed that the MLA could make some changes—and indeed it did. In this hope, I make these untimely suggestions.

I am myself a translator. I recently finished a translation of Aimé Césaire's *Une saison au Congo*.[5] And, because there is no market demand for it, I have put aside in a long-term way the project of translating Assia Djebar's *Loin de Médine* into Bengali for the Bangladeshi women's movement. I translate as an act of transgression, because I cannot not do it, always aware that it levels the text. Walter Benjamin was not allowed to become a university teacher. If things had fallen otherwise, one wonders if he would have dismissed the reader so easily. I also engage in the plurality indicated in the title of our forum. With Palgrave and with Hosam Aboul-Ela's able coeditorship, I am running a translation series, Theory in the World, which brings non-Euro-US texts into English. We will soon celebrate the appearance of our first translation, the Brazilian theorist Mariolena Chaui's *Resistance and the World*. I am at the moment engaged in organizing the translation of Arindam Chakrabarti's *Deho, Geho, Bondhutto*, a text in my native language. We focus on transgressions and impossibilities—rather than acknowledge the normative.

There are therefore no statistics in my presentation. My dear friend and ally Kenneth Prewitt, a distinguished social scientist at Columbia University, talks about the way in which a set of statistics is calculated in order to come to what is basically an English word—a species of translation. Once the statistics are established, Prewitt pointed out, it is easy to endow them with all the aura of the word in the history of the language. The word of the moment, he told me, is *progress*. Once you know the statistics, you know if there has been progress. My friends in rural India show the power of this logic in accepting the absence of development.

We need a deep change of mind in order to thrust the contextualization of the global into its own repeated displacement, into its supplement. Otherwise the equation of globalization and Americanization continues as the task or burden of translation. We forget then that the phonetic elements of languages do not translate—that is also an abstraction. I am often told that when I speak in my mother tongue, it sounds beautiful—it is a legitimation by reversal of the argument behind the word *barbaros*. Meaningless sounds, whether ugly or beautiful. In place of such culturalist exoticization of the MLA, the task of the translator as member might be to rethink the current workaday definition of translation and try to make translation the beginning, on the way to language learning, rather than the end.

I close with Abderrahman Sessako's 2006 film *Bamako*. In one scene, a Malian Muslim woman swears by Allah in a secular African symbolic court judging the World Bank. A global context. Unlike all the other witnesses, she will not be shown any further in the film. In other words, this particular limit-case will not translate into a Euro-specific practice, although the practitioners are African and the country calls itself secular. In another scene, a traditional healer is dismissed by court protocol but later reappears to sing most movingly. My colleague Mamadou Diouf tells me that the song is incomprehensible even to the Malians who crowd the compound. Here is an entry into the abstract task of translation: the court of law, engaged with world governance even if inhabited by fellow Africans in a good cause, is faced by an incomprehensible traditional desire to supplement, literally beside the task. Tradition here remains undecidable, incomprehensible, not immediately usable unless, through social translation, as in W. E. B. DuBois's long-ago practice in *Souls of Black Folk*, it is actively translated—as DuBois did the Negro spiritual—into European notation. He managed the text so that by its end, the performative had been translated into performance, and the entire text was managed by that move.[6] If you were born in a world of so-called less-taught languages, pick up the challenge, make a decision. It will not happen if you merely crave power. And it will not emerge from the appropriative benevolence of the languages that are perennially taught. Raymond Williams, who certainly could not imagine a globalized world, nor did he take note of gender, gave us this invaluable clue: the dominant ceaselessly appropriates the emergent and rewards it as part of the thwarting of its oppositional energy, channeled into a mere alternative (121–27). Losing that which is to come in the future anterior for mere institutional rewards will break our promise to the philosophers of the future.

## POSTSCRIPT

The Tower of Babel is our refuge. In Derrida's reading, it is a God who asks men, his children, to translate, and not to translate, at once ("Des Tours" 118). Babel/Bavel is His name. Long ago I argued that when God becomes history and the sacrifice is gendered, the Mother's hand is not arrested into the making of a covenant, comparing Toni Morrison's *Beloved* with the story of Abraham and Isaac (*Critique* 305). Here I substitute "other people's children" for the messianic singular—by way of the thesis that every language can be an instrument for moving into the phenomenal. This thought for me is grasped before one's desire to undo historical damage to one's own mother tongue (the objection invariably brought to the plea for imagining equivalence).

If the effort to imagine the equivalence is rethought as "other people's children" as equivalent to my own, we have x-rayed comparative literature—translating before translation—into the semiotics of reproductive heteronormativity at its most impersonal.[7] Derrida chose hymen and marriage as his concept-metaphors for translation. I speak of reproductive heteronormativity upstream from sexual contract or preference, as the irreducible. It is the baseline coding assemblage at our disposal. Reproduction from difference as the norm is the irreducible; upstream from straight/queer/trans as phenomenally understood. *Hetero*- here is the antonym of *auto*-. The queer use of childbearing, for example, is an important extramoral use of difference. Language is always already (re)produced in difference; so are capital and translation. Examining the specificities of each reproduction, we see the predicament of phenomenal reproduction (sex-gender systems) in each.

Translation in these understandings marks being/becoming-human. Do animals translate? Elsewhere I have quoted Oedipus's lament: "O marriages, marriages, you put us in nature, and putting us back again, reversed the seed, and indexed fathers, brothers, children, kin-blood mingled, brides, women, mothers, a shameful thing to know among the works of man. . . . "[8] Derrida cites Porphyry on the Roman Crassus: "A lamprey [toothed eel] which belonged to the Roman Crassus would come to him when called by name [*onomasis kaloumene*], and had such an effect on him that he mourned when it died, though he had earlier borne with moderation the loss of three children" (*Animal* 85).

Even if we recognize that the Law of the Father (the very mark of being/becoming human) staged in *Oedipus* is also a longing to follow our animality, we who belong historically to a sector of the human that accessed the Law through a language less taught in the United States will not want to humanize that longing into Crassus's eel's ability to translate human speech, will not want to follow a cited animal incorrectly, by translating capital/English's call for translation as if it were our proper task/name, even if our master mourns for us.[9]

NOTES ═══════════════════════════════════════════

1. See the opening of Spivak, "Translation."

2. "It would be bad natural history to expect the mental processes and communicative habits of mammals to conform to the logician's ideal" (Bateson 180).

3. This definition of the untranslatable, in Barbara Cassin's dictionary, was provided to me by Alessandra Russo.

4. I am revising this piece at Mahatma Gandhi University in India, and it fills me with despair that, as India rises, not only are the humanities dispensed with as excess baggage but the idea of teaching more than English and the local language is not even remotely entertained outside the megacities.

5. The haunting footprint of that experience of translating is to be found in my "Who Killed Patrice Lumumba?"

6. I have developed this in my DuBois lectures of November 2009, forthcoming from Harvard University Press.

7. For an analysis of rationalizing social formation by reproductive heteronormativity, see Ambedkar. Although he is ostensibly speaking of caste formation, the argument applies to group formation in general.

8. *Oedipus the King* (lines 1403–07). My translation is as literal as possible, to show that Oedipus reproaches marriage for the reversed inscription of human kinship, which makes incest possible (Spivak, "Tracing").

9. Derrida's taking up the untranslatable French pun in *suis*, first-person singular for both "to be" and "to follow," as a stable essential description of being human, and a "mad pursuit" of the animal in search of questions too complex to summarize here, is relevant to my use of this final example (*Animal* 78).

# WORKS CITED

Ambedkar, B. R. "Their Mechanism, Genesis and Development." *Castes in India: The Essential Writings of Ambedkar.* Delhi: Oxford UP, 2002. 241–62. Print.

Bateson, Gregory. *Steps to an Ecology of Mind.* Chicago: U of Chicago P, 2000. Print.

Becker, Alton. *Beyond Translation.* Ann Arbor: U of Michigan P, 1996. Print.

Benjamin, Walter. "The Task of the Translator." *Illuminations.* Trans. Harry Zohn. New York: Schocken, 1968. 69–82. Print.

———. *The Work of Art in the Age of Its Technical Reproducibility.* Trans. Michael Jennings. Cambridge: Harvard UP, 2008. Print. Trans. of *Das Kunstwerk im Zeitalter seiner Technischen Reproduzierbarkeit.*

Cassin, Barbara, ed. *Vocabulaire européen des philosophies: Dictionnaire des intraduisibles.* Paris: Seuil, 2004. Print.

Chakrabarti, Arindam. *Deho, Geho, Bondhutto.* Calcutta: Anustup, 2008. Print.

de Man, Paul. "Conclusions on Walter Benjamin's 'The Task of the Translator': Messenger Lecture, Cornell University, March 4, 1983." *Yale French Studies* 97 (2000): 10–35. Print.

Derrida, Jacques. *The Animal That I Am.* Trans. David Wills. New York: Fordham UP, 2008. Print.

———. *"Des Tours de Babel."* Trans. Joseph Graham. *Acts of Religion.* Ed. Gil Anidjar. New York: Routledge, 2002. 101–34. Print.

———. *Rogues: Two Essays on Reason.* Trans. Pascale-Anne Brault and Michael Naas. Stanford: Stanford UP, 2005. Print.

DuBois, W. E. B. *The Souls of Black Folk.* 1953. Electronic Text Center, U of Virginia Lib., Sept. 1996. Web. 29 June 2010.

"Entretien avec Ernesto Laclau et Étienne Balibar." *Rue Descartes* 67 (2009): 78–99. Print.

Forbes, Jack D. *Black Africans and Native Americans: Color, Race, and Caste in the Evolution of Red-Black Peoples.* Oxford: Blackwell, 1988. Print.

Marx, Karl. "The Eighteenth Brumaire of Louis Bonaparte." *Surveys from Exile.* Trans. David Fernbach. New York: Random, 1974. 143–249. Print.

Spivak, Gayatri Chakravorty. *A Critique of Postcolonial Reason: Toward the History of a Vanishing Present.* Cambridge: Harvard UP, 1999. Print.

———. "Race before Racism: The Disappearance of the American." *Edward Said and the Work of the Critic: Speaking Truth to Power.* Ed. Paul Bové. Durham: Duke UP, 2000. 51–65. Print.

———. "Rethinking Comparativism." *New Literary History* 40.3 (2009): 609–26. Print.

———. "Tracing the Skin of Day." *Undated: Nightskin.* Dubai: 1x1 Art Gallery, 2009. 20. Print.

———. "Translation as Culture." *An Aesthetic Education in the Age of Globalization.* Cambridge: Harvard UP, forthcoming.

———. "Who Killed Patrice Lumumba?" Conf. on Translating Postcolonial into French. Columbia U. 26 Mar. 2010. Keynote address.

Williams, Raymond. *Marxism and Literature.* New York: Oxford UP, 1977. Print.

# Practicing and Theorizing Translation: Implications for the Humanities

## BRETT DE BARY

I thank Catherine Porter for inviting me to participate in this forum, and I congratulate her on the success of the theme "The Tasks of Translation in the Global Context," which generated more than fifty panels for the 2009 convention, bringing so many distinguished translators, scholars, and theorists to Philadelphia and to this discussion.

As a scholar with a long-standing commitment to the practice of translation, Porter has articulated a number of concerns and recommendations in her MLA newsletters and other publications during her presidential year, recommendations that the scholars at this panel generally endorse. What Porter calls "the global context" of our work applies with particular urgency today to the work of the translator. She urges that there be emphatic support for the teaching of foreign languages in humanities curricula in the face of budgetary retrenchment and that the value of translation, a hitherto underutilized arena of scholarly collaboration, be acknowledged. She urges that translation be recognized as scholarly activity in decisions about hiring, tenure, and promotion. Finally, she notes that much more broadly based public support is needed for the kinds of translation activities that might reverse the import-export imbalance, according to which less than four percent of books published in the United States each year are translations. The last fact is an unmistakable manifestation of the severe economic asymmetries that define the contempo-

*The author is professor of Asian studies and comparative literature at Cornell University. A version of this paper was presented at the 2009 MLA convention in Philadelphia.*

PROFESSION

rary global context as well as a manifestation of one of the most powerful and persistent colonial legacies.

The more specific aim of this forum, however, is to open for discussion several pressing questions of a largely scholarly nature that have to do with translation: What is the significance of translation studies as an emerging field in our profession? How might we rigorously assess the potential of translation studies to generate new work and provoke fruitful new activity in the humanities? Is the troubled (and troubling) distinction between theory and practice pertinent to translation, or might a reconceptualized translation, precisely, challenge that distinction? Does the study of translation offer anything new to the humanities, and—if, for some, such a question betrays an overly historicist bias—how otherwise do we assess its importance?

I offer a few thoughts, a few generalizations, in response to the four papers presented at this forum:

Translation studies, less developed in the United States academy than in many other sites (neighboring Canada is just one), has the potential to pose complex historical, interpretive, and theoretical questions for the humanities.

The problem of translation is intimately related to matters of language, yet current reconceptualizations also take translation to be paradigmatic of sociality—that is, relationality per se. As such the study of translation has become a site for radical political critique.

Since they concern relationality, the practice and theory of translation inevitably involve negotiating hierarchized differences. As Porter has suggested, the invisibility of the translator remains a powerful convention. The ideological insistence that translation is ancillary may be because close consideration of translation, as a process and as a mode of subjectivity, renders the notion of sovereign subject (including sovereign nation) untenable.

Work on translation is offering new approaches to the theorization of difference and comparability, but we must be attentive to how such theorizations are themselves subtly differentiated and even in contest with one another.

At its best, work on translation should challenge not only the commonsense notion of interlingual boundaries (between unitary national or other languages) but also institutionalized boundaries of discipline and genre.

The four papers articulate and enact new approaches to translation. In my discussion, I note their commonalities but will also be concerned with differentiating them from one another.

I begin with Verena Conley, whose paper explicitly raises the question, Why translation now? While it is not uncommon in translation scholarship to deplore the dominance of global English, Conley suggests that, with a shift of perspective, we might more productively apprehend our era as one where people are "living in translation." Languages themselves have been deterritorialized and put in constant contact with one another. The space of their coexistence, according to Conley, should be characterized in terms of networks rather than bounded and discrete language towers. She rejects the bias that would see the metaphor of translation as static and topological, a concern she shares with Naoki Sakai. Drawing on the poststructuralist intervention into translation theory, Conley rejects the communication model of the translated message passing unchanged through neutral space. According to Jacques Derrida, the translated and the translating are not separable, are not exterior to each other. Translation is a traversal, not an arrival.

For Conley, then, at a moment when globalization entails the accelerated mobility of peoples, the process of translation must be apprehended not as an arrival but as movement between. She reminds us, moreover, that in many instances the movement of globalization corresponds to a history of decolonization and thus manifests the linguistic traces of long periods of living under the language of the colonizing other. Indeed, she proposes that, whether it is the result of colonialism or not, it is multilingualism, or living in translation, that is the norm for many populations, rather than monolingualism. Whether in the work of Samuel Beckett, Kateb Yacine, or Atiq Rahimi, our consideration of form, texture, and style in literary studies has been diminished insofar as monolingual assumptions have led us to neglect the problematic of translation, which opens up an approach to the text as double writing. When living in translation, one can never consider one language uniquely one's own. Conley thus calls on today's intellectuals, and quite specifically on theorists, to adventurously disidentify with their "own" languages and actively negotiate, rather than disavow, the world of translation we live in.

While Verena Conley defines the global context of our forum's title as a way of assessing the specificity of the task of the translator today, Tom Conley problematizes the very figures of connectivity that yield a perspective of history as progression. He writes that it is *we* "who imagine a linear chronology when our eyes scan the words from left to right. . . . Implied is a model based on a 'life of forms of art.'" Reflecting on his own work of translating Gilles Deleuze's *The Fold: Leibniz and the Baroque*, Tom Conley invokes the line as fold ("At once an organic and inorganic force, it moves ahead ceaselessly, it coils on itself, it turns and curves about . . .") to explore the same inseparability of *translated* and *translating* that Verena Conley's essay broaches. For Tom Conley, the line, at once organic and inorganic, "identifies thinking as a process coextensive with writing and drawing." As Conley asserts with Joachim du Bellay, writers must think spatially.

It is the shape of writing that conveys the style. Although Tom Conley does not self-consciously foreground the problem of nonequivalence in translation, he underscores the difference of the English word *line* from *ligne*. It must be what Walter Benjamin (in "The Task of the Translator") would call the *mode* of meaning of the French *trait* that prompts Conley to interpret *line* also as "style," asserting (as Benjamin himself did), that it was not the message or the translated (Deleuze's philosophical claims about Leibniz) that bedeviled him as a translator of *The Fold* but the style. He tells us that Deleuze, moreover, frequently referred to style as *une manière de penser* ("a manner of thinking"). Eschewing historicism, Conley seems to approach the problematic of translation formally, if we allow for the materiality of language and the organic/inorganic nature of the line. Interestingly, it is precisely this formalism that endows his concept of translation with a provocative antigenre, antidisciplinary force: for the translator, facing "a tsunami of lines"—"Nine times the book's title is furrowed in the first five sentences, literally *pli sur pli*"—the practice of translation is itself theoretical, *une manière de penser*. Conley would situate the task of the translator precisely on the *line* that conventionally separates the interiority of thinking from the supposed exteriority of writing.

Naoki Sakai is a scholar and practicing translator who publishes his theoretical writings in both English and Japanese, in a mode he calls "heterolingual address." To address an audience in more than one language, as Sakai sees it, is to abandon the assumption that communication (i.e., transmission of the message or translated) is guaranteed among bounded language communities, which are usually taken to be national language communities. Heterolingual address always assumes, among the addressees, the presence of the foreigner, the one who may not understand. Sakai's work, like Derrida's, has sought to expose the logical antinomies underlying the boundary concept of interlingual translation, usually taken to be translation between two national languages, as "translation proper," in Roman Jakobson's sense. In my view, this notion of interlingual translation is still pervasively and uncritically invoked in American translation studies. Sakai also dismantles the logic underlying the modern nationalist assumption of isomorphism among national subject, national language, and native speaker, showing how it relies on a questionably binarized regulative schema, that of "cofiguration." Thus he joins Verena Conley in asserting that languages are not one's own. His work combines formal analysis of philosophical logic with historicization. Japanese history offers one of many resources for exposing the specifically modern, ideological nature of contemporary understandings of translation. Chinese writing had been employed for many centuries in Japan as simply another register of writing. Yet the invention of the notion of Chinese as a foreign language to be translated was a precondition for the emergence of Japanese conceptions of the national in the eigtheenth century.

Sakai joins both Verena Conley and Tom Conley in defining translation as movement and rejecting static representations of it. Yet he takes up the problem of spatialization with an emphasis different from Tom Conley's. As a process of bordering, translation can only be movement, like that of a pen tracing a line on paper. The dominant notion of translation as a transfer between two preexisting entities is a static, spatialized representation that erases the temporality of translation as movement, of translation as the very process of bordering that allows two languages to be differentiated. By historicizing and criticizing this spatialized metaphor of translation, Sakai shows how it has been subtly implicated in the violence of modern classificatory systems and their differentiations involving nationality, ethnicity, and race.

Gayatri Spivak joins our panel as a scholar for whom theoretical work and the practice of translation have been inseparable. If she begins her remarks with references to works by Paul de Man and Benjamin, which by now have become canonical in Euro-American translation studies, it is only to reopen to question their language, which has been subjected to deadening repetition and recitation. She takes on the question we thought had been settled for translation studies, that of our relation to the original. But is it, after all, inconsistent with a Benjaminian sense of translation to expose the text to the test of historical difference and see if it survives? Like Verena Conley, Spivak turns to the "global context" of our panel title to indicate that historical difference. She asks us to recall that de Man translated Benjamin's *Aufgabe* not as "task" but as "giving up" on the original, asserting that, "we have . . . no access to it, so for all intents and purposes there never has been one" (91). Spivak asks pointedly if this apparent nonchalance toward the original was possible only in a Euro-specific context—that of deconstruction. Today's global context, she suggests, calls for new inflections of the task of the translator, at a time when the encounter with the linguistic difference of the original may be more jeopardized than ever in the face of the intensifying abstractions and standardizations of capital.

Spivak does not draw a distinction between origin and original in her remarks. But I would suggest that this deconstructive distinction is maintained in the important clarifications she sets forth later. Why, we may ask, does a speaker who calls on intellectuals to be "custodians of the world's wealth of languages" then insist puzzlingly that their task is "to translate before translation?" Here, I see Spivak hewing to deconstruction's rigorous critique of the origin while insisting on the political urgency of encountering the Tamil or Gikuyu original as textured, concrete linguistic materialities. Like Sakai, she is vigilant in the refusal to endorse any nationalistic notion of a native language or native speaker, reminding us that it is, after all, in a state of "helplessness . . . before history" that we acquire a "first dwelling in language." This is why Spivak emphatically refuses to frame her call for reevaluation of the original in what she terms the "spontaneous-artificial opposition." Her acknowledgment of the individual language speaker's helplessness before history accords with a Derridean sense that we have no direct access to the origin of language, which is always made available to us through a fundamental mediation or translation. Her call for translation as activism is thus doubled: custodial in relation to a practical responsibility for less commonly taught languages, on the one hand, yet deconstructive in its reminder that "translation before translation" is prephenomenal or "upstream" from verbal translation, certainly not involved with the merely phonetic sense of linguistic difference that may be a disguised form of exoticism. Only such an awareness can awaken us to the potential of language learning as an essentially philosophical task, even a revolutionary praxis.

The catachrestic impulse in Spivak's gesture comes as a thought-provoking conclusion to our panel. Spivak asks us to distance ourselves from some of the deconstructive moves of poststructuralist translation theory without jettisoning it entirely. In demonstrating the often unrealized progressive potential of deconstruction for politics, she is one of the few who have begun to show us what possibilities a truly postdeconstructive era in the Euro-American academy might offer. But for translators and translation studies in the global context, even this sense of "our era" in the Euro-American academy must be subjected to uncompromising and far-reaching decentering. This is, I agree, an equally urgent political task.

## WORK CITED

de Man, Paul. *The Resistance to Theory*. Minneapolis: U of Minnesota P, 2006. Print.

# Philosophical Translation and Untranslatability: Translation as Critical Pedagogy

## EMILY APTER

During a period of economic downturn in which there has been much hand-wringing about the vulnerability of the humanities to accusations that it lacks unifying paradigms or a clear, consensual vision of what it studies, translation studies, or what I think of as the translational paradigm, has emerged as a viable rallying point. Translation is national and cosmopolitan in purview. In a way that is neither coercive nor artificial, it fords the divides between world lit and theory, between Western and non-Western literatures. As a subject field, it is accessible to academics and nonacademics alike. As one of the oldest technologies of communication and diplomacy, it has a distinguished history. As a professional training, it can even produce measurable outcomes. And it is relevant politically: to the struggle against Globlish by nonmajority languages; to plurilingual education in officially monolingual states; to far-flung literacy communities; to the economics of publishing and competition for cultural legitimation; to legal intellectual property disputes pertaining to copyright, plagiarism, and piracy; and to strategies of international security—specifically, the weaponization of language in cyberwar. Little wonder then that the publication of books in translation studies has grown exponentially in the past ten years, accompanied by a spike in university programs emphasizing the theory and practice of translation.

As I argued in my book *The Translation Zone*, translation has historically been a mainstay of comparative literature in all its disciplinary guises,

The author is professor of French and comparative literature at New York University. A version of this paper was presented at the 2009 MLA convention in Philadelphia.

 PROFESSION

from early periods to the contemporary moment. Translation has emerged as a catalyst for disparate yet coherent pedagogies because it effectively conjugates classical and Renaissance traditions of philosophy, philology, humanism, and *translatio studii* with exilic humanism (associated canonically with the work of Leo Spitzer, Erich Auerbach, and Edward Said); with post-Sputnik intellectual developments in linguistics, machine translation, and deconstruction; and with cultural translation (advanced by Lawrence Venuti, Jill Levine, Tejaswini Niranjana, Gayatri Chakravorty Spivak, Mary Louise Pratt, Lydia Liu, and Robert Young, among others).

Recently there is evidence of renewed attention to philosophical translation. Symptomatic of this tendency is a panel titled "Translation of Philosophy / Philosophy of Translation," organized by Ben Van Wyke for the 2010 American Comparative Literature Association Conference. The brief concisely articulates major issues at stake:

> For at least the past thirty years or so, questions of translation have been moving to the fore in philosophy. Far beyond traditional concerns that have focused merely on the accuracy of translated philosophical texts, translation is fast becoming one of the most fundamental tropes for the very workings of philosophy. According to Derrida, for example, whose work has played a profound role in making this connection explicit, "the origin of philosophy is translation or the thesis of translatability."
> . . . Not only [have] philosophy and comparative literature been paying increasing attention to translation, but certain areas of translation studies have also been inspired by philosophy, especially by many tenets of post-Nietzschean notions of language and their implications for this practice. However, philosophic ponderings on the trope of translation often ignore certain realities related to the actual practice. . . .
> What can philosophy learn from translation studies? How can philosophy be used to help us view and/or practice translation? If translation is at the origin of philosophy, can there be a philosophy of translation?

The final question begs answering in the affirmative. Yes, let there be a philosophy of translation: a branch of philosophy that recognizes translation as an important heuristic; that enters the problem of translation into traditional philosophical subfields (metaphysics, epistemology, ethics, logic); and that philosophizes translation as a medium of writing, thinking, and producing rather than as a loose metaphor for transcoding, interpreting, or transcribing.

## PHILOSOPHICAL TRANSLATION

Philosophy in translation studies has routinely referred to professional practice, as in "What is your philosophy of translation?" Are you a

literalist in the doctrinal Hebraic, Qur'anic, and mystical Christian traditions, seeking to preserve to the maximum the original letter of the sacred
text? A word-for-wordist who proceeds by rendering textual segments at
the same rank (morpheme, word, group, clause, sentence)? A partisan of
the German Romantic tradition (spanning August Wilhelm von Schlegel
and Friedrich Schleiermacher to Walter Benjamin), who construes literalism as a form of foreignized cultural translation? Or do you subscribe to a
philosophy of free translation in the tradition of Jerome and Boethius, according to which the faithful translator is the one faithful to God "but not
to the individual words of God's Word" (Robinson 113)? In other words, a
sense-for-sense practitioner of unbounded (or mixed-rank) translation or
a poet playing with translation loosely in imitation and pastiche? For all
the rich research these opposing traditions have inspired, what interests
me most is something more pointed: What does it mean to think translation as a kind of philosophy, or as a way of doing theory and its history?

Such questions prompt reflection on the full impact of translation
on the making of cross-continental philosophy and theory. The intra-
European and transatlantic transfer of texts, while often acknowledged,
has yet to be accounted for as part of theory's archival remit. A prominent
development in this as yet unwritten translation history would doubtless
be the halting constitution, over more than three decades, of a corpus of
English versions of difficult texts composed in French (by Derrida, Lacan,
Foucault, Deleuze, Irigaray, Kristeva, Rancière, Badiou, et al.). With each
contribution to this intellectual horizon, the translators play a pivotal role
in the history of theory. Translational apprenticeship, as a way of learning and teaching philosophy and theory, has always been recognized, but
such work warrants more explicit foregrounding as a critical pedagogy in
the humanities.[1]

If a particular text chosen for translation clearly influences the course of
theory, so too does the date of the text's translation, especially where there
is discrepancy in periods. The general rule seems to be that the greater
the time lag between a text's original publication and its translation, the
greater the chance the text will be misread or creatively recontextualized.
In early texts by Gilles Deleuze, Félix Guattari, Giorgio Agamben, Judith
Butler, and Alain Badiou for example, tectonic shifts between the moment
of their cultural production and the reception of their translation led to
new semantic colorations of key words like "difference," "the sensible,"
"biopolitical," "publicity" (*Öffentlichkeit*), "gender," and "evental." Words,
say, that had specific resonance with situationism, French Maoism, or May
'68 ("situation," "logics of revolt," "conjuncture") come to be substantially
resignified by the time they reach the early 2000s, whether in Žižekian

Leninism or the Badiouvian postneoliberal "Communist hypothesis" (Badiou). My point here is that in studying the history of translation within the history of philosophy and theory, we are not just performing a philological or intellectual exercise. By gauging the deformations, reformulations, and temporal *décalages* of translated works, we are doing philosophy.

The contemporary foregrounding of philosophical translation owes much to the landmark volume *Difference in Translation*, a collection of essays edited by Joseph F. Graham and published in 1985. Here we find essays by Philip E. Lewis, Cynthia Chase, Richard Rand, Alan Bass, Jacques Derrida (his important reading of Benjamin's "Task of the Translator," "Des Tours de Babel"), and the late and much missed Barbara Johnson. As an ensemble, the collection marks a moment in the history of deconstruction in which translating, instead of being something assumed— what critics do as part of their training—is activated as theory. In the words of the book's editor, "We might set translation as a test for claims about deconstruction or any other disruptive effects of discourse" (Graham, Introduction 17). Noting that Derrida's work "has always already been (about) translation," Johnson offers a nuanced summary of how for Derrida translation emerged as a way of doing philosophy:

> Derrida's rearticulation of philosophy and translation is obviously not designed to evacuate meaning entirely. But his concept of textuality displaces the very notion of *how* a text means. What goes on in every text far exceeds what can be reduced to so-and-so's "thought." Derrida's own ingenious translations, such as that of Hegel's *Aufhebung* by *la relève*, are attempts to render all the often contradictory meanings of a term in such a way that crucial logical complexities are not oversimplified. It is quite often by finding the pressure points previously lost in translation that Derrida rearticulates philosophy with itself. (145)

The rearticulation of philosophy with itself enables something quite miraculous: it eases the difficult passage of natural language into philosophy, characterized by Derrida as the "violent difficulty in the transference of a non-philosopheme into a philosopheme" (Johnson 146). This difficult transference is keenly felt in Derrida's treatment of the word *pharmakon* ("Pharmacie" and "Plato's Pharmacy"). "No, it is not a *pharmakon*, . . . it is rather a *pharmakon*," to borrow Peggy Kamuf's phrase in her analysis in this issue of *Profession* of Derrida's "Plato's Pharmacy."[2] Kamuf fixes on Derrida's identification of the invisible pivot, the Greek-to-Greek translation of philosopheme-*pharmakon*, whereby an apparent nontranslation translates nonetheless. Jonathan Rée tracks a similar operation in Martin Heidegger's *Dasein*:

> In most contexts *Dasein* is equivalent to the English "existence" (for example in the Darwinian "struggle for existence"), but in *Being and Time* there is a distinct concept of *Existenz* which had a stronger claim on that word. It could also be translated, in some ways very faithfully, as "being-there," except that this might reactivate the metaphysical connotations that Heidegger was determined to avoid. So Macquarrie and Robinson were obliged to invent an artificial expression to serve as *Dasein*'s counterpart in English. That new English word was "Dasein" (with a capital initial but no italics; plural: "Daseins"; possessive: "Dasein's"), and it was duly included in their index of English expressions.                (232)

"No, it's not *Dasein*, it is rather Dasein." What we have here is a distinct case of fidelity to the original in which the target is same and othered—which is to say, philosophized.

Johnson is fascinated by philosophy's fidelity to philosophy by means of this othering process of translation. The philosopheme taps into its own foreignness and contacts its correlative in another language. That the quilting point of untranslatables is where philosophy happens suggests that philosophy answers to untranslatability even as it attempts to cross over into translation. As Johnson, glossing Heidegger, puts it:

> The bridge of translation, which paradoxically releases within each text the subversive forces of its own foreignness, thus reinscribes those forces in the tensile strength of a new neighborhood of otherness. Yet all travelers on that bridge are answering a summons that repulses them at every step, a summons reminiscent of the sign Lautréamont sets up in front of Maldoror, containing a warning that is received just a moment too late to be heeded: "Vous, qui passez sur ce pont, n'y allez pas." "You, who are crossing over this bridge, don't get to the other side."      (148)

With the help of Lautréamont, Johnson inadvertently moves translation theory, identified throughout *Difference in Translation* with such topics as abusive translation, the property of the proper name, signature, fidelity, and prosthesis, to the arena of what might be called the translational interdiction or first-order untranslatability: "You who attempt to cross this bridge will not pass." This ban on passing from one language to another may be read not just as an example of the philosopheme's obstacle course but also as an idea that has particular resonance today in efforts to rethink theological and secular criticism. It suggests a bound of sacrosanction, a theology of translation, a "saving difference" (an expression used by Harold Bloom that I am détourning), which is a difference believed in because it saves or preserves the untranslatable.[3] Bloom seems most concerned with staging a scene of primal injunction whose caption might read: "Thou Shalt Translate Me." Such a command, in exacting submission from its addressee, corresponds to what he calls "God's condescension, his accommodating gift of his Election-love ('*ahabah*')," whereby "the human receiver [of God's book, whether in Scripture or in nature] incorporates and makes himself one with the Divinely given cipher" (51, 52).

## THE TRANSLATIONAL INTERDICTION

If the duty to translate is rooted in Bloom's writing in the cipher of the Hebrew Bible and its secular reinscription in the aesthetics of Romanticism, one could say that in more recent philosophy and theory, the duty to not translate is derived from Islamic tradition and more generally from principled opposition to facile computations of cultural equivalence. I am thinking here of Abdelfattah Kilito's injunction "Thou shalt not translate me," a title Kilito used for a lecture that plays off titles in his work: *Tu ne parleras pas ma langue* (*Thou Shalt Not Speak My Language*) and "Défense de parler ma langue" (rendered as "Thou Dost Not, and Shalt Not, Speak My Language"). A chapter begins:

> One day I realized that I dislike having foreigners speak my language. How did that happen? I used to think of myself as an open-minded, liberal person who wished unto others what he wished unto his kin. Furthermore, I used to think it my duty to endeavor as best I could to make my language radiate its brilliance, to increase the number of its learners, and so forth. But that noble goal disappeared when I realized that I dislike having foreigners speak my language.    (*Thou Shalt* 87)

Kilito then recounts the time he spoke Arabic with an American woman whose uncanny mastery of the language made him squirm. When she uses the Moroccan colloquial term *wallahila*, it strikes him as transgressive: "Did she realize that *wallahila* contains the word 'Allah,' and that she let herself so easily tread on rough terrain? She referred, probably without knowing it, to a faith that apparently was not hers. I leave this question open" (92). The question in question circles through the problem of sacred language used in ignorance; so does the issue of broken trust among native speakers in the face of foreign entry into their language world.

Through lessons and anecdotes of translational travesty, Kilito formulates something like the divine right of untranslatability. In "Du balcon d'Averroès" ("Averroës's Balcony"), a pastiche of Jorge Luis Borges's 1949 fiction "La busca de Averroes" ("Averroës's Search"), he gives us a parable of the untranslatable. Just as in Borges's tale, where Averroës emerges as the father of untranslatability theory (he discovers that Greek concepts of tragedy and comedy are untranslatable in Arabic), in Kilito's short story he is cast, at least initially, as the author of an untranslatable Arabic phrase that comes to the narrator in a dream. This phrase, *lougha-touna-l-a'jamiyya*, includes the root *ajam*, meaning "non-Arab" or "barbarian," and is rendered in French as "notre langue étrangère" (literally, "our foreign tongue") (158). The enigmatic sense of the expression obsesses the narrator: it refers to the common barbarian tongue for both Arabs and Greeks (i.e., Persian), to a native language as foreigners speak it, to foreignized or othered speech in one's native tongue, to the experience of being unhomed in the mother tongue, and to many other meanings besides. The phrase seems to guard the trace of an *Ursprache*—a sacred, originary language that will reveal the origin of philosophy.

Suspecting that philosophy has been lost in translation, the narrator stages a spectatorial encounter in which a faceless Averroës (standing for philosophy) and the narrator's translator (standing for translation) confront each other in a de Chirico–like dream setting: a courtyard overlooked by one opaque and three transparent windows. This face-off is interrupted when a fight breaks out between the translator and the narrator. The former accuses the latter of insulting the Arabic language, calling him to account for repressing the attribution of the little phrase to Averroës (an attribution he claims to have discovered in a work by the narrator on the picaresque novel that he, the translator, translated into Arabic). "Tu n'as pas lu ma traduction parce qu'elle est en arabe," he rebukes him (161; "You did not read my translation because it is in Arabic" [trans. mine]). The hapless narrator learns that he has betrayed his own text by betraying Arabic. In the end he makes amends, restoring Arabic to its position of glory as a singular God language: the origin and end of all languages, the master original and master target both.

The narrator ultimately solves the mystery of his phrase. Pursuing a chain of associations that leads from Borges (whose Averroës is horrified by the danger to classical Arabic posed by the colloquial mixture of Spanish and Arabic spoken by Spanish street kids) to Noah's ark (where the Deluge is taken as a metaphor for the catastrophic loss of Arabic), he traces the phrase to the preface of a renowned Arabic dictionary, *Lisane al-'arab*, whose author, the thirteenth-century Egyptian scholar Ibn Manzour, was the first to apprehend fully that Arabic was becoming an endangered language. Taking up Manzour's cause (and in defiance of his feckless translator, who in a strange turnaround now speaks to him only in French), the narrator assumes the mantle of Arabic defender, becoming, as it were, a champion of the translational interdiction. Though the story's message is elusive—it seems to be satirizing Arabocentrism and by extension all forms of cultural nationalism (manifest, say, in the recent prosecutions of insults to Turkishness)—it nonetheless uncovers the moral structures of guilt and betrayal that hold the translational prohibition in place and that theologically underwrite the complex cathexes of writers to their languages.

Waïl S. Hassan, in his translator's introduction to *Thou Shalt Not Speak My Language*, sets the context for Kilito's protective barrier around Arabic. He reminds us that the "sacred book of Islam is, from the perspective of the faithful, untranslatable because it is considered the literal word of God; human beings are incapable of exhausting its meaning, let alone transposing it into other languages" (xix). Hassan recalls too that in much Islamic tradition, translators are readily held to be apostates and heretics; a class of interpreters worthy of punishment but also of redemption. Emphasizing the folk etymologies clustering around the Arabic words for translator—*mutarjim, turjuman, tarjamah,* terms that in fact redound etymologically to the Turkish *tercümen,* itself an Ottomanized version of the ancient Babylonian word for "interpreter," *targumannu,* later Europeanized as *dragoman*—Hassan notes that the phonetically similar but etymologically unrelated Arabic word *tarjamah*

> shares the root verb *rajama,* which means "to stone to death," with a sizable constellation of words that include *rajm* (killing, beating, battering, reviling), *rajam* (well, cavity, hole in the ground, oven), *rujum* (shooting stars), *rajeem* (cast with stones, damned, an epithet of Satan, and also driven away, reviled, insulted), *rujmah* (grave and tombstones). The verb *rajama* also appears in expressions like *rajm bil-ghayb* (conjecture, soothsaying) and *kalam marjum* (uncertain or unreliable speech). *Tarjamah* therefore carries connotations of alienated speech that have the flavor of falsehood, damnation, and death, but also possibilities of survival, narration and understanding. (x)[4]

*Thou Shalt Not Speak My Language* articulates in a casual idiom the fearsome, possessive requirements of owning Arabic. To own Arabic is to assume its untranslatability, its status as an Adamic language.

In an earlier book, *La langue d'Adam* ("The Language of Adam"), Kilito stipulates that Babil, or plurilingual confusion, should be regarded no longer as punishment for humankind's hubris but instead as a divine sign, a manifestation of God's intention to mark and preserve linguistic difference among people.[5] Monolingualism, particular to each language and composing the diversity of languages, becomes something to have and to hold in reverence. Such an idea runs patently counter to the reigning orthodoxy of linguistic pluralism so commonly embraced by comparative literature and world literature programs. Kilito's bid for monolingualism risks sounding anticomparatist or, at worst, xenophobic, but it seems

directed at safeguarding the sacred in language, particularly as the sacred resides in the singularity of poetry. Arabic poetry is Kilito's model
untranslatable—even more than the Qur'an—for a poem, in passing from
one language to another, loses rhyme, and once rhyme is sacrificed, poetry
turns into something other—which is to say, prose.[6] Translation, according to Kilito, cuts the poetic thread, the very same thread that organizes
and regulates the cosmos. His injunction "Thou shalt not translate me"
rests on a heightened awareness of translational taboo—of translation's
potential for violating sacred tongues or the private language of prayer
and recitation. But it skirts the issue of ecclesiastical censorship imposed
by institutions of clerical power. The case of John Wycliffe's English bible
(1382), the use of which became an offense punishable by death, starkly
reveals how the politics of sacred language becomes imbricated in the
politics of religious institutions, particularly when what is at issue is control over clerical and lay instruction.[7]

The sanctity of the language of Holy Writ is freighted with the oldest
questions of Judeo-Christian hermeneutics: In what language did God
originally speak? Did Adam speak the same language before and after the
Fall? If Latin is the language by which God's word is transmitted, and
if it is decreed untranslatable, how was this policy reconciled with the
fact that the Latin bible was known to be a translation of Old Testament
Hebrew and New Testament Coptic and Greek? Such questions continue
to resonate in contemporary debate. Are religious exponents of prayer or
religious ceremonies in the original adhering to what Wai Chee Dimock
calls "an orthodox and fetishizing claim about untranslatability," or are
they deferring to faith in untranslatability as the guarantor of, as Lawrence Rosenwald put it, "the idea of a sacred language distinct from its
secular alternative" (Dimock and Rosenwald)? These questions of translation and theology have moved to the center of philosophical translation
as it works through problems of messianism, fedeism, orthodoxy, doctrinal fidelity, the bounds of secular law, tolerance, ethical neighboring,
the right to offend, literalism, and linguistic monotheism.

## DICTIONARY OF UNTRANSLATABLES

My own keen interest in the untranslatable as both problem and paradigm
arose from collaborative work on the English edition of Barbara Cassin's
2004 *Vocabulaire européen des philosophies: Dictionnaire des intraduisibles* (whose
current working title is "Dictionary of Untranslatables: A Philosophical
Lexicon"). Both a history of philosophy and a massive translation exercise,
the dictionary engaged philosophical translation concretely in experimental

formal registers. It fell somewhere between Diderot and D'Alembert's *Encyclopédie, ou Dictionnaire raisonné des sciences, des arts et des métiers* (1751–66), with articles ranging over such topics as electricity, Africans, sex, monarchy, humankind, and stocking manufacture, and Reinhart Koselleck's *Geschichtliche Grundbegriffe*, a dictionary of political and social concept-history (2004). Unlike these comprehensive counterparts, the *Vocabulaire* aimed to create a multilingual rubric. Though the master language was French and the orientation was toward the Hellenic, scholastic, Enlightenment, and German European traditions, there was a concern to move away from Euro-ontology, as stamped by phenomenology and the French Heideggerians. Cassin was interested in what she called a "metaphysics of particles" (Discussion). Though subject theory was duly represented, the idea was to replace ontological nationalism with an approach that emphasized the shapes of language assuming a national silhouette or personality. Accordingly, entries compared and meditated on the specific differences furnished to concepts by Basque, Catalan, French, Greek, Romanian, Danish, Finnish, Classical Greek, Latin, German, English, Spanish, Hungarian, and Polish. What made the *Vocabulaire* unique was the effort to rewrite the history of philosophy through the lens of the untranslatable, itself identified as a term that was frequently left untranslated as it transferred from language to language (as in the examples of *polis, Begriff, praxis, Aufheben, mimesis, feeling, lieu commun, logos, matter of fact*) or that was constantly subject to mistranslation and retranslation (especially evident in such entries as *subject, translation, world, truth, sense, sovereignty,* and *categories*).

In conceptualizing the original project, Cassin was particularly committed to activating philosophy as medium and life-form. Entry terms were treated neither as static nominalism nor as universals but as live speech acts. Opposed to the model of the dictionary as a concept-mausoleum, Cassin treated words as free radicals, as *parole in libertà*. She devised the construct of *lemmes* (directionals, signposts) as navigating devices that encouraged an aleatory rather than telos-driven *mode d'emploi*.

The *Vocabulaire* significantly defines philosophical translation as the fulcrum of a new untranslatability studies in seven ways.

First, it reinforces the philosophical-theoretical dimension in translation studies, which has tended to emphasize literature. It provides a concrete way of doing philosophy. In the spirit of Derrida's 1979 seminar "The Concept of Comparative Literature and the Theoretical Problems of Translation," it prompts us is to address a key question: Is the right to philosophy a right to translation ("Concept")?

Second, it offers heightened awareness of theologies of untranslatability that emphasize reasons not to translate. Kilito's injunction constitutes a branch of study for philosophy and translation history that investigates laws ensuring that sacred languages be left in a state of nontranslation.

Third, it induces a productive confrontation between Continental and Anglo-analytic traditions. The French *Vocabulaire* actually has quite a bit of analytic philosophy already in it, but it is often skewed in favor of Continental perspectives. In the forthcoming English edition, the decision was made to preserve this skew, on the grounds that part of the project's interest for an anglophone readership was its demonstration of where Continental and analytic philosophy disagree irreconcilably.

Fourth, because the English edition will probably reach a wider readership than the French, I and my coeditors, Jacques Lezra and Michael Wood, hope that as a result the entries will be transformed: contested, refined, and expanded. We are optimistic that by virtue of its reception in Asia, South Asia, Africa, the Middle East, and Latin America, the *Vocabulaire* will serve as an experimental model for future comparatisms and for philosophizing in non-European languages. Ideally the project would be extended to non-European philosophical traditions, while conserving the relay between Europe and non-Europe and the focus on translation, so that the work does not become a generalist encyclopedia of world philosophy. Transferred from print to the electronic medium, the *Vocabulaire* could also be used as a plurilingual wiki: open to all cultural users, live, interactive, and continuously self-updating. The philosophical untranslatable in this respect would emerge as a kind of self-translating machine of the humanities.

Fifth, the project affords an example of how to use translation for collaborative pedagogy. As a work of translation, on translation, and in translation, which interrogates Babel as, in Derrida's words, "the translation of translation" ("Des Tours" 165), it invites analysis of editorial decisions pertaining to the contrivance of particular thesaural systems. It also prompts critical scrutiny of how, paradoxically, translators have translated the untranslatable and where they have run into trouble. (One quickly realizes, for example, that the *contresens*—itself an untranslatable term that can mean "a reversal of intention," "an error," "an opposite sense"—is the gold standard of translation mistakes.) Another great quandary is posed by homonymy. Cassin argues that the Aristotelian refusal of homonymy—which would insist, for example, that "hello cannot mean go to hell," on the principle of noncontradiction, which stipulates that words cannot simultaneously have and not have the same meaning—is contested by the Sophists. Noting that the Aristotelian philosophers' "ban on contradiction is, *mutatis mutandis*, as structuring as the prohibition of incest," Cassin emphasizes the importance of the Sophists, who "play on homonymy in order to shake the univocality of meaning which the principle of all principles demands" ("Philosophising").

Sixth, in addition to serving as a prototype of collective, multiauthored labor, the *Vocabulaire* occasions reflection on how the untranslatable carries in it a philosophy of languages together. What we find in this book is philosophy cast as a political theory of community, built up through the transference and distribution of semantic units that are irreducible, exceptional. The places where languages touch reveal the limits of discrete national languages and traditions. We obtain glimpses of languages in paradoxically shared zones of nonnational belonging at the edge of mutual unintelligibility. Such zones encompass Glissantian opacities (untranslatable nubs located at the edges of spoken and written expression); bilingualism that owns up to the condition of unownable, unclaimable linguistic property; and syntactic *folie* (elaborated by Foucault, Derrida, and Deleuze in the multiple guises of perverse grammatology, nonsense worlds, *schizo-langue*, and crack-up).[8]

Seventh, the *Vocabulaire* should encourage curricular initiatives in the form of courses, colloquiums, and cross-institutional degree programs. Such initiatives might be particularly important for comparative literature as a field called to devise substantive ways of doing deep language work with a theoretical cast. Comparative literature arguably derives its raison d'être from the constant revision of vocabularies of cultural reference. The *Vocabulaire* enables this revisionism because to think the untranslatable is to rethink national units of comparison. The focus on the untranslatable might serve to wean comparative literature from a soft international diplomacy model and from its tendency to search for similarity and identity, screen out disagreement, and avoid direct encounters with insecurable knowledge.

## NOTES

1. Jonathan Rée makes the following case for the importance of translation in the history of philosophy: "In the English language in the twentieth century, . . . many of the finest translations are philosophical, and many of the greatest works of philosophy are translations. Miller's version of Hegel's *Phenomenology*, published in 1977, is brilliant; its only clear drawback is that it has overshadowed the very different but no less marvelous translation by Baillie, dating from 1910. Then there is the meticulous work of several dedicated translators of Husserl, and a remarkable sequence of parallel texts (German and English on facing pages), which began with C. K. Ogden's edition of Wittgenstein's *Tractatus* in 1922, and continued in J. L. Austin's version of Frege's *Foundations of Arithmetic* and G. E. M. Anscombe's of Wittgenstein's *Investigations*. Norman Kemp Smith's commanding version of the *Critique of Pure Reason*

has been read ragged by thousands of students since it was first published in 1929, but hardly any serious weaknesses have come to light. . . . Probably the most magnificent achievement of all, though, is Macquarrie and Robinson's version of Heidegger's *Being and Time*, whose publication in 1962 marked an epoch in the history of philosophy in English" (232).

2. Kamuf writes: "According to the myth Socrates recounts, an Egyptian demigod presented to the king of the gods his invention of writing, calling it a *pharmakon* and praising all the benefits it would bring humankind. The king responded in effect, No, it is not a *pharmakon*, as you pretend; it is rather a *pharmakon*, and you have been deluded by your fondness for this invention of yours. It will not benefit men but deprive them of the benefit they now realize by having to exercise their memories. Between the first and second iteration of the word, the value or meaning of *pharmakon* and thus of writing turns, as Derrida puts it, 'on its strange and invisible pivot.'". . . It is thus already a scene of interpretative translation, from Greek to Greek, where the king gets to decide both what the other *meant to say* and what he *did not say* but *should have said*—in other words, the truth about writing. At stake, then, in transposing into another language this pivotal play is not just the repetition of a same word bearing different and indeed opposable meanings but also the point of view *in* the text from which the true value of writing is decided. What is brought out by Derrida is the reproduction by translation of the point of view and the interpretation of the king."

3. The phrase "saving difference" is coined by Bloom in his response to Derrida's notion of *différance*: "Writing, as Derrida tropes it, both keeps us from the void and, more aggressively (as against voicing), gives us a saving difference, by preventing that coincidence of speaker with subject that would entrap us in a presence so total as to stop the mind" (43).

4. My thanks to David Bellos for his comments on the rich etymological history associated with the Arabic terms for "translator" and "translation."

5. Kilito writes: "Dissemination in space, diversity of languages and colors: that's a positive thing, the concretization of God's design. The confusion of languages is not a malediction, it is a divine sign, like dispersion in space. God installs diversity in his creation, and it is an effect of his merciful will that men are finally disseminated, evidently so as to populate and fructify the planet" (my trans.).

6. Enlisting the ancient philosopher al-Jahiz, Kilito writes, "He is of the opinion that 'poetry cannot, and should not, be translated. When translated, its rhyme is disrupted, its meter ruined, its beauty lost, and its wonder fades'" (*Thou Shalt* 27).

7. A contemporary example of the translational interdict as a form of religious censorship and persecution is the extension of the *fatwah* from Salman Rushdie to the translators of his *Satanic Verses*. The Japanese translator was stabbed to death in 1991. The book's Italian translator was injured in an attack in 1991, the Turkish translator in 1993.

8. On poetic opacity, see Glissant.

# WORKS CITED

Apter, Emily. *The Translation Zone: A New Comparative Literature*. Princeton: Princeton UP, 2006. Print.

Badiou, Alain. *L'hypothèse communiste*. Clamecy: Nouvelles Éditions Lignes, 2009. Print.

Bloom, Harold. *A Map of Misreading.* Oxford: Oxford UP, 1975. Print.

Cassin, Barbara. Discussion of Cassin's *Vocabulaire européen des philosophies*, with Emily Apter. New York U Humanities Initiative. 16 Feb. 2010.

———. "Philosophising in Languages." Trans. Yves Gilonne. Trans. of "Violence de la traduction: Traduire l'intraduisible." *Vingt-deuxièmes assises de la traduction littéraire (Arles 2005).* Paris: Actes Sud, 2006. 167–79. Print.

———. *Vocabulaire européen des philosophies: Dictionnaire des intraduisibles.* Paris: Seuil, 2004. Print.

Derrida, Jacques. "Le concept de littérature comparée et les problèmes théoriques de la traduction." MS. Jacques Derrida Papers MS-C001, box 14, folder 1, U of California, Irvine. Trans. as "Who or What Is Compared? The Concept of Comparative Literature and the Theoretical Problems of Translation." Trans. Eric Prenowitz. *Discourse* 30.1-2 (2008): 22–53. Print.

———. "Des Tours de Babel." Graham, *Difference* 165–207.

———. "La Pharmacie de Platon." *La dissémination.* Paris: Minuit, 1972. 69–199. Print.

———. "Plato's Pharmacy." *Dissemination.* Trans. Barbara Johnson. Chicago: U of Chicago P, 1981. 61–172. Print.

Dimock, Wai Chee, and Lawrence Rosenwald. "Translation and Empire." *Rethinking World Literature.* Dimock, 7 Jan. 2010. Web. *Facebook* forum.

Glissant, Edouard. *Poétique de la relation.* Paris: Gallimard, 1990. Print.

Graham, Joseph F., ed. *Difference in Translation.* Ithaca: Cornell UP, 1985. Print.

———. Introduction. Graham, *Difference* 13–30.

Hassan, Waïl S. "Translator's Introduction." Kilito, *Thou Shalt* vii–xxvi.

Johnson, Barbara. "Taking Fidelity Philosophically." Graham, *Difference* 142–48.

Kilito, Abdelfattah. "Du balcon d'Averroès." *Le cheval de Nietzsche.* Casablanca: Le Fennec, 2007. 155–79. Print.

———. *La langue d'Adam.* Casablanca: Toubkal, 1999. Print.

———. *Thou Shalt Not Speak My Language.* Trans. Waïl S. Hassan. Syracuse: Syracuse UP, 2008. Print.

———. *Tu ne parleras pas ma langue.* Trans. Francis Gouin. Paris: Sindbad, 2002. Print.

Rée, Jonathan. "The Translation of Philosophy." *New Literary History* 32.2 (2001): 223–57. Print.

Robinson, Douglas. "Free Translation." *Routledge Encyclopedia of Translation Studies.* Ed. Mona Baker. London: Routledge, 1998. 113–16. Print.

Van Wyke, Ben. "Translation of Philosophy / Philosophy of Translation." *Seminar Themes. Creoles, Diasporas, Cosmopolitanisms: ACLA Annual Meeting, 2010.* Amer. Comparative Lit. Assn., n.d. Web. 15 June 2010.

# Passing Strange:
# The Laws of Translation

PEGGY KAMUF

*In memory of Barbara Johnson*

To speak of translation as a passage seems to require no passage beyond the literal, proper, or strict sense of the word. In Latinate languages at least, the respective nouns and verbs—*translation/translate, traduction/traduire*, and so forth—mark a movement that bears or leads across, a transferring or ferrying from shore to shore. This movement is transitive: the ferry carries passengers and gives passage to those free agents called meanings, which cannot or should not be stopped at the borders between natural languages. Such commonplaces all seem to circulate without metaphor, transgression, or trespass between that movement called translation and another called passage, as if from one to the other there were in fact no passage, as if the passage from one idea to the other described an impossible movement leading nowhere. In French one could say it is as if *il ne se passe rien* when translation is figured as passage. But this brings into view, in however passing a manner, another figure that ought not to be in the picture at all, which is the figure of the impasse, of no passage, or aporia. How is it that one can so quickly be ferried between the opposing shores of the same figure? That question only plunges one back into the waters where the opposition seems to sink in some curious medium that can keep a channel open between a thing and its opposite, between passage and im-

The author is Marion Frances Chevalier Professor of French and professor of comparative literature and English at the University of Southern California. A version of this paper was presented at the 2009 MLA convention in Philadelphia.

 PROFESSION

passe, and at the same time block any passage between them. Between passage and impasse, in other words, there is at once passage and impasse.

What, then, is this passing strange medium that can suspend logical contradiction in its fluid mixture? How to think translation beginning from such a medium that suspends a meaning from its contrary and in which the very possibility of passing *a* meaning enters an impasse? I begin by referring these questions back to a text that remains indispensable for any thinking of translation today.

First published in 1968, Jacques Derrida's essay "Plato's Pharmacy" is a long reflection in writing on the problem of translation as it is inaugurally framed for Western philosophy by the text of Plato. The problem of translation, which is to say, a problem of passage. Early on in "Plato's Pharmacy," Derrida announces the problem that "we will be dealing with": "With this problem of translation we will be dealing with nothing less than the passage into philosophy" ("Pharmacie" 80; "Plato's Pharmacy" 71–72; trans. slightly modified). The passage into philosophy is a problem from the moment a strange logic can link concepts to their signifiers. For, as initiated by the Platonic legacy, philosophy has to presume the reducibility of the signifier and thus of any particular, natural language system—which is to say, it presumes the translatability of its concepts. The passage into philosophy, therefore, passes not just in practice or in fact by way of translation, because it must do so not only in the sense of the passage from one language to another, but already within a same language, from a nonphilosopheme into a philosopheme.

These two passages are both put into difficulty, or turn into impasses, by what Derrida reads as the effects of *writing*, which is to say, of a *pharmakon*, this term by means of which Plato designates writing in the *Phaedrus*. To be sure *pharmakon* does not carry the sense of writing in any dictionary of ancient Greek one might consult. Like every good writer, Plato is engaged in translating, negotiating passages, operating substitutions between given points in his idiom. Hence he will write a scene of the dialogue in which one character and then another figures "writing" as *pharmakon* and asserts that its meaning or its value is that of a *pharmakon*—in other words, "remedy," "recipe," "poison," "drug," "philter," and so forth. As this scene is meant to highlight an essential dispute as to the evaluation of writing (as distinct from speech and living memory), a passage has to be opened between contrary meanings of the same term, between, on the one hand, meanings like "remedy" and "recipe" and, on the other, those of "poison" and "drug." This intralinguistic passage appears to leave the extralinguistic translator little choice but to translate, for example, here as remedy and there as poison, which seals off the passage that has been opened up by Plato's writing between these contradictory senses. The translator seems obliged to separate out one meaning from the other, thereby *deciding* between them according to the inaugural gesture of the Platonic text that is staging precisely this decision as to the value or meaning of the *pharmakon* and thus of writing. That decision is inaugural, therefore, not only for the evaluation of writing but also for that presumed annex and servant of writing called translation, whose object from then on will be to block the passages writing opens in order to save meaning from the ravages of an essential ambiguity.

The point is that this task does not befall the Western tradition of translation by accident; rather, it is inscribed in the legacy of the Platonic text, which programs both the passage and the impasse, both the linking of opposites and the interruption of that link in a decision to keep *logos* safe from the passe-partout nature of writing. This tradition bequeaths its condemnation of writing and enlists translation to enforce it. I quote from "Plato's Pharmacy":

> [T]his blockage of the passage among opposing values is itself already an effect of "Platonism," the consequence of something already at work in the translated text. . . . All translations into languages that are the heirs and depositaries of Western metaphysics thus produce on the *pharmakon* an *effect of analysis* that violently destroys it, reduces it to one of its simple elements by interpreting it.
> ("Pharmacie" 111–12; "Plato's Pharmacy" 98–99)

If this indictment of a certain tradition of translation seems unreasonably harsh, one needs to recall the scene. According to the myth Socrates recounts, an Egyptian demigod presented to the king of the gods his invention of writing, calling it a *pharmakon* and praising all the benefits it would bring humankind. The king responded in effect, No, it is not a *pharmakon*, as you pretend; it is rather a *pharmakon*, and you have been deluded by your fondness for this invention of yours. It will not benefit men but deprive them of the benefit they now realize by having to exercise their memories. Between the first and second iteration of the word, the value or meaning of *pharmakon* and thus of writing turns, as Derrida puts it, "on its strange and invisible pivot" (97; 109). It is thus already a scene of interpretative translation, from Greek to Greek, where the king gets to decide both what the other *meant to say* and what he *did not say* but *should have said*—in other words, the truth about writing. At stake, then, in transposing into another language this pivotal play is not just the repetition of the same word bearing different and indeed opposable meanings but also the point of view *in* the text from which the true value of writing is decided. What is brought out by Derrida is the reproduction by translation of the point of view and the interpretation of the king.

This indictment of tradition and its inheritance from the king's decisive interpretation bids one to think about another relation between translation and original text, one that forgoes the king's legacy forbidding access to the strange medium from which emerges the anagrammatic writing ascribable to the greatest works of tradition. I want to try to evoke this other relation, even though—and I underscore this point—it will always remain impossible to realize or actualize such a relation. This impossibility, however, does not pose an absolutely limiting condition. If it did, there would be little sense in even speaking about it.

What would this other relation look like? Well, quite simply, like an utterly faithful translation in every respect, replicating in the target language all the same entries and to their entire extent from the source language on top of which the original sits. It would be an exact reproduction of all the links by means of which the original drills into its source, except that the source language would be replaced by the target language and the translation would send its probes down from coordinates that can be mapped only in the translating language. We may suppose that Walter Benjamin was thinking about this other relation when he wrote, in "The Task of the Translator," "Unlike a work of literature, translation does not find itself in the center of the language forest, but on the outside facing the wooded ridge; it calls into it without entering, aiming at this single spot where the echo is able to give, in its own language, the reverberation of the work in the alien one" (76; "Aufgabe" 16).

When Benjamin's essay is judged enigmatic or cryptic, as frequently it has been, perhaps it is in part because Benjamin is also evoking this other, impossible relation between original and translation. His descriptive and even prescriptive formulas for translation leave out of account almost altogether the representative function of translation, the duty to re-present in the other language the meaning, the information, which has been bequeathed to interpretive translation as its primary, if not its sole, object. His search for a "theory that looks for other things in a translation than reproduction of meaning" (78) is bound to appear implausible, if not impossible, when measured against the tradition in which faithfulness is first of all and even exclusively fidelity to *interpreted* meaning—and thus ultimately fidelity to the point of view of the king, whose decisions will have the violent force of that authority.

Yet to what, if not meaning (i.e., interpretation), can translation remain faithful? How can it be faithful without reserve to the text itself, to all its articulations in the vast reserve of its language? Since Benjamin appears to be thinking about only translations of poetic texts, one may wonder if it is this restriction that gives him license to neglect meaning in translation. But what of a philosophical or any other presumably nonpoetic text? Would not nearly everything risk being lost if a translator approached it under this other dispensation, to render not first of all meaning but the writing from the storehouse of the *pharmakon*—which is to say, from the reserve of that paradoxical, uncertain, and polysemous name for writing in a specific language that Derrida has retrieved from the Platonic legacy?

At this point, another aspect of the problem arises: the difference between philosophic and poetic texts is an indissociable part of the legacy that determines translation as first of all an interpretation of meaning. This is an immense question, but one can get close to its root by posing writing as what is at issue there. On the one hand, the poetic text disseminates a voice in writing; cast on the waters of a language and set adrift, it calls to translation as if to a harbor in which to drop anchor before sailing off again on the new ocean of this other language. On the other hand, philosophy's call to translation would appear to emanate not from its writing in some language or other but from meanings that appeal to be given other names in other languages. Ultimately the appeal is made by concepts meant to stand free of any one natural language, in the medium of universality rather than particularity. The measure of the distinction between poetry and philosophy is taken perhaps nowhere more clearly than in translation when it is called on by the one or the other to be faithful.

In speaking of another model of faithfulness, however, one has to keep in mind yet a third albeit impossible kind. To illustrate it, one could take another hint from Benjamin, who famously asserts in the final lines of his essay that "[t]he interlinear version of sacred texts is the prototype or ideal of all translation" (82). Without taking the time to sketch a reading of this conclusion of the essay,[1] I will simply say that the necessity of this gesture appears to arise because translation stands under the laws defining ethical relations in general, provided that by "ethical" one understands everything that concerns responsibility and response to others, which would place translation squarely in its domain. We commonly acknowledge this ethical sense when we speak of the faithfulness or fidelity of translations and likewise of their betrayals, or else of doing or failing to do justice to the other language, the other writing, of respecting or failing to respect the original, and so forth. These modes of speaking about translation are not mere figures of speech that extend ethical categories outside their proper determination. On the contrary, the relation with alterity in general, including with those other animals presumed incapable of speech, has its condition of both possibility and impossibility in what is called translation. It is thus not at all by way of analogy or figure that faithfulness, justice, respect, and, let us add, hospitality are given as laws to translation.

To draw out these laws very rapidly, I return to the work of Derrida. One could take up Derrida's own reading of Benjamin's essay, "Des tours de Babel," so as to draw out the laws of translation in terms of the double bind installed when Yahweh commands Shem both to translate his name but above all not to translate it. This double bind situates the dilemma in which violence and respect can characterize both gestures, translating and not translating. It urges the question, Is it more or less violent to appropriate the other in my language than to refrain from doing so out of respect, but also thereby to refuse every approach, every contact, every comparison—in short, every hospitality? There is here an antinomy, a contradiction in the law of reason. But there is yet a further way to think about this. Rather than as only a contradiction within the law, one has to consider the tension as well as the connection between two different kinds of laws to which translation, like every ethical relation, must answer. This tension cannot be resolved by collapsing the difference between the two orders; indeed, that the difference remain impossible to reduce is the necessary condition on which each may exert the effect of a law. Derrida formalizes this distinction as that between conditional laws and an unconditional law in his later writings on gift, forgiveness, justice, and hospitality. To these names for ethical relations or acts, one should add the relation of translation, which is already implied in each of the others. Like justice or hospitality, then, translation would be subject to conditional or conditioned laws, on the one hand, and, on the other, to the unconditional law, which would be the command to produce an utterly faithful translation in every respect, a faithfulness without reserve to the textuality of the other text, even though such unreserved fidelity is impossible.

To clarify this a little further, let's pretend to speak by way of analogy with hospitality and consider first its unconditional law, hospitality without conditions or limits. An unconditionally hospitable host would withhold nothing from a guest, to the point of dissolving or reversing the very distinction between them. The unconditional law prescribes a hyperbolic transgression of every defining trait by which we think we can recognize this thing called hospitality; it thus quickly may come to resemble a kind of monstrosity or crime: usurpation, invasion, the overriding of every threshold between any one and any other, not only the threshold of the private *chez soi* but also of national territories and their border controls.

It would transgress, *à la limite*, all those conditional, practical, historical, customary, and locally specific laws that regulate hospitality and contain its hyperbole in some bounds. Yet, conditional, customary hospitality, in its limitation, displays another kind of monstrosity, that of oxymoron: it is hospitality but only conditionally, up to a point, the point at which it reverses into a withdrawal or refusal of hospitality, or even into aggressive allergy and hostility. There is thus a kind of double transgression, whereby both the absolute law and the contingent, conditioned laws must transgress against each other, through the steps of what Derrida has dubbed the "pas d'hospitalité" ("Pharmacie" 75).

Reciprocally transgressive hospitality, its absolute law transgressed by its conditioned laws and vice versa, is not all one is summoned to think with this distinction. One must also account for the no less reciprocal *necessity* of the two orders. The unconditional law needs the conditioned laws if it is not to remain abstract and illusory and thus risk being perverted into its opposite. It must, that is, become concrete and conditioned, historical. But likewise reciprocally, the conditional, historical laws would always risk being perverted into something else if they were not, as Derrida writes, "guided, given inspiration, given aspiration, required, even, by the law of unconditional hospitality" (Derrida and Dufourmantelle 79).

These laws of hospitality are not just analogous to but continuous with or implied by laws of translation, both unconditional and conditional. Hospitality's laws are also and indissociably expressed in the terms of a translation across language difference, which is difference not only between so-called natural languages but within a so-called same language, between idioms and signatures, and even between human language and the languages of nonhuman living beings. *Like and as* hospitality, then, translation answers to limited and contingent laws—which is why, and this is all too obvious, its practices are neither historically nor socioculturally invariant. But also, and this may seem at first less obvious, it must answer to its singular and unyielding unconditional law: the impossibility of a faithfulness without reserve.

Without any further semblance of analogy, we could say simply that the unconditional law is required so that, despite its pervertibility, language can continue to name and to translate, for example, "hospitality" without blocking passage of the unconditioned, hyperbolic other. Every translator knows this law thoroughly from the experience of coming before it and reading its demand for absolute, impossible fidelity. The demand is the text's and its unconditional law is written.

# NOTE

1. A longer version of this paper puts forward a reading of the end of Benjamin's essay. See Kamuf.

# WORKS CITED

Benjamin, Walter. "Die Aufgabe des Übersetzers." *Gesammelte Schriften*. Vol. 4.1. Ed. Tillman Rexroth. Frankfurt am Main: Suhrkamp, 1972. 9–21. Print.

———. "The Task of the Translator." *Illuminations*. Trans. Harry Zohn. New York: Schocken, 1969. 69–82. Print.

Derrida, Jacques. "La pharmacie de Platon." *La dissémination*. Paris: Seuil, 1972. 69–197. Print.

———. "Plato's Pharmacy." *Dissemination*. Trans. Barbara Johnson. Chicago: U of Chicago P, 1981. 61–171. Print.

———. "Des tours de Babel." *Psyché: Inventions de l'autre* I. Paris: Galilée, 1998. 203–35. Print.

Derrida, Jacques, and Anne Dufourmantelle. *Of Hospitality*. Trans. Rachel Bowlby. Stanford: Stanford UP, 2000. Print. Trans. of *De l'hospitalité*. Paris: Calmann Lévy, 1997.

Kamuf, Peggy. "Passing Strange: The Laws of Translation." *Nottingham French Studies* 49.2 (2010): 80–91. Print.

# Translation, Empiricism, Ethics

LAWRENCE VENUTI

My case study is drawn from the work of a contemporary translator, Arthur Goldhammer, who is currently a senior affiliate of the Center for European Studies at Harvard University. During the past thirty years, Goldhammer has written English versions of over a hundred French texts in art history, literary theory and history, and philosophy and history of science. By far the bulk of his work falls in the field of social history, monographs and edited volumes by such historians as Philippe Ariès, Georges Duby, Emmanuel Le Roy Ladurie, Jacques Le Goff, and Pierre Nora. It would be no exaggeration to say that countless readers are greatly in Goldhammer's debt.

This remark, however, is an honorific cliché when said of any translator's work, and it sheds no light on what is at stake in translating. We might rather ask, In what does a reader's debt to a translator consist, a debt that clearly exceeds any translation fee (which is paid, in any case, by a publisher)? Can the debt to Goldhammer be reduced to his making intelligible to Anglophones over a hundred French texts? Is it possible to think of translation as a gift that does not incur a debt or participate in a contract, whether with a publisher or a reader? In what would the translator's gift consist and how can it be appreciated beyond debt or contract, whether to the foreign text or culture or to the receiving culture? Can answers to these questions lead to thinking about translation that removes, diminishes, or perhaps redefines the neglect and misunderstanding that it continues to suffer today?

*The author is professor of English at Temple University. A version of this paper was presented at the 2009 MLA convention in Philadelphia.*

         PROFESSION

These questions consider translation vis-à-vis Jacques Derrida's exploration of the paradoxes involved in gift giving. Goldhammer, like most professional translators, is likely to see such speculation as irrelevant. "Translation is hard enough," he has said, "without hamstringing yourself with theoretical *partis pris*" (*How to Do Things*). In lectures where he has set out his own understanding of his approach, his gambit is to analyze verbal choices from various translations. "Together," he tells his audience, "we can walk through some of the questions distilled from daily practice" (*Translating*). The examples he gathers—all instances of outright error or failures to transfer the precise nuance of a word or phrase—point to one overriding question, namely, whether the translation reproduces the style of a literary text or the meaning of a scholarly text. A telling metaphor reveals the concepts underlying Goldhammer's approach. Translation, he asserts, is "like fielding a ground ball: it's almost impossible to explain in words how you do it, and anyone who tried to follow such a description would look pretty foolish on the ballfield. But any spectator can see when the job is being done well" (*Translating*).

This metaphor does assume a theory, the epistemology known as empiricism. According to Antony Easthope's succinct but dissenting account (88–89), empiricism might be said to consist of three key assumptions:

A real object or process is not constructed for knowledge but given, autonomous from the knowing subject, and on observation that object or process yields a knowledge that is free of illusion and prejudice.

The linguistic and cultural forms by which reality is known are transparent and do not materially affect the subject's observation or knowledge.

The subject too is not constructed but autonomous from any process of construction, always free to know, so that knowledge derives from the correspondence between subject and object.

In line with these assumptions, Goldhammer asserts that a good translation can be instantly perceived as such by any reader, and this union of knowing subject and object of knowledge is unmediated by the subject's cultural formation, so that the nature and value of the translation need no description, explanation, or justification, which in any case are "almost impossible" to provide and in the end "pretty foolish."

Insofar as empiricism is characteristic of British and American cultural traditions, emerging with such thinkers as Francis Bacon, Thomas Hobbes, and John Locke and evident, as Easthope shows, not only in philosophical speculation but also in history, poetry, and literary journalism, it produces a distinctively anglocentric image of translation—commonsensical, pragmatic, ultimately anti-intellectual. Under scrutiny, its limitations become apparent. If it is valid, one must wonder why academics, publishers, and readers have not recognized translation as a valuable cultural practice by rewarding it at tenure-and-promotion considerations, issuing a steady stream of translated texts, and reading them with an informed appreciation of their status as second-order creations, as translations. One must wonder why as a rule academics fail to remark on the translations that they use in their research and teaching, going so far as to quote and comment on the translation as if it were the source text. Goldhammer is an extremely accomplished translator, but he cannot present an account of his work that illuminates it for his colleagues, his publishers, or his readers, and so he is powerless to remedy the continuing marginality of translation or to improve its effectiveness as an essential practice in cross-cultural exchange.

Empiricism is a central problem here because it gives rise to a concept of language as direct expression or reference, leading to an instrumental model of translation as the reproduction or transfer of an invariant contained in or caused by the source text, whether its form, its meaning, or its effect. In *An Essay concerning Human Understanding* (1689), Locke assumed the instrumental model in describing translation as "chang[ing] two words of the same signification one for the other" (3.4.9), where the "same signification" refers to a semantic invariant. Instrumentalism continues to guide a great deal of translation practice and research as well as translator training. It is the dominant understanding of translation everywhere today, even among scholars who look at their work as far removed from empiricism because deliberately or explicitly grounded in other theoretical discourses.

To advance the understanding of translation, we must replace instrumentalism by thinking that is hermeneutic. On the materialist assumption that language is creation thickly mediated by linguistic and cultural determinants, a hermeneutic model treats translation as an interpretation of the source text whose form, meaning, and effect are seen as variable, subject to inevitable transformation during the translating process. This is to suggest not that no formal or semantic correspondence exists between the source and translated texts but that any such correspondence results from an interpretive labor that is decisively determined by the translating language and culture. Translating never gives back the source text unaltered. It can only inscribe an interpretation, one among many possibilities, through lexical and syntactic choices that can alter source-textual features like meter and tone, point of view and characterization, narrative and genre, terminology and argument.

The translator inscribes an interpretation by applying a third category, which mediates between the source language and culture, on the one hand, and the receiving language and culture, on the other, a method of transforming the source text into the translation. This third category I call an interpretant, deriving it from Charles Peirce's semiotics. Peirce makes clear that the interpretant constitutes a "mediating representation" between a "sign" or signifier and its "object," where the object is itself a representation, a content or signified (53–54; cf. Eco, *Theory* 69). In Peirce's theory, as Umberto Eco observes, "a sign can *stand for* something else to somebody only because this 'standing-for' relation is mediated by an interpretant" (15). As examples of interpretants, Eco lists a dictionary definition, an encyclopedia entry, a visual image, and a translation into other language, showing that the interpretant functions as a means of performing a semantic analysis: it is a code or theme that invests the sign with a certain intelligibility by transforming it into another chain of signifiers ("Peirce's Notion" 1469; see also Eco, *Theory* 70–71). Eco's discussion becomes somewhat misleading when he lists a translation as an interpretant, insofar as every translation, as I am arguing, requires the application of an interpretant as an essential condition of its existence. With this qualification we can see that interpretants too can precipitate an endless chain of interpretants, codes used to analyze the interpretants in processes like translation.

Peirce himself suggestively compares the notion of an interpretant to translation. He remarks that he relies on this notion "because it fulfills the office of an interpreter, who says that a foreigner says the same thing which he himself says" (53–54). Note that here the interpreter does not merely interpret or orally translate a foreigner's speech but "says" in some unspecified way that his interpretation has met the formal requirement of adequacy or equivalence. An interpretant, it would seem, might be not only thematic in relating a signifier to a signified but formal in indicating the structural nature of the relation.

In translation, the interpretant is a principle of mediation and transformation that is both formal and thematic. Formal interpretants include a concept of equivalence, such as a semantic correspondence based on current dictionary definitions, or a concept of style, a distinctive lexicon and syntax related to a genre. Thematic interpretants are codes: they may be specific values, beliefs, and representations; a discourse in the sense of a relatively coherent body of concepts, problems, and arguments; or a particular interpretation of the source text that has been articulated independently in commentary. Interpretants are fundamentally intertextual and interdiscursive, rooted primarily in the receiving situation even if they incorporate source-cultural materials to some extent. The translator's application of interpretants recontextualizes the source text, replacing intertextual and interdiscursive relations in the source language and culture with relations in the translating language and culture that are built into the translation.

To explore the usefulness of the hermeneutic model, I consider Goldhammer's 1992 translation *The Village of Cannibals*. The French text is the historian Alain Corbin's account of the social and political motives behind an incident of rural violence in nineteenth-century France: a nobleman in the Dordogne was tortured and burned to death by a crowd of peasants. Goldhammer, while making adjustments that conform to the structural features and linguistic norms of English, generally maintained a semantic correspondence according to current French-English dictionaries in a transparent style characteristic of British and American academic history. In fact, his choices recast Corbin's writing in a recognizably academic form. Thus Goldhammer used such formulaic words and phrases as "flourished," "played a crucial role," and "the crux of the matter," all of which are free renderings that deviate from the French text. The word "flourished," employed in the sentence "This myth flourished through much of the nineteenth century," renders "se révélera d'une grande solidité" (in a closer version, "will exhibit great stability"), while the phrase "played a crucial role" renders "constitue un élément décisif" ("constitutes a decisive element") (*Village of Cannibals* 3; *Village des cannibales* 11). Similarly, "the crux of the matter" was used to translate the French word "l'essentiel," which can be Englished as "the essential [thing]" or "the essential [point]" without adopting an academic formula (7, 12; 16, 22). These departures point to Goldhammer's application of a specific formal interpretant in his translation: the stylistic conventions of academic historical writing in anglophone cultures.

Similar conventions underlie Goldhammer's handling of Corbin's frequent use of the term *l'imaginaire*, although here a thematic interpretant can also be perceived: the philosophical code of empiricism. *L'imaginaire* can be closely rendered into English as "the imaginary," but Goldhammer consistently replaced it with such words as "image," "imagination," "imagery," "fancy," even "propaganda" (see *Village des cannibales* 12, 13, 33, 37, 124, 134, 141, 150; *Village of Cannibals* 4, 5, 20, 55, 89, 97, 102, 109). Thus Corbin's assertion that "Il faut le massacre pour que se réalise pleinement la métamorphose ou, plutôt, pour que s'opère la totale incarnation des figures hostiles imposées par l'imaginaire" (66) might be given a close rendering as follows:

> The slaughter was necessary for the metamorphosis to be fully achieved or, better, for the total incarnation of the hostile figures imposed by the imaginary to take place.

Goldhammer, however, translated freely:

> It took a murder to bring about the full metamorphosis of the "Prussian" from figure of the imagination to incarnation of evil.  (46)

In replacing *l'imaginaire* with "the imagination" and related words, Goldhammer's translation draws the sharp distinctions between fact and fiction, truth and falsehood, reality and appearance on which empiricist epistemologies are based.

Yet Corbin's use of the term *l'imaginaire* can be interpreted very differently, according to a materialist genealogy. This genealogy would stretch back at least to Jacques Lacan's 1949 essay "The Mirror Stage As Formative of the Function of the I," where the first moment in the formation of human identity is called the "imaginary phase" but is nonetheless real, "an ontological structure of the human world" that establishes the basis for the subsequent construction of subjectivity through interpersonal relationships and in language (2). During the 1960s, this psychoanalytic concept was given a social application, when Louis Althusser relied on Lacan to rethink the Marxist concept of ideology, not as political ideas or false consciousness but as a representation embodied in social practices, at once imaginary and lived, active in forming class identities and in mystifying real social relations ("Ideology" and "Marxism"). At roughly the same time, the political theorist Cornelius Castoriadis formulated the imaginary as a concept of social analysis that bears even more directly on Corbin's use of the term. The "social imaginary," according to Castoriadis, "is not an image *of*. It is the unceasing and essentially *undetermined* (social-historical and psychical) creation of figures/forms/images, on the basis of which alone there can ever be a question *of* something" (3). In Castoriadis's thinking, the materialism assigned to the concept by Lacan and Althusser comes to the fore such that the imaginary not only is indistinguishable from but also creates reality. Corbin's argument that the murdered nobleman came to embody the peasants' social imaginary might thus be seen as giving the concept the same ontological status that it has in Castoriadis's work.

Philippe Carrard has criticized Goldhammer's translation for its departures from Corbin's French text, particularly in "simplifying his theoretical apparatus" (81). The matter is more complicated, because Goldhammer's translation cannot be judged simply as inaccurate or incorrect. He has offered an interpretation that is neither incompetent nor arbitrary by applying a distinctive set of formal and thematic interpretants. His interpretation included the idea that, as he put it in an interview,

Corbin is not "a particularly theoretically self-conscious historian" but rather one who takes "a more literary, intuitive approach." Corbin himself examined Goldhammer's translation in unusual detail, sending the translator five pages of handwritten notes. Goldhammer explained that "nearly all the comments had to do with the 'weight' and 'coloration' of specific word choices. [Corbin] didn't raise any issues of theoretical interpretation/misinterpretation" (Message).

Accustomed as we are to disallowing authorial intent as a reliable standard of interpretation, we might well be suspicious of Corbin's assessment of the translation. Yet the fact remains that whether Corbin deploys the concept of *l'imaginaire* with rigorous consistency can be questioned, primarily because the historical incident he addresses raises the issue of delusion. It involved a false attribution to the victim: the crowd of peasants accused the nobleman of shouting "Vive la République!" and of being a Prussian, although at the murderers' trial neither accusation was found to be true. Corbin argues that the nobleman was transformed into a scapegoat by the peasants' social imaginary, a contradictory ensemble of antiaristocratic, antirepublican, and proimperial sentiments, but he occasionally uses the term *fantasmes* ("fantasies") to describe the gap between their collective anxieties and the identity and actions of their victim (e.g., see Corbin, *Village des cannibales* 119, 120). Goldhammer has in effect chosen to emphasize Corbin's use of terms like *fantasmes* instead of assigning a specifically French conceptual density or intertextual relation to his use of *l'imaginaire*. In setting up this choice as the equivalent of the French text, the translator has performed the "abstraction" that Althusser saw in empiricist truth claims, a procedure in which essential data are separated from the inessential on the basis of a privileged epistemology and in which a real object is reduced to a partial object of knowledge (Althusser and Balibar 34–43).

Goldhammer's translation thus reflects a deep investment in empiricist discourse. On the one hand, the assumption that language is transparent communication led Goldhammer to reject any jargon that too noticeably departed from current Standard English, the most familiar form of the language and therefore the most seemingly transparent. On the other hand, the assumption that historical writing discovers an objective truth based on facts led him to avoid theoretical concepts that posited the difficulty, if not impossibility, of distinguishing between textuality and reality and that thereby put into question the historian's objectivity. He inscribed the French text with the empiricism that continues to dominate British and American academic history and informs his own instrumental theory of translation.

How, then, should Goldhammer's translation be evaluated? The instrumental model is of no help here. The invariant that it assumes is contained in or caused by the source text—its form, meaning, or effect—becomes the sole criterion of accuracy and therefore fundamentally determines the value of the translation. Yet Corbin's text, particularly his use of the term *l'imaginaire*, can support at least two conflicting interpretations inscribed by two different translations. The hermeneutic model offers a more incisive and comprehensive account, because it treats any formal and semantic correspondence as partial and contingent: partial, because it is incomplete in re-creating the source text and slanted toward the receiving language and culture; contingent, because it is fixed by one among other possible interpretations, each of which establishes a criterion of accuracy that varies among receiving cultural constituencies, social situations, and historical moments.

Because translating always submits the source text to a transformation, a translation cannot be evaluated merely through a comparison to that text without taking into account the cultural and social conditions of the translator's interpretation. The evaluation must be shifted to a different level, a level that seems to me properly ethical: in inscribing an interpretation in the source text, a translation can stake out an ethical position and thereby perform an ideological function in relation to competing interpretations. Here I draw on Alain Badiou's thinking, specifically his concept of an ethics that challenges institutionalized knowledges and communitarian interests and pursues cultural innovation and social equality. Badiou's ethics raises a number of questions, not the least of which is his antipathy toward the communitarian, as if every social grouping were exclusionary or repressive, enforcing conformity and domination (73–74). I want precisely to worry this point in his thinking, treating as unethical not knowledge that serves any communitarian interest whatsoever but only knowledge affiliated with a group that has achieved such dominance in an institution as to exclude or marginalize the competing knowledge of other groups. A translation in the human sciences, then, might be evaluated according to its impact, potential or real, on academic disciplines in the translating culture; according to whether it challenges the styles, genres, and discourses that have gained disciplinary authority; according to whether it stimulates innovative thinking, research, and writing and alters the course of the institution.

I would therefore question translators who conceive of their role as the importation of foreign thinking without affecting the smooth operation of the academic institutions where that thinking is to be received. Goldhammer has advocated such a role, arguing that "scholarly prose is written for consumption primarily by a scholarly community, and the translator must respect the linguistic norms of the target community" (*Translating*). But Goldhammer has done much more: he has assimilated Corbin's French text to the styles and discourses that are invested with the greatest authority among British and American academic historians. His translation professes a greater sense of responsibility toward this audience than toward Corbin's project or French historical discourses. This is the crucial sense in which anglophone academic historians are in Goldhammer's debt.

The mostly positive reviews that greeted the translation, reviews that favorably received Corbin's work and only rarely mentioned Goldhammer's, demonstrate that the translation was successful according to the empiricist terms that the translator shared with his main academic audience. In a typical review that appeared in the *Times Literary Supplement*, Robert Tombs, a specialist in French history at Cambridge University, praised Corbin's text as providing a "startling picture of some of the grim realities of rural life, narrated simply and sensitively, and translated plainly, so that the horrors of the act of retribution still emerge starkly amid the theoretical exegesis." Tombs's investment in empiricist history is evident in his preference for a "simple" narration that is not complicated by "theoretical exegesis." To call Goldhammer's translation "plain" also fits this bill, given its seeming transparency, but Tombs seems entirely unaware of the strongly assimilative nature of the English version, which reduces the term "plain" to a naive understatement.

Let us rather imagine a translator who assumes an oppositional stance in his or her work, a translator who is an intellectual in Edward Said's sense, "skeptical, engaged, unremittingly devoted to rational investigation and moral judgment" (20), refusing any complacency or quiescence in relation to authoritative cultural and social institutions like the academy and the publishing industry—even when the translator is employed by them. This translator will be constantly alert to the differences that comprise foreign languages, texts, and cultures, constantly engaged in signaling those differences to constituencies and institutions in the receiving situation, and constantly inventive in finding the linguistic and cultural means to make a productive difference in that situation. Such a translator gives us the basis of a relentless interrogation of the academic status quo. The resulting translation is not given or recognized as a gift, whether to the foreign text and culture or to the receiving situation, and it is not written with the expectation of a reward, insofar as it aims at a radical questioning of the rewarding institution, of the hierarchy of values, beliefs, and representations housed in that institution. This translation—need I say?—is not likely to be received with gratitude, which it does not seek, but it may construct a new intellectual community that did not previously exist and that, when the translation has done its interrogative work, will set it aside, its work done, its critical moment past. Is this translation with a hammer, initiating a transvaluation that establishes a new critical orthodoxy? Or is this translation that is self-consuming, that sacrifices itself in its very reception, eventually superseded? Can it be both, so that we remain trapped in yet another cliché, although now revised, the notion that translation is a thankless task?

## WORKS CITED

Althusser, Louis. "Ideology and Ideological State Apparatuses." *"Lenin and Philosophy" and Other Essays*. Trans. Ben Brewster. London: Monthly Rev., 1970. 127–86. Print.

———. "Marxism and Humanism." *For Marx*. Trans. Ben Brewster. London: New Left, 1977. 219–47. Print.

Althusser, Louis, and Étienne Balibar. *Reading Capital*. Trans. Ben Brewster. London: New Left, 1970. Print.

Badiou, Alain. *Ethics: An Essay on the Understanding of Evil*. Trans. Peter Hallward. London: Verso, 2001. Print.

Carrard, Philippe. "Taming the New History: Alain Corbin and the Politics of Translation." *History of the Human Sciences* 6 (1993): 79–90. Print.

Castoriadis, Cornelius. *The Imaginary Institution of Society*. Trans. Kathleen Blamey. Cambridge: MIT P, 1998. Print.

Corbin, Alain. *Le village des cannibales*. Paris: Aubier, 1990. Print.

———. *The Village of Cannibals: Rage and Murder in France, 1870*. Trans. Arthur Goldhammer. Cambridge: Harvard UP, 1992. Print.

Derrida, Jacques. *Given Time: 1: Counterfeit Money*. Trans. Peggy Kamuf. Chicago: U of Chicago P, 1972. Print.

Easthope, Antony. *Englishness and National Culture*. London: Routledge, 1999. Print.

Eco, Umberto. "Peirce's Notion of Interpretant." *MLN* 91 (1976): 1457–72. Print.

———. *A Theory of Semiotics*. Bloomington: Indiana UP, 1976. Print.

Goldhammer, Arthur. *How to Do Things with Style*. 24 Jan. 1997. Center for European Studies, Harvard U, n.d. Web. 9 Feb. 2010.

———. Message to the author. 4 Oct. 2004. E-mail.

———. *Translating Subtexts: What the Translator Must Know*. Center for European Studies, Harvard U, n.d. Web. 9 Feb. 2010.

Lacan, Jacques. *Écrits: A Selection*. Trans. Alan Sheridan. New York: Norton, 1977. Print.

Locke, John. *An Essay concerning Human Understanding*. Ed. Peter H. Nidditch. Oxford: Oxford UP, 1975. Print.

Peirce, Charles S. *The Writings of Charles S. Peirce: A Chronological Edition, 1867–1871*. Vol. 2. Ed. Edward C. Moore. Bloomington: Indiana UP, 1984. Print.

Said, Edward W. *Representations of the Intellectual*. New York: Random, 1994. Print.

Tombs, Robert. "Roasting a Fine Pig." *Times Literary Supplement* 16 Oct. 1992: 22. Print.

# Teaching in— and about—Translation

## SANDRA BERMANN

Comparative literature and translation have long been intersecting fields. And translations have long been integral to the teaching of comparative literature. But recently the use of translations in our classrooms has become far more pervasive. This development is not surprising, given the increasing range of texts being taught in comparative literature—and given the increasing importance of translation in a world transformed by globalization, war, and migration. Ours is by any standard a culturally interwoven and interdependent world. Whether we are watching the news or reading a favorite novel, translation is part of our everyday lives. But translation's effects on literary education are, I believe, just beginning to be explored. Helping our students think *about* translation as they read a growing number of works *in* translation can create modes of teaching— and learning—that are more keenly attuned to the particular languages, literatures, and cultures of our planet. It is one of the ways we can prepare our students for life in a global, polylingual world.

There are some clear disciplinary reasons why comparative literature might want to teach not only in but also about translation, now more than ever before. I begin by describing the history of comparative literature's growing connections to translation and translation studies. I then turn to ways in which translation is transforming the field of literary studies more generally through its attention to three areas: translation and lan-

The author is Cotsen Professor of the Humanities, professor of comparative literature, and chair of the Department of Comparative Literature at Princeton University. A version of this paper was presented at the 2009 MLA convention in Philadelphia.

     PROFESSION

guage, translation and world literature, and translation and collaboration. In conclusion, I consider how these issues might be incorporated more fully into the university curriculum.

## Disciplinary History

Comparative literature is often described as the transnational and interdisciplinary study of literature. As Haun Saussy reminds us, its interests reach outward, encouraging encounters with other literatures, media, and disciplines. At the same time, it is a field with a theoretical bent, engaged in ongoing analyses of what we do as well as how and why. Translation is important to comparative literature because it not only extends literary study to new cultures, languages, and texts; it also opens the field to important theoretical reflections. This dual role of translation in comparative literature, and in literary study in general, is relatively new.

In the 1960s and much of the 1970s, comparative literature still focused almost exclusively on a historical study of the major European literatures. These were read, whenever possible, in the original language. But in the later twentieth century, thanks in large part to new interest in cultural studies and postcolonial studies and responding to changes in the material world as well, the field extended its geolinguistic reach. Its emphasis on language learning did not decrease. But with its growing investment in languages, literatures, and cultures from many parts of the globe, far more translations entered the classroom. At the same time, the field's increased commitment to interdisciplinary work brought intersemiotic translations—film, music, theater, dance, photography, and digital representation (Bernheimer, *Comparative Literature* 21–48).

In this vastly expanded zone of late-twentieth-century comparative study, which I have elsewhere called the "and zone," comparative literature encountered, with new eagerness and insight, the discipline of translation. True, comparative literature was, from the first, accompanied by translation. But for most of its twentieth-century history, translation as a field of practice or theory remained unexplored, largely because the comparatist was, after all, meant to read texts only in the original.

By the time comparative literature turned explicitly to the use of translation in the 1990s (see Bernheimer, "Bernheimer Report"), translation had itself emerged as a distinct disciplinary field. Coming into its own in the 1960s and 1970s (Bassnett, *Comparative Literature* and *Translation Studies*), translation studies grew in importance as the material and social structures of our world became more global, with the spread of financial, information, and military networks; with an increasing migration of peoples; and with war (Apter). As the century came to a close, the role of translation could be seen in the growing use of translations in literature courses, particularly in world literature. It could also be tracked in the growing number of theoretical questions it posed. Comparative literature became a major site for reading in translation but also for reflecting on a series of new theoretical issues. Comparative literature is already a different discipline thanks to this encounter.

Translation's effects have been primarily interrogative rather than prescriptive. Three particular sets of questions recur with unusual frequency. I describe them briefly here, moving from the micro level of translation and language to the question of translation and world literature, then finally to institutional matters of translation and collegial collaboration. Joining them all is a heightened awareness of polylingualism and, with it, the increasing importance of dialogue both within and outside the academy. Unlike some theoretical reflections, those of translation have both philosophical and practical implications—for our universities and the profession as a whole.

## TRANSLATION AND LANGUAGE

Translations are texts in which other languages can be heard—whether as distant echoes or as distinct dialogues. In either case, translations emphasize the play of other and self, different and same, stranger and host as they ask us to rethink what we mean by "a language." Roman Jakobson's definition of three modes of translation—interlingual, intralingual, and intersemiotic—already suggested the interplay not only of signs but also of sign systems. Jacques Derrida's meditations on translation develop a more thoroughly differential perspective, emphasizing the polysemous and dialogic quality of all languages, if most clearly the postcolonial ones.

Theorists today, from Edouard Glissant to Homi Bhabha to Paul Bandia and others, are extending and transforming these inquiries as they draw attention to notions of linguistic and cultural doubleness, hybridity, or heteroglossia that arise very pointedly in a postcolonial and globalized world. Thinking about translation in these contexts challenges conventional ideas about language itself as well as about the writing—and reading—of literary texts. As Glissant makes clear, several traditions can and usually do lie embedded in what we call a single language. An awareness of the importance of oral literatures, creoles, vernaculars, and the multilingualism that in fact affects the histories of all languages and literatures deepens—and changes—what we mean by "language" (see esp. 89–120).

Thinking about language and languages in such theoretical terms suggests some of the challenges of translation as well as its role in literary and cultural history. As translations and translators frequently remind us, linguistic translation means cultural translation. Yet no matter how well prepared and carefully wrought, no matter how deep the linguistic and cultural knowledge of the translator, translation does not and cannot reproduce its already complex source. Rather, it negotiates with it, transforming culture through culture, languages through languages. Translation allows a text to live on in another culture and time (Benjamin). But translation also questions and disrupts a text from a new cultural standpoint, raising unanticipated questions in the cultures that now read it.

In ways such as these, the language of translation suggests—and in some sense embodies—the dialogue and the complex ethical choices that guide the study of texts in a global, cross-cultural, and cross-disciplinary context. As Antoine Berman writes, an ethic of hospitality inhabits the work of translation. A dialogue exists there between a stranger and a self, a linguistic-cultural other and a linguistic-cultural same. A stranger—indeed, strangers—inhabit its text. It is the job of the translator and the privilege of the reader to begin to explore this otherness.

## Translation and World Literature

Growing interest in a more global range of readings—particularly visible in world literature programs in the United States and abroad—raises both challenges and hopes. Might the teaching of world literature, in its many translations, promote that conversation of languages and cultures that engages students and readers with the narratives, poetries, and complex histories of our globe's often conflicting geolinguistic sites? And might this conversation lead to a more respectful and responsible relationship among cultures?

The increasing presence of world literature courses on our campuses is particularly promising if they can be taught with keen awareness of the specificity of languages and cultures implicit in each text. Such teaching can prevent our too easily homogenizing or generalizing these readings. Thinking about translation keeps attention focused on textual issues. Moreover, teaching literatures with an awareness of language and translation introduces historical dimensions that emphasize the political and social questions affecting them. Such questions are implicit in David Damrosch's definition of world literature as "any literary text that circulates outside its context of origin" (4). How in fact does a text circulate? What is its translation history?

Translation histories inevitably have very worldly dimensions. Political, informational, financial, technical, religious issues all affect the act, even the possibility, of translation as well as a text's eventual dissemination and reception. We'll want to know how various texts have been translated, by whom and for what purposes—political, literary, economic, religious. Questions can arise about how such translations affect original-language authors and the languages in which they write. We can also consider why some translated texts remain so very difficult, if also so very important to understand.

In asking these questions, issues of inequality become salient. Some languages are never translated at all. Are there situations in which not to translate might be seen as the best cultural translation? Considering such questions brings specific socioeconomic, political, and religious issues to the fore. Ngũgĩ wa Thiong'o speaks of translation as ideally a conversation, a dialogue of equals to which we might aspire as we rethink relations in our globalized world. Is this ideal at all possible? Could it lead to a more constructive and responsive global consciousness? Although translation offers the potential to create a less hierarchical conversation among different world cultures large and small, such a conversation will depend on understanding the risks, difficulties, and power relations that translation entails. We can teach this understanding as we teach texts in translation.

## TRANSLATION AND COLLABORATION

On the macro level of institutional planning, translation can elicit very practical efforts of collaboration—bringing the dialogue intrinsic to the language of translation to an interpersonal, interinstitutional, and at times international level. Increasingly, collaboration affects our teaching. Using translations to reach different cultures and disciplines in our courses, we collaborate with colleagues, and often with students, of different linguistic and cultural expertise.

Collaboration can also create new courses and programs that focus on the question of translation and underscore its importance to literary analysis and to the real world. Here opportunities to teach about translation have the advantage of drawing together colleagues from many divisions of the university and disseminating the humanistic knowledge of language and interpretation more broadly on campus. Here the relational qualities associated with translation are staged as well as interpreted. Here new and unforeseen theoretical and practical questions tend to arise. For translation is a topic that inevitably shuttles between issues in the everyday world and those in the academy. It encourages us to think about the skills we teach as well as the attitudes we instill in young people about to set out into a global, interdependent world.

## Practicum

Though comparative literature courses may be particularly well situated to focus on translation issues, any course in which a translation is used and in which there is time to discuss it in some detail can become a site for raising translation's linguistic and textual questions in concrete form. As students read a translation, be it of Rainer Maria Rilke or Sor Juana de la Cruz, they might be asked to experiment with a translation of their own—producing it independently or in collaboration with those who know the pertinent language. If the language is unknown to most students, they can work with a line-by-line translation provided by the professor. Another effective strategy is to compare several translations of a short text to underscore each translator's different interpretive priorities. Both modes allow students and professors to engage with questions of the languages and practices of translation. And both prepare the class well for other sorts of comparative topics.

World literature courses or other courses bringing together texts from different cultures easily prompt linguistic, historical, and political questions. The course syllabus can provide an entry: How has the presence or absence of published translations affected what we read in the course? Who has decided what is translated and what is available on our bookshelves, in our libraries, and on the Web? How has translation been perceived in different periods of history and by different language and cultural groups? The story of the linguistic and cultural transmission of a text (such as *One Thousand and One Nights* or Dante's *Inferno*) can illuminate both the complex trade routes of a given text and what we mean by world literature. Such linguistic and cultural transit can provide the basis of an entire course, allowing students to note how texts move beyond their original literary or cultural context to affect other cultures while being transformed in turn. Such studies could also focus on contemporary texts. Works by a figure such as Amitav Ghosh, where translation is sometimes simultaneous with original-language publication, can provide intriguing discussions about world literature and its texts today.

Collaboration in the form of team teaching for world literature courses can and often does bring together scholars from different disciplines and linguistic backgrounds. Some world literature projects are already reaching beyond individual campuses to involve scholars in international as well as interinstitutional collaborations. The result is a heightened awareness of linguistic and cultural specificity in courses that are by nature broad, that often move quickly.

Collaboration in other sorts of courses might also prove fruitful. One of the most dramatic ways to teach not only in but also about translation is to create new courses and programs that focus on translation itself. Translation studies is a growing field in the humanities, and it is often through programs in translation that its questions can affect the university curriculum most directly. Translation can be linked to theoretical and practical issues both. From such work, the translators and interpreters called for by a recent MLA report might even emerge (MLA Ad Hoc Committee).

Though there are still few programs in the United States that train professional interpreters and translators and only a few graduate programs in the field so far, an increasing number of departments are developing courses and programs on the undergraduate level. There are several ways to approach this curricular change, but the simplest is to create a course emanating from a department of comparative literature (or the humanities, or another language and literature department) that would be intended for a broad population of students.

One could also combine this central course with other offerings already taught in literature departments and elsewhere in the university, in order to structure a program joining several departments and a broad set of colleagues. From my experience working with Michael Wood to create Princeton's Program in Translation and Intercultural Communication, I know this can be a particularly exciting—and economical—way to extend teaching in and about translation to other divisions of the university. If time and resources exist, one might establish a center for translation, as has been done in a number of Canadian and European universities, one that could offer courses from the undergraduate level to the graduate and professional levels.

Any of these alternatives extends the study of translation to more university students and colleagues. Such programs can have deep and positive effects on campus and off. They underscore the importance of language learning, sending students to study abroad and take courses in language and literature departments. They also lead to initiatives in the less frequently taught languages. As Gayatri Spivak has taught us, the deep learning of languages and cultures remains one of the best preparations for reading as well as writing translations—and this learning ought not be only of the languages we most commonly teach (*Death* 9–12, 106n12; "Politics"; and "Translating").

As students pursue the study of languages and cultures, as they think about translation in the university and in the everyday world, they often engage in volunteer translation projects and develop their own translation workshops on campus. For faculty members in interdepartmental translation programs, the challenging ideas gained from colleagues in disparate fields are a major attraction. All concerned learn much about the politics of language in our world and the power relations that affect translation in particular. They also suggest ways in which translation can be part of our work both in and outside the academy.

If our students, faculty members, and administrators develop a greater awareness of and respect for translation in the twenty-first century, we will come one step nearer to understanding the languages, cultures, and histories of our world, and more translations, translators, and readings will engage with the questions and new interpretive possibilities that translation poses. Encouraging these trends through research, teaching, and curricular innovation, comparative literature can contribute importantly—and visibly—to an innovative, humanities-oriented university education.

## NOTE

Parts of this essay were presented at the ADE-ADFL seminar in June 2009; some have also appeared in expanded form in my ACLA Presidential Address, "Working in the And Zone."

## WORKS CITED

Apter, Emily. *The Translation Zone: A New Comparative Literature*. Princeton: Princeton UP, 2006. Print.

Bandia, Paul. *Translation as Reparation: Writing and Translation in Postcolonial Africa*. Manchester: St. Jerome, 2008. Print.

Bassnett, Susan. *Comparative Literature*. Oxford: Blackwell, 1993. Print.

———. *Translation Studies*. Rev. ed. London: Routledge, 1991. Print.

Benjamin, Walter. "The Task of the Translator: An Introduction to the Translation of Baudelaire's *Tableaux parisiens*." Trans. Harry Zohn. Venuti 75–85.

Berman, Antoine. *The Experience of the Foreign: Culture and Translation in Romantic Germany*. Trans. S. Heyvaert. Albany: State U of New York P, 1992. Print.

Bermann, Sandra. "Working in the And Zone: Comparative Literature and Translation." *Comparative Literature* 61.4 (2009): 432–46. Print.

Bernheimer, Charles. "The Bernheimer Report, 1993: Comparative Literature at the Turn of the Century." Bernheimer, *Comparative Literature* 39–48.

———, ed. *Comparative Literature in an Age of Multiculturalism*. Baltimore: Johns Hopkins UP, 2004. Print.

Bhabha, Homi. *The Location of Culture*. New York: Routledge, 1994. Print.

Damrosch, David. *What Is World Literature?* Princeton: Princeton UP, 2003. Print.

Derrida, Jacques. *Monolingualism of the Other; or, The Prosthesis of Origin*. Trans. Patrick Mensah. Stanford: Stanford UP, 1998. Print.

Glissant, Edouard. *Poetics of Relation*. Trans. Betsy Wing. Ann Arbor: U of Michigan P, 1997. Print.

Jakobson, Roman. "On the Linguistic Aspects of Translation." Venuti 138–43.

MLA Ad Hoc Committee on Foreign Languages. *Foreign Languages and Higher Education: New Structures for a Changed World*. New York: MLA, 2007. PDF file.

Ngũgĩ wa Thiong'o. "The Language of Languages." *To Be Translated or Not to Be: PEN/IRL Report on the International Situation of Literary Translation*. Ed. Esther Allen. Barcelona: Inst. Ramon Llull, 2007. 131. Print.

Saussy, Haun. "Exquisite Cadavers Stitched from Fresh Nightmares." *Comparative Literature in an Age of Globalization*. Ed. Saussy. Baltimore: Johns Hopkins UP, 2004. 3–42. Print.

Spivak, Gayatri Chakravorty. *Death of a Discipline*. New York: Columbia UP, 2003. Print.

———. "The Politics of Translation." Venuti 369–88.

———. "Translating into English." *Nation, Language, and the Ethics of Translation*. Ed. Sandra Bermann and Michael Wood. Princeton: Princeton UP, 2005. 93–111. Print.

Venuti, Lawrence, ed. *The Translation Studies Reader*. 2nd ed. New York: Routledge, 2004. Print.

# Teaching Baudelaire,
# Teaching Translation

JONATHAN CULLER

In Nicholson Baker's novel *The Anthologist*, Paul Chowder, a poet and anthology maker, describes encountering poems in the *New Yorker* or another magazine:

> You locate the poem, because you're naturally curious to see what this week's or this month's trawl is. . . . There it is. You take in the title—"Way Too Much." Way too much: Okay! And then you check the name of the writer—hmm, Squeef Corntoasty, never heard of him. Or: I sure have seen Squeef Corntoasty's name popping up in a lot of places lately. Or if it says "translated from the Czech by Bigelow Jones," forget it, you instantly move on, because translations are never any good.
>
> Well, wait—that's not fair. That's ridiculously unfair. I've read some wonderful translations. . . . But my heart does droop when I see that it's a translation. (68–69)

We say poetry is what gets lost in translation—an adage that suggests the hapless lot of the translator. Translating poetry is a mug's game. Most enterprises offer at least some hope of success, but the translator of poetry operates in a context where failure is defined as inevitable. Doomed to struggle with the differences between languages and with the material of languages themselves, you have little hope of producing something that will be praised. The most you can hope for, it seems, is that people will take enough notice of your translation to point out the aspects of the original that it fails to capture.

*The author is Class of 1916 Professor of English and professor of comparative literature at Cornell University. A version of this paper was presented at the 2009 MLA convention in Philadelphia.*

One context in which this problem can be turned to advantage—not to the advantage of translators, I'm afraid, but at least to someone's advantage—is the pedagogical one. When I teach a course on Charles Baudelaire, I generally get quite a few students who want to take a course with me but whose French is weak and who need the help of translations. My policy has been that the state of their French is their problem, not mine—I'm not going to stop to translate. But I have found that the presence of linguistically challenged students and the introduction of translations into the discursive space of the classroom can actually be pedagogically beneficial. If we look at a translation or translations alongside a poem by Baudelaire, questions about the effectiveness and accuracy of a translation are a spur to discussion. The students with a better knowledge of French are happy to display this for the benefit of their less fortunate peers. And, particularly important for me, the route through translation provides an easy way to raise questions about formal features of the poems, which in ordinary discussions either get neglected or else require an insistence by the teacher that seems fussy and pedantic. Usually, when discussing a poem, asking questions about the meter or rhyme scheme seems an academic distraction from the interpretive question of what the poem means, but since formal patterning—meter, rhyme, other sorts of phonological repetition—is one dimension on which poem and translation will differ markedly, the subject comes up naturally when translation is in play. Questions about the choices affecting rhythm, meter, rhyme, and phonological patterning are immediately relevant. They are not easy to answer, but they are unavoidable. Moreover, commenting on something that a translation missed seems less high-stakes to students than offering an interpretive comment to a large seminar. Translations can also generate disagreement more easily than discussion about the poem itself. If these days students are less inclined to disagree with one another in class than they used to be, disagreeing about a translation seems to involve less of a challenge to the other person.

Above all, comparing translations highlights features of the original. If we are discussing Baudelaire's "Correspondances," whose famous first stanza runs

> La Nature est un temple où de vivants piliers
> Laissent parfois sortir de confuses paroles;
> L'homme y passe à travers des forêts de symboles
> Qui l'observent avec des regards familiers.          (11)

we might compare first some prose translations. Keith Waldrop, winner of the National Book Award, translates the first stanza: "Nature is a temple whose columns are alive and often issue disjointed messages. We thread our way through a forest of symbols that peer out, as if recognizing us" (14). Clive Scott offers a version "that tries to push prose as close to a verse translation as it can": "Nature is a temple: from time to time, its living pillars sibylline, let slip bewildering words. We pass along these aisles, through symbols forest-thick, followed by eyes that know our minds" (159–60). Scott's version is more engaging, doubtless because of the half rhymes or assonances that give the passage some structure (*time-sibylline-minds, aisles-eyes*) and because of the more clearly articulated rhythm (Scott says he is trying to create a text with "a firm bearing rhythm" [160]), and it boldly marks the *confuses paroles* as "sibylline," unclear yet enigmatic and potentially prophetic rather than simply disjointed (Baudelaire's rhyming of *paroles* and *symboles* is relevant here). Scott also makes a choice about *regards familiers*, which is ambiguous in the French—familiar to us, or overly knowing—rendering in a different way ("know our minds") some of the uncanniness that in the French may stem from this ambiguity. Waldrop's "thread our way" is a skillful rendition of *passe à travers*, which most verse translations do not try to capture, but his "as if recognizing us" not only is clunky but strangely introduces an "as if" focused on action rather than on the uncanny quality of these symbols. His "peer out," however, while somewhat awkward, especially with the transposition of *forêts* into the singular, does hint at the paranoia that may lurk behind this verse of Baudelaire's (think of Nerval's "Crains, dans le mur aveugle, un regard qui t'épie" ["Fear in the blind wall a look that spies on you" (my trans.)]). But both these translations, perhaps because of the normalizing pull of prose, shift the third person to the first-person plural, from *l'homme* to "we," which is out of keeping with the deliberate impersonality of the poem (as contrasted with, say, Baudelaire's sonnet "Obsession," which translates this impersonal situation into psychological terms: "Grands bois, vous m'effrayez comme des cathédrales" (75; "Woods, you scare me like cathedrals" [my trans.]).[1] Though the translators might argue that today "man" is tied to presumptions of male privilege that are irrelevant to the poem (though certainly not to Baudelaire in general!), still the insertion of a first-person pronoun in a poem distinctive for its lack of them transforms the poem in a significant way.

How do these compare with verse renderings? Roy Campbell, Francis Cornford, James McGowan, Allen Tate, and Richard Wilbur all use "man," the appropriate term to oppose to *Nature* in the parallel structure Baudelaire sets up and a term that may be less ideological in verse than in normalizing prose.[2] William Crosby offers "mankind," which could in principle be a good solution, despite its breaking of the parallelism, though his future tense, "Here mankind will cross by" either projects a singular future event, which is something quite different, or imagines a destiny with an unclear "cross by":

> Nature is a temple where the living pillars
> Permit from time to time confused words to escape;
> Here mankind will cross by, where symbols take the shape
> Of forests gazing on his progress like familiars.　　　(29–31)

His choice brings out, by deviating from the original, the fact that Baudelaire's sonnet imagines not a singular passage but a general condition of passage through a world rendered enigmatically meaningful. The hexameter that Crosby uses in lines 2 and 3, though capturing the balance that often marks the French alexandrine, seems long in English, replete with extra syllables. Richard Howard and Richard Wilbur give us rhymed pentameter quatrains that share something of the effect of Baudelaire's alexandrines, which do not often divide into equal hemistiches.

> The pillars of Nature's temple are alive
> and sometimes yield perplexing messages;
> forests of symbols between us and the shrine
> remark our passage with accustomed eyes.　　　(Howard 15)

> Nature is a temple whose living colonnades
> Breathe forth a mystic speech in fitful sighs;
> Man wanders among symbols in those glades,
> Where all things watch him with familiar eyes.
> 　　　　　　　　(*Baudelaire in English* 19 [trans. Wilbur])

Comparing those two translations, I would quarrel with Howard's "forests of symbols *between* us and the shrine," which projects a divine center that is precisely lacking in Baudelaire's nature as temple, though Howard's "and sometimes yield perplexing messages" is more economical than Wilbur's fanciful "Breathe forth a mystic speech in fitful sighs." Is anything gained by imagining the *confuses paroles* as sighs? One could go on; the point is that this sort of comparison is a good way into both the meaning and the formal features of a poem.

But the approach I have been discussing still assumes that one knows what the original means and then examines translations to see how far and in what ways they fall short. Scott in his wonderful, difficult book *Translating Baudelaire* suggests that we ought to think about translation differently. Instead of assuming that we know what the source text means, can we not imagine that "the translator does not draw meaning out of the source text and embody it in another language but instead confers

meaning on the source text by using another language" (177)? Marilyn
Gaddis Rose has argued that translation should be more widely used as an
instrument of literary criticism. Attempting to put a poem into another
language helps us get inside literature; it forces us to consider meaning
in a new way, producing an "interliminal" space of possible meanings: attempting a translation helps us discover what the source text might mean
—which is faithful to the most elementary use of translations to discover
the meaning of texts we cannot read in the original (13, 7). Scott goes
further in his experiments of conferring meaning by changing one fixed
form into another—translating the sonnet "À une passante," for example,
into a villanelle and "Le balcon," a poem written in five-line stanzas where
the fifth line repeats the first, into a rondeau. "The process of translation
itself," Scott writes, "provides an opportunity to put these forms under
much greater expressive pressure, to oblige them to carry more emotional
freight, and ultimately to test their capacities . . . how well will a villanelle
withstand the strains of a Baudelairian sonnet? And what counter-claims
will a villanelle wish to make on that sonnet, and will they be justified,
and could they be enhancing?" (97)—a provocative question.

Here is Baudelaire's sonnet:

> La rue assourdissante autour de moi hurlait.
> Longue, mince, en grand deuil, douleur majestueuse,
> Une femme passa, d'une main fastueuse
> Soulevant, balançant le feston et l'ourlet;
>
> Agile et noble, avec sa jambe de statue.
> Moi, je buvais, crispé comme un extravagant,
> Dans son œil, ciel livide où germe l'ouragan,
> La douceur qui fascine et le plaisir qui tue.
>
> Un éclair... puis la nuit !—Fugitive beauté
> Dont le regard m'a fait soudainement renaître,
> Ne te verrai-je plus que dans l'éternité ?
>
> Ailleurs, bien loin d'ici ! trop tard ! *jamais* peut-être !
> Car j'ignore où tu fuis, tu ne sais où je vais,
> Ô toi que j'eusse aimée, ô toi qui le savais!          (92–93)

Amid the deafening traffic of the town,
Tall, slender, in deep mourning, with majesty,
A woman passed, raising, with dignity
In her poised hand, the flounces of her gown;

Graceful, noble, with a statue's form.
And I drank, trembling as a madman thrills,
From her eyes, ashen sky where brooded storm,
The softness that fascinates, the pleasure that kills.

A flash . . . then night!—O lovely fugitive,
I am suddenly reborn from your swift glance;
Shall I never see you till eternity?

Elsewhere, far off! Too late! never, perchance!
Neither knows where the other goes or lives;
O you whom I would have loved! O you who knew it!
                    (MacIntyre 157; trans. of final line modified)

Scott gives us two villanelle versions. A less radical free-verse villanelle "enacts the poet's attempt to transform a set of aural pressures and disorders [as in 'La rue assourdissante autour de moi hurlait'] into an exclusivity of the eye." But his rhymed villanelle translation is an extraordinarily bizarre rendering that highlights a number of issues: this villanelle, for instance, projects the encounter not "as a unique, once-and-for-all event, but as something repeated, habitual, as a kind of Muybridgean cinematic sequence, a series of frames slightly differentiated from each other, where the repetition itself takes the woman away, confirms her in an otherness" (99). This sense of the poem as rendering something habitual corresponds with Albert Thibaudet's prescient celebration of this sonnet—anticipating Walter Benjamin's take on it—as having become "consubstantiel à la poussière dorée du boulevard" ("part and parcel of the golden dust of the Parisian Boulevards"), so that male Parisians, as they stroll along eyeing the women who pass by and away forever, repeat the final alexandrine to themselves to savor their urban experience (22; my trans.). This villanelle may also better convey the sense of the theatricality of the street, downplaying the cliché of the romantic encounter that the sonnet form helps mythify, with its very irritating, deludedly narcissistic final clause, "ô toi que le savais!"

Scott's fearless translation reads:

Her motion elastic, her furbelows Stygian—
Marooned on a refuge, by the din of the street,
My whole self convulsed as she passed callipygian,[3]

Her figure as svelte as her cadence was Phrygian
And legs statuesque and galbous and fleet.
Her motion elastic, her furbelows Stygian,

An hypnotic *douceur* and Salome's religion
Were locked in her look which I drank till replete;
My whole self convulsed as she passed callipygian,

Her eyes full of storm and so hauntingly strygian.[4]
Was she grieving *grande dame* or a whore on her beat,
Her motion elastic, her furbelows Stygian?

And then she was gone, slick-fast as a widgeon,[5]
To beyond all beyond, to where none ever meet.
My whole self convulsed as she passed callipygian,

Too late, but she knew, this canny Parisian,
That love at last sight puts the city on heat,
Her motion elastic, her furbelows Stygian.
My whole self convulsed as she passed callipygian.          (97–98)

This version highlights the linking in the Baudelairean canon of the widow and streetwalker, both of whom signal an emptiness: one of loss, the other of mutual degradation. The *passante* causes a rebirth in the poet that is not just a rekindling of sexual desire but also already nostalgia for imagined loss. This translation also reduces the "hollow amplitude" of Baudelaire's tenth and eleventh lines—"Ne te verrai-je plus que dans l'éternité?"—a grandiloquence that undermines the complex specificity and drama of the encounter (Scott 98–99). But this translation is a daring gamble, especially since the Baudelairean rhymes, which include a rare *rhyme-léonine*, *majestueuse-fastueuse*, become in English the sequence *stygian, callipygian, Phrygian, strygian*, not to mention *widgeon*. In English, multisyllabic rhymes, especially when linked with dactyls, push verse toward doggerel. But Scott shrewdly notes that translation can capture the temporality of a text in a way interpretation cannot. Here the translation gives the taste of nineteenth-century doggerel, of Baudelaire's belief that a poet should know all the rare rhymes of his language, and of the modern fortunes of this text, with the Benjaminian "love at last sight" (101). At any rate, it is a bold interpretive gesture that captures readers' attention and provokes a reaction.

Radical translations, conferring meaning on the original, strengthening some features, bringing others to prominence, encouraging a certain irreverence in the face of the original, can thus promote a good discussion.

## NOTES

1. For discussion of "Obsession" as a reading or translation of "Correspondances," see de Man; Culler.
2. For Cornford, Tate, Campbell, and Wilbur, see *Baudelaire in English* 16–19.
3. *Callipygian* means "having shapely buttocks."
4. *Strygian*, from the French *stryge*, means "vampire."
5. *Widgeon* is a species of duck.

## WORKS CITED

Baker, Nicholson. *The Anthologist*. New York: Simon, 2009. Print.

Baudelaire, Charles. *Les Fleurs du Mal.* Paris: Gallimard, 1975. Print. Vol. 1 of *Œuvres complètes.*

*Baudelaire in English.* Ed. Carol Clark and Robert Sykes. Harmondsworth: Penguin, 1997. Print.

Crosby, William H., trans. The Flowers of Evil *and* Paris Spleen. By Charles Baudelaire. Brockport: BOA, 1991. Print.

Culler, Jonathan. "Reading Lyric." *Yale French Studies* 69 (1985): 98–106. Print.

de Man, Paul. "Anthropomorphism and Trope in the Lyric." *The Rhetoric of Romanticism.* New York: Columbia UP, 1984. Print.

Howard, Richard, trans. *Les Fleurs du Mal.* By Charles Baudelaire. Boston: Godine, 1982. Print.

MacIntyre, C. F., trans. *One Hundred Poems from* Les Fleurs du Mal. By Charles Baudelaire. Berkeley: U of California P, 1947. Print.

McGowan, James, trans. *The Flowers of Evil.* By Charles Baudelaire. Oxford: Oxford UP, 1993. Print.

Nerval, Gérard de. "Vers dorés." *Les chimères.* Geneva: Droz, 1966. 79. Print.

Rose, Marilyn Gaddis. *Translation and Literary Criticism: Translation as Analysis.* Manchester: St. Jerome, 1997. Print.

Scott, Clive. *Translating Baudelaire.* Exeter: U of Exeter P, 2000. Print.

Thibaudet, Albert. *Intérieurs: Baudelaire, Fromentin, Amiel.* Paris: Plon, 1924. Print.

Waldrop, Keith, trans. *The Flowers of Evil.* By Charles Baudelaire. Middletown: Wesleyan UP, 2006. Print.

# Teaching Poetry in Translation: The Case for Bilingualism

In my seminars on the historical avant-garde, I regularly include a unit on Russian poetry and the visual arts because I take these to be among the signal accomplishments of the early twentieth century. My knowledge of Russian is limited: some twenty years ago, in preparation for the writing of my book *The Futurist Moment*, I enrolled in a summer crash course in Russian at the University of California, Irvine. I lived in the dorm as Masha, was not allowed to speak English (a rule that kept me very silent!), and after a six-week period could read short passages with the help of a dictionary. Having mastered the Cyrillic alphabet, I could make my way through the Russian section of the stacks and look up Russian bibliography.

Avant-garde manifestos—for example, those of Velimir Khlebnikov and of Kasimir Malevich—do not suffer much in translation; the poetry is another matter. Even the best translations cannot convey the structure, much less the sound of a Khlebnikov or Vladimir Mayakovsky poem. Bilingual editions, especially those with texts on facing pages, are useful, but they are also expensive to produce, and so it is a blessing that we now have, readily available and free of charge, a number of excellent Web sites where we can hear and read the poetry in question and study its relation to the artist's books in which much of it was originally published. What is required of the student—and can be accomplished—is a minimum knowledge of Cyrillic: there are now many sites on the Internet that the student can use in identifying translations of titles or captions.

*The author is Sadie Dernham Patek Professor of Humanities, emerita, at Stanford University. A version of this paper was presented at the 2009 MLA convention in Philadelphia.*

Consider Mayakovsky's famous early poem "A vy mogli by?" ("And You, Could You?"), which first appeared in the artist's book *Trebnik troikh* ("The Missal of the Three") in 1913. It was "A vy mogli by?" that Mayakovsky recited at what turned out to be the last reading he gave before his suicide on 14 April 1930. In response to a student heckler at the Institute of National Economy in Moscow, he declared, "Any proletarian ought to understand this poem. If he doesn't he's simply illiterate. You should study. I really want you to understand my things." But the audience, increasingly cool to anything other than socialist realism, remained skeptical (Brown 21–22; Seldes 138–39).

A recording of Mayakovsky reading "A vy mogli by?" is available, with an English translation, at Penn Sound (Mayakovsky). On the Russian Web site *Poeziia avangarda*, this recording, rather scratchy, is followed by two others: Valery Sherstyanov (2000) and Sergei Biryukov (2003), both MP3s produced in Germany. When we study the poem in class, I play all three versions, while putting on the screen the written text, both in the Cyrillic of the original (Mayakovsky and Lissitzky, *Dlia golosa* 41) and in a transliteration based on the United States Library of Congress system:

| | |
|---|---|
| Я сразу смазал карту будня, | Ia srázu smázal kártu búdnia, |
| плеснувши краску из стакана; | plesnúvshi krásku íz stakána. |
| я показал на блюде студня | Ia pókazál na bliúde stúdnia |
| косые скулы океана. | kosýe skúly ókeána. |
| На чешуе жестяной рыбы | Na chéshué zhestiánoi rýbi |
| прочел я зовы новых губ. | prochél ia zóvy nóvykh gúb. |
| А вы | A vý |
| ноктюрн сыграть | noktiúrn sygrát' |
| могли бы | moglí by |
| на флейте водосточных труб? | na fléite vódostóchnykh trúb? |

I added accent marks to the transliteration because the poem's metrics are so central to its meaning. Here are two English translations: the first is Edward Brown's literal one, the second, Peter France's, the version used in the beautiful facsimile edition of Mayakovsky and El Lissitzky's *For the Voice*:

### But Could You?

I color-smeared the chart of everyday
splashing paints on it from a drinking glass;
on a dish of fish aspic I showed
the slanted cheekbones of the ocean.
On the scale of a tin fish
I read the message of fresh lips.
And you—
Could you play a nocturne
On a downspout flute?           (Brown 21–22)

### & You Could You?

I have blurred the map of every day,
set paint out of the paint-pot splashing,
I have shown in aspic on a plate
the slanting cheekbones of the ocean.
In a metallic fish's scales
I have read the call of future lips.
And you,
could you
a nocturne play
on the flute of waterpipes?
(Mayakovsky and Lissitzky, For the Voice 41)

At one level, Mayakovsky's is a fairly straightforward lyric, as he told the suspicious student. The poet announces his power to transform the everyday into art, to transform so humdrum a thing as a dish of fish aspic into the slanted cheekbones of the ocean, to see metallic fish scales (a logo used on shop signposts) as a woman's lips. And now, turning suddenly to the audience, he asks, "And what about you? Can you play a nocturne on a downspout flute? Can you make music on an ordinary drainpipe?"

Mayakovsky's miniature futurist manifesto hardly seems remarkable: it insists that the urban landscape with its drainpipes and street signs can become the stuff of the new poetry. Scholars have searched for visual analogues to the specific images: Juliette Stapanian-Apkarian, for example, insists that the poem is based on cubist still lifes that have the same elements—a pot, a glass, a plate of fish, and a musical instrument—as in Georges Braque's *Still Life with Herring* (1909–11) or *Still Life with Violin and Jug* (1909–10) (106–07). But the image of the plate of fish aspic as the slanting cheekbones of the ocean is surely more surrealist than cubist; indeed the whole poem is protosurrealist: the fish-scale lips, for example, anticipate Man Ray's image of Lee Miller's giant lips floating in an empty blue sky in his 1934 painting *Observatory Time* (here I show the image in class).

But the visual analogy is finally less important to an understanding of the poem than is its brilliant use of metrics. The Russian poem, we see in the transliteration, begins as a regular iambic tetrameter quatrain rhyming *abab*—a stanza Aleksandr Pushkin might have written. But no sooner does the poem establish its verse parameters than it defies them. The second quatrain begins normally (lines 5–6), but the next three lines look on the page like free verse, the norm not reasserting itself until the final line. But this description is not accurate: listen again to the recitation, whether by Mayakovsky or the other two readers, and it becomes clear that lines 7–9 constitute a single iambic tetrameter line, broken into three parts—

A vý /noktiúrn sygrát' / moglí by

And you / a nocturne play / could you

Read this way, the lines constitute the second rhyming quatrain (*rybi, gub, vi, trub*), and the poem's ten lines count as eight.

But why the broken line with its semblance of free verse? Uncannily, Mayakovsky's poem enacts structurally what is being said; it presents its lyric subject as capable of transforming the plumbing of traditional verse and making it sing. The aggressive challenge to those in the poet's audience (And you—what can you do?) is presented prosodically as well as semantically. Then, too, "A vy mogli by?" is tightly structured phonemically: consider the intricate sounding of "*Ia srazu smazal kartu . . . krasku iz stakana*" as well as the witty rhyming of *budnia* (weekday, humdrum) with *studnia* (aspic) and further along of *gub* (lips) with *trub* (pipes).

No English translation can render this complex sound play. The versions above are unrhymed, as is the translation "And Could You?," by Ilya Kutik and Andrew Wachtel:

> I suddenly smeared the weekday map
> splashing paint from a glass;
> On a plate of aspic
> I revealed
> the ocean's slanted cheek.
> On the scales of a tin fish
> I read the summons of new lips.
> And you
> could you perform
> a nocturne on a drainpipe flute?

This translation has the virtue of stressing the suddenness and spontaneity of the poetic act: the word *srazu* ("suddenly," "at once") is simply left out in the Brown and France versions. But there are also attempts to render Mayakovsky's quatrains in rhymed verse. Here are two exemplars randomly culled from the Internet:

### BUT COULD YOU?

> I blurred at once the map of humdrum,
> by splashing colours like a potion;
> I showed upon the dish of jelly
> the slanted cheekbones of the ocean.
>
> Upon the scales of metal fishes
> I read the new lips' attitude.
> But could you now perform a nocturne
> Just playing on a drainpipe flute?

### So Could You?

At once I smeared all routine
by spilling paint in my place;
I took a plate of gelatin
and formed an ocean's jagged face.
I picked the summons of fresh youth
off rusty glint of fish scale tin.
So could you take a drainpipe flute
and play a nocturne on a whim?          ("Mayakovsky")

Superficially, these quatrain poems sound closer to the original, but the need for rhyme forces the translator to add unnecessary words, as in "the new lips' attitude," or to invent such flaccid alternatives for new lips as "the summons of fresh youth." The "map of humdrum," "splashing colours like a potion," and "ocean's jagged face" are not accurate or even suggestive translations of Mayakovsky's phrasing. Notice, moreover, that the aggressive challenge of "And you" in line 7 is totally lost in both rhymed versions.

To translate Mayakovsky's stanzas from a Russian rich in rhymes into a much less inflected and hence difficult-to-rhyme English is all but impossible. What bilingual study does is precisely expose the gap between the original and the translation, a gap that testifies to the poet's subtlety and skill. The best English translation of "A vy mogli by?" I've come across is by the Scottish poet Edwin Morgan, who has translated many Russian poets and here renders Mayakovsky in Scottish:

### Ay, but can ye?

Wi a jaup the darg-day map's owre-pentit—
I jibbled colour fae a tea-gless;
ashets o jellyteen presentit
to me the great sea's camshach cheek-bleds.
A tin fish ilka scale a mou
I've read the cries a new warld through't.
But you
wi denty thrapple
can ye wheeple
nocturnes fae a rone-pipe flute?          (19)

Read aloud, Morgan's version should not offer many difficulties to the anglophone reader: *fae* (lines 2, 10) means "from"; *ashets* (line 3) is an adaptation of French *assiette*, meaning "plate"; "camshash" (line 4) is "crooked"; "mou" in line 5 is short for "mouth." This poem's guttural, alliterative, and consonantal Scottish, in any case, is much closer to the Russian than is standard English, and Morgan is sensitive to the important break in line 7 ("But you") as well as to Mayakovsky's rhymes. Morgan's version is the only one of the six cited here that really gives the feel of the original.

To compare the various translation alternatives of "A vy mogli by?" provides an entrance into Mayakovsky's poetics. To examine what can and does go wrong in translation practice and to see how wanting even the best translation will be is to enlarge one's sense not only of one little Russian poem but of poetry in general.

Another form of translation is available to us for Mayakovsky—the visual translation performed by Lissitzky. In the late autumn of 1922, when Mayakovsky was in Berlin, he collaborated with Lissitzky on a book called *Dlia golosa* (*For the Voice*), which submits thirteen of Mayakovsky's best-known poems to Lissitzky's brilliant graphic design. Mayakovsky later praised this little (7.5" × 5.25") book as "technically a perfect example of typographic art" (Railing 12–14). In 2000, the British Library in conjunction with MIT Press made a boxed facsimile of *For the Voice*, containing the Russian book, an English translation, and a book of scholarly essays providing commentary on the poems and visual prints.

Figure 1 The layout for "A vy mogli by?"

The little book (both in Russian and English versions) has a thumb index with visual symbols and shortened titles. On the verso page, an image of typecase elements relates to the subject of the poem using heavy bars between lines of type or at an angle to the type; the recto page contains the poem, rendered expressively in large letters. The typeface is sans serif, and the letters are black and red on a white ground (fig. 1). Lissitzky's translation of Mayakovsky's poem is extremely interesting. The verso presents a grid structure filled with question marks and, in the lower boxes, letters for the alternate letter forms for the *b* of *by* ("would") and the *v* of *vy* ("you"). The red question grid is overprinted by a monumental *A* and an equally large question mark. While *a* in Russian is usually translated as "but," it also means "and." The boldface letters are Lissitzky's choice, but in France's version the giant A is translated with an ampersand so that the single, isolated letter of the original can be rendered by a comparable English one. The resulting ideogram is the artist's conception of the poem. He begins with an empty grid, in keeping with Mayakovsky's map of the everyday, and produces his own order—an order then violated by the entrance of question marks.

A visual translation of a verbal text as remarkable as Lissitzky's is rare. In most instances of teaching poetry in translation, there are hardly likely to be many available visual translations or counterparts. Still, Mayakovsky's poem can provide a useful paradigm. Ideally, any poem should be read in its language of composition, poetry being, as Robert Frost so famously quipped, what is lost in translation. But since, practically speaking, many of the world's great poetries are now available to our students only in translation, we must rise to the occasion by never pretending that a translation is more than a good reproduction of a painting; it is not the painting itself. True, as translators often tell us, a translation of poem X by poet Y may well be a new poem in its own right; it may even be an improvement on the original. But if our first concern as teachers is to introduce our students to poetry outside the anglophone box, then let us hear and look at the original. The materiality of the poem in question is always central, even in translation.

## WORKS CITED

Brown, Edward J. *Mayakovsky: A Poet in the Revolution*. Princeton: Princeton UP, 1973. Print.

Kutik, Ilya, and Andrew Wachtel, eds. *From the Ends to the Beginning: A Bilingual Anthology of Russian Verse*. Dept. of Slavic Langs. and Lits., Northwestern U, 21 Mar. 2003. Web. 30 June 2010.

"Mayakovsky." Trans. Dina Belyayeva. *Ordinary Finds*. 19 July 2009. Tumblr, n.d. Web. 27 July 2010. Blog. <i12bent.tumblr.com/search/Mayakovsky>.

Mayakovsky, Vladimir. "And Could You?" Penn Sound, U of Pennsylvania, 23 Jan. 2006. Web. 30 June 2010.

Mayakovsky, Vladimir, and El Lissitzky. *Dlia golosa*. London: British Lib., 2000. Print. Facsim. of the 1923 Russian ed. Vol. 1 of MIT P ed. of *For the Voice*.

———. *For the Voice*. Trans. Peter France and Martha Scotford. London: British Lib., 2000. Print. Vol. 2 of MIT P ed. of *For the Voice*.

Morgan, Edwin M. *Wi the Haill Voice: Twenty-Five Poems by Vladimir Mayakovsky*. Oxford: Oxford UP, 1922. Print.

Railing, Patricia, ed. *Voices of the Revolution: Collected Essays*. London: British Lib., 2000. Print. Vol. 3 of MIT P ed. of *For the Voice*.

Seldes, Barry. "Sensibilities for the New Man: Politics, Poetics, and Graphics." Railing 138–58.

Stapanian-Apkarian, Juliette. "Modernist 'Vision' in the Poems of Mayakovsky." Railing 72–129.

# Disability and Language

## *Introduction*

### PETRA KUPPERS

In my disability culture classroom, the first few weeks circle, traverse, query, and play with the languages of disability. What do you call these people? Is there a "these people," and, if there is, what do they share? What do you call them if you are one of them, and, if you are not, what does the *them* say about an *us*?

This group of essays grew not out of my classroom but out of the discussions of the Committee on Disability Issues in the Profession and our long-standing agenda of offering nonableist language to our colleagues in the field. But, productively rather than frustratingly, we could never quite agree on the right terms. Many of us who served on this committee over the years saw the question of disability's languages as the juice of our field. The questions, the uncertainties, the tensions are more often than not the creative heart of our endeavors. So in introducing these essays on why disability's languages are of interest to us as teachers and professionals, I return to my classroom and to the effects of introducing language's and culture's plasticity.

In those first few weeks of my semester, the pedagogical agenda is to own discomfort, to live with uncertainty, to understand the seriously playful potential of language. This is a literary and cultural studies classroom, after all, so we discuss not only different models of disability but also concepts of queering, drag and resistance, reclamation and survivance, audiences and reception, poetics and phenomenology (for some initial readings on issues like these, see Snyder, Brueggemann, and Thomson, one of the first humanities-based collections in disability studies; in the field of rhetorics,

*The author is associate professor of English, theater, and women's studies at the University of Michigan, Ann Arbor.*

see Wilson and Lewiecki-Wilson; and for an introduction to the current state of the field, see Davis). After a few weeks, most students settle down to the real labor of understanding disability's cultural places in our world, and they stop fretting too much about whether or not they use words that might inadvertently offend. What about *differently abled, Down syndrome child, wheelchair-bound, mad, freak, exceptional*? Why do some people prefer *person with a disability* and others *disabled person*? Are people without a disability *nondisabled people, normal*, or *TAB* (temporarily able-bodied) (Wendell)? As we hash these questions out, we agree on a few base issues: as long as we are respectful and patient with ourselves and others, it's OK to experiment, to try out language in one's mouth, and listen all the way to the end to find out if there's discrimination, paternalism, or pathos in the undertones (and we get to sense the audist language in this sentence—that is, language that understands spoken word and audio input as the dominant form of communication). As long as we take seriously the charge to be aware, ask questions where we are unsure, and call one another out when we note words that make us uncomfortable, we are involved in a worthwhile social justice project. Together, we are honing our ability to understand how we communally make meaning and how our languages shift.

One of the most important learning goals of these weeks is a budding understanding that there are no fixed answers out there and that language changes just as our cultures do. After a while, in that classroom, it's no longer always necessary to pull out references about the vibrations of the words, this echoed prosody, as students pick up on the origins and frameworks for terms. Is a term more likely used in a service environment, in a care facility, by parents of disabled children? Is it a self-identifying label? Is it used by a first-, second-, or third-generation activist? Who is the audience for the term? We begin to understand that words are relational, wielded differently at different times by different people for different purposes. These insights are built on earlier disability studies scholarship, on the foundational work of social scientists and academics who articulated the disability movement's political positions from the 1970s on, like Vic Finkelstein, Harlan Hahn, and Irving Zola. Zola traces how issues of naming are central to the creation of a minority discourse around disability, both in line with and divergent from other minority identity models.

The Committee on Disability Issues in the Profession invited three authors to write on the topic of language and disability, and each presents some of the relational, shifting grounds of disability's language(s), and the disagreements and challenges of the field.

In many disability culture classrooms around the nation, classes begin by reading Simi Linton's "Reassigning Meaning." The chapter begins:

> The present examination of disability has no need for the medical lan-
> guage of symptoms and diagnostic categories. Disability studies looks
> to different kinds of signifiers and the identification of different kinds
> of syndromes for its material. The elements of interest here are the lin-
> guistic conventions that structure the meanings assigned to disability
> and the patterns of response to disability that emanate from, or are at-
> tendant upon, those meanings. (8)

Unpacking this paragraph is good material for a lecture hour. Teachers can use specific, local, or topical examples and decline them through
the various stages of Linton's text. Michael Bérubé, Margaret Price, and
Kristen Harmon all offer material for such a discussion: they chart how
linguistic conventions affect responses to disability and how activists, or
just ordinary people, in turn speak back to the meanings that labels have
attached to them.

These essays begin in strife. The particular landscapes of disability
they address—cognitive disability, neurodiversity and mental health, and
Deafness—are undergoing language change in disability studies itself,
not only in the wider social world.

Bérubé, who has written extensively on the insights that life with his
son Jamie, diagnosed with Down syndrome, has afforded him, speaks to
the tensions among and beyond the different models of disability that have
created the first wave of disability activism. The social model locates disability at the meeting place of personal impairment and a disabling social
world; the medical model locates disability in individuals and employs various techniques to normalize them. From here, things get complicated, and
Bérubé asks what the price of this complexity might be. (For a provocative
perspective, a full etiology and critique of social model language, see also
Shakespeare and Watson.) Price speaks from the position of someone who
is labeled. She feels the force of the different words for disabilities of the
mind and sees the need for coalition politics and strategic messiness. She
addresses changing medical terms. That medicine changes and transforms
its vocabulary undermines any sense that science holds permanent answers
for stable labels. Harmon carefully attends to the multiple group allegiances
and nuances of language surrounding *Deaf*, delineating a changing and
morphing political rhetoric in her community. She shows, like Price, how
recent cultural change and a postdeafened movement create a constructive
and generative messiness. Together, these essays show culture in flux, language in shift, and the politics that surround and influence disability.

When I speak at conferences, or even when I wheel into my classroom
on the first day, no one challenges me anymore on my terms of preference: *disabled woman, wheelchair user*. If I am pressed to be more specific,

if someone wants to know what's the matter, I might go as far as to say, "mobility impairments, pain and fatigue issues." I explain why I do not disclose medical labels; I do not intend to stabilize the power of medical regimes, historical diagnostic racism, and misogyny, choosing instead to align myself with political labels, as a disability culture activist. There's privilege in the ability to refuse to state the diagnosis. I launch myself into the public sphere with one of the most recognizable implements of disability, the wheelchair, a symbol ubiquitous on parking signs and Americans with Disabilities Act (ADA) references. People with invisible impairments, on the other hand, often have a much harder time getting accommodations and averting unwelcome intrusions, a problem that swings in the background of the essays here: who speaks for whom, why, and how are access issues as much as my ramps are.

There are so many more issues around language and disability that fuel contemporary disability studies: critiquing the old yarns about the unspeakability of pain, unfolding the complexity of speech difference and linguistic citizenship, discussing cultural difference and disability labeling, changing a discourse of disability rights to one of disability justice.

In the lifetime of students in our classrooms today, the world has shifted: in 1990, the ADA came into force, after decades of campaigning. Everybody working in disability studies today has experienced in some form the world-changing impact of this act: ramps, speaking elevators, curb cuts, parking places, the growth of American Sign Language as a recognized language in university settings, a slowly growing popular cultural visibility of disability as a lived experience. As scholars and teachers in the modern languages, we are part of this change, and we can make change happen. The baseline of language discussions around disability is that we are embarked, we are growing, we have a hopeful agenda, we are self-critical and self-reflexive, and we are interdependent, embodied, and powerful.

So there we are, at the beginning of the twenty-first century, with people-first language like *people with disabilities* and with the more politicized group identification that the phrase *disabled people* implies for many (and, just in case you are looking for answers, these two descriptors are least likely to offend today). And there are other words, before the PWD and the DP: *cripple*, *retard*, *spaz*, *dumb*. They provide the deeper sediment for this discussion around terms; they hold pain and, rarely, newly recovered pride. Literature and language scholars have begun to mine the representations of disability in ways that do not merely renounce oppressive structures but also find play in them. The swing in our words is part of the energy of the discovery projects made in disability and Deaf activism, disability and Deaf studies, and disability and Deaf arts. Much cultural camaraderie is expressed in the improvisatory uses we make of our old and new terms. These language fights are not about political correctness or head-on oppositions: they speak to the creativity of people who live with difference, about the ability to swerve out from under textual fixing and a word's hail.

## WORKS CITED

Davis, Lennard, ed. *Disability Studies Reader*. 3rd ed. London: Routledge, 2010. Print.

Finkelstein, Vic. *Attitudes and Disabled People*. New York: World Rehabilitation Fund, 1980. Print.

Hahn, Harlan. "Towards a Politics of Disability: Definitions, Disciplines and Policies." *Social Science Journal* 22.4 (1985): 87–105. Print.

Linton, Simi. "Reassigning Meaning." *Claiming Disability: Knowledge and Identity*. New York: New York UP, 1998. 8–33. Print.

Shakespeare, Tom, and N. Watson. "The Social Model of Disability: An Outdated Ideology?" *Exploring Theories and Expanding Methodologies: Where Are We and Where Do We Need to Go? Research in Social Science and Disability*. Ed. S. Barnartt and B. Altman. Vol. 2. Amsterdam: JAI, 2001. 9–28. Print.

Snyder, Sharon H., Brenda Jo Brueggemann, and Rosemarie Garland Thomson, eds. *Disability Studies: Enabling the Humanities*. New York: MLA, 2002. Print.

Wendell, Susan. *The Rejected Body: Feminist Philosophical Reflections on Disability*. New York: Routledge, 1996. Print.

Wilson, James C., and Cynthia Lewiecki-Wilson, eds. *Embodied Rhetorics: Disability in Language and Culture*. Carbondale: Southern Illinois UP, 2001. Print.

Zola, Irving. "Self, Identity, and the Naming Question: Reflections on the Language of Disability." *Social Science and Medicine* 36.2 (1993): 167–73. Print.

# Term Paper

## MICHAEL BÉRUBÉ

Recently I was asked, at a conference on cognitive disability, why my paper had employed the term *disability*. I replied by referencing my entry on *disability* in *New Keywords*, in which I pointed out that although the word retains some sense of stigma when applied to persons, it simply means "inoperative" when applied to objects—as when we speak of disabling a smoke detector or a function on a computer. The question wasn't simply about terminology, however; in the course of my talk, I'd pointed out that although the social model of disability has done important cultural and political work over the past few decades and that the general public (and much of the medical profession) still needs to grasp the distinction between individual impairments and the idea of disability as the social organization of impairment, it is easier to adopt the social model when it comes to ramps and curb cuts, closed captioning and Braille than when it comes to cognitive or intellectual disability. It's one thing to demonstrate that physically impaired person X is disabled by a doorway too narrow for her wheelchair, quite another to demonstrate that cognitively impaired person Y is disabled by a built environment that overtaxes his intellectual capacities. Because it's possible that cognitively impaired person Y would be disabled by *any* built environment, the social model of disability has its limits when it comes to dealing with people with intellectual disabilities.

Had I been wearier or in a more combative mood, I might have replied, more simply, that it is not really remarkable for a speaker to use the term *disability* at a conference titled "Cognitive Disability: A Challenge to

*The author is Paterno Family Professor in English Literature and Science, Technology, and Society at Penn State University, University Park.*

PROFESSION

Moral Philosophy." I'm glad I didn't, for it turned out that the questioner opposed the use of the term in any and all circumstances, preferring instead *difference*.

But I often wonder whether such disputes over terminology are arguments about a difference without a distinction. Because my younger son has Down syndrome, there are certain motor and cognitive tasks he has trouble with; does it matter whether we ascribe these to disability or to difference? When all the deck chairs on the terminological *Titanic* are arranged properly, Jamie will still need help in tying his shoes, and he still won't understand money very well.

I had a similar sinking feeling during a committee meeting not long ago in which people argued over whether to use the phrase "people with Down syndrome." Usually, such people-first phrasing is de rigueur, on the grounds that people with disabilities are people first; "person with Down syndrome" therefore sounds more humane, less stigmatizing, than "Down syndrome person." However, the opponents of the locution "people with Down syndrome" argued that the phrase unfortunately suggests that people with Down syndrome are completely defined by Down syndrome, as if Down syndrome is all they have.

At that point, I began to fear that we had become much too clever at this kind of thing. Consider it an occupational hazard of faculty members who work in language and literature—or, indeed, of faculty members in general. There isn't a word or a phrase we can't weigh in the scales and find wanting, and we're even capable of taking the logic that led to the general acceptance of a term like "people with Down syndrome" and turning it on its head so that people-first terminology somehow sets people at a discount. Yet there is a case to be made for preferring the term "autistic person" to "person with autism," just as there is a case to be made for the reverse.

Now, I'm just a soul whose intentions are good: oh Lord, please don't let me be misunderstood. I don't think it's pointless to argue over the terminology of disability; I'm not suggesting that we revert to *Mongoloid idiot* and *cripple*, and I wouldn't want to see the Individuals with Disabilities Education Act (IDEA) restored to its original title, the Education for All Handicapped Children Act. Nonetheless, I don't quite see the point of renaming the IDEA the Individuals with Differences Education Act, since I think that would take an already amorphous and elusive term, *disabilities*, and dissolve it entirely into water vapor.

So which terminological battles are worth fighting, and on what grounds? In recent years I've found that there are deep divisions in the disability community with regard to what would seem to be more substantial matters. The cases of Terri Schiavo and *Oregon v. Gonzales* (involving the constitutionality of Oregon's physician-assisted suicide law) revealed that there are many people with disabilities who favor greater autonomy for people with disabilities unless those people's wishes do not correspond to their own; that there are some people with disabilities who regard every dying person as a person with a disability; and that there are many people with disabilities who rightly fear that statutes like Oregon's will lead us to a slippery slope at the bottom of which waits Peter Singer. (Singer functions in these debates as a conversation stopper, a terminus ad quem where the Benthamite imperative to reduce suffering meets the ableist assumption that all people with disabilities are suffering.) I already knew that there was no consensus, among people with disabilities, with regard to the ethics of prenatal screening. Aren't these debates—about who should enter the world and how we should leave it—more important than squabbles over language? Or are there nontrivial relations between squabbles over language and struggles over life and death?

A decade ago, Nancy Fraser's *Justice Interruptus* got a chilly reception from some left intellectuals who believed that her distinction between the politics of recognition and the politics of redistribution subordinated the former to the latter—as if dehumanization should matter to the left only when it has economic effects. Fraser didn't help her cause among queer theorists by consigning homophobia to the recognition end of the continuum. "To be sure," Fraser wrote, "gays and lesbians also suffer serious economic injustices; they can be summarily dismissed from paid work and are denied family-based social-welfare benefits. But far from being rooted directly in the economic structure, these [injustices] derive instead from an unjust cultural-valuational structure" (18). Judith Butler famously replied that harm to gays and lesbians was not "merely cultural." Following in Butler's wake, some theorists have argued that it is best to assume, lest anyone make the mistake of taking homophobia too lightly, that there are *no* nontrivial relations between the politics of recognition and the politics of redistribution, if indeed it is possible to separate the two, even analytically.

One wonders how that debate would look from the perspective of disability studies. On the one hand, the stigma attached to disability involves recognition harms that almost always have material effects—if we understand *material*, as Fraser urged us to do, as distinct from and irreducible to the economic sphere. On the other hand, it is not clear to me that the phrase "people with disabilities," or even the term *disability* itself, involves a recognition harm. Debates over disability terminology suggest to me that it is indeed exceptionally difficult to distinguish recognition harms from redistribution harms. Fraser's attempt to adjudicate the cultural left versus reformist left debates of the 1990s may be inadequate to the kinds of harms involved in the dehumanization of people with disabilities. At the same time, some debates over disability terminology appear to me to be inconsequential (not merely cultural but, rather, merely trivial), leading me to believe that the important difference to bear in mind is not that between recognition harms and redistribution harms but that between substantial harms and insubstantial harms.[1]

I imagine that we continue to engage in debates over terminology because we fear that everything related to disability involves a potential recognition harm. Allow me to make this point obliquely. The last time I taught Erving Goffman's *Stigma: Notes on the Management of Spoiled Identity* (a text that has become as important for disability studies as for queer theory), I couldn't help noticing that at certain moments in Goffman's text, the most heterogeneous conditions are yoked by violence together, as when Goffman writes that "ex-mental patients and expectant unmarried fathers are similar in that their failing is not readily visible" (48) and that "a woman who has had a mastectomy or a Norwegian male sex offender who has been penalized by castration are forced to present themselves falsely in almost all situations" (75). What's going on in these weird passages? I think Goffman is winking at us, as one of the wise: he knows that stigma has a temporal dimension, that social opprobrium, like everything else, can be historicized. He just doesn't get around to saying so explicitly until the closing pages of his book, when he suggests that "when, as in the case of divorce or Irish ethnicity, an attribute loses much of its force as a stigma, a period will have been witnessed when the previous definition of the situation is more and more attacked" (137). Divorce and Irish ethnicity aren't discrediting attributes any longer; likewise, mastectomy and unwed fatherhood have lost much (though not all) of the stigma once attached to them. Mental patients and sex offenders, by contrast, continue to be stigmatized, and many people might add that sex offenders are properly stigmatized. My point—and, I think, Goffman's implicit point—is not only that stigma has a history but also that different forms of stigma move at different speeds. It is possible, for instance, to find openly gay men and women in elective office—something that was unimaginable at the time *Stigma* was published.

Yet disability remains deeply and widely stigmatized. I often suspect that cognitive disability is the slowest-moving of the stigmas and will remain a subject of horror and avoidance for decades to come. That's why my questioner was right, in the end, to challenge me about the term *disability* and about my insistence on the limits of the social model: most of the world hasn't caught on to the social model yet and still regards *disability* as definitively discrediting. I ruefully remarked, later in that question-and-answer period, that I had recently seen a 5K fund-raising run advertised under the heading "Autism: The Race for the Cure" and had bitterly suggested to my disability studies students that "Race for the Cure" fits on fliers and posters—and in minds—more readily than "Race for the Reasonable Accommodation." We argue about terminology, in other words (and it is always about speaking in other words), because we don't yet know which fights to pick and which battles we can actually win. Perhaps someday, when physical and cognitive disabilities have finally lost much of their stigmatizing force, we'll be able to look back and determine which arguments about language made a difference and which were simply clever language games. Until then, we work in the dark, we do what we can.

## NOTE

1. I make this argument at greater length in *The Left at War* (215–18): "Whatever the drawbacks to Fraser's recognition/redistribution formulation, the point remained that there needs to be *some* threshold for what counts as a 'significant' form of politics, or all forms would be equally important—or equally trivial. That is not to say that redistribution politics (or Rorty's 'reformist left') is necessarily or by default more important than recognition politics. There are many trivial forms of financial, electoral, and regulatory politics; not every issue in civil procedure or zoning law is a Constitutional matter. Conversely, there are many critical forms of recognition politics, the struggles over abortion and gay rights are fundamental to American culture and society. It is only to say that patriarchy does not fall whenever a young female undergraduate decides to spell 'womyn' with a y, and that Camille Paglia's complaints about the ethnic stereotyping of Italian-Americans in *The Sopranos* do nothing to improve the quality of people's lives. And it is to say that it is sometimes difficult beyond measure to try to measure the impact of recognition politics: some recognition harms may not affect the politics of redistribution for many years, or only in a circuitously indirect manner; and certainly no one who seeks social justice should be compelled to refrain from remarking recognition harms until the appropriate redistribution harms have been duly tabulated and recorded" (218).

## WORKS CITED

Bérubé, Michael. "Disability." *New Keywords: A Revised Vocabulary of Culture and Society*. Ed. Tony Bennett, Lawrence Grossberg, and Meaghan Morris. Malden: Blackwell, 2005. 87–89. Print.

———. *The Left at War*. New York: New York UP, 2009. Print.

Butler, Judith. "Merely Cultural." *Social Text* 52-53 (1997): 265–77. Print.

Fraser, Nancy. *Justice Interruptus: Critical Reflections on the "Postsocialist" Condition*. New York: Routledge, 1996. Print.

Goffman, Erving. *Stigma: Notes on the Management of Spoiled Identity*. New York: Simon, 1963. Print.

# Mental Disability
# and Other Terms of Art

## MARGARET PRICE

It's difficult to put language to disabilities of the mind. I am always struck by the discomfort people feel when they try to talk about this subject. "I don't know the right word for it," they hesitate, or, "This probably isn't the PC way to say it, but. . . ." This concern is separate from the problem of hate speech as applied to mental disabilities; terms like *psycho* and *nuts* are common, even in the supposedly enlightened halls of academe. For the present essay, I am concerned with the question of naming mental disability when the intent is respectful—for even then it is a knotty question.

Why is it so hard? Our difficulty in naming disabilities of the mind does not arise from a lack of words, for we have dozens, including *mentally ill, crazy, retarded, mad, intellectually disabled, neuroatypical, cognitively disabled, psychiatric system survivor, mentally challenged, psychiatric services consumer,* and *idiot.* Nor does our difficulty arise from a lack of historical context, for philosophers have striven for thousands of years to explain this sort of impairment. Aristotle wrote at length about the effect of black bile, which in his view inspired a predisposition to melancholy as well as gifts in areas including statesmanship and the arts (Radden 58). Finally, the struggle does not arise from obscurity, since mental disability is one of the most common conditions in the world. According to the National Institute of Mental Health, one in four American adults "suffer[s] from a diagnosable mental disorder in a given year" (*Numbers*), and the World Health Organization estimates that globally hundreds of millions of people each year are affected

*The author is associate professor of English at Spelman College.*

by mental, neurological, or behavioral disabilities (*Mental Health*). In statistical terms, we could almost say that mental disabilities are normal.

Yet still we struggle to find the words. In this piece, I explain some of the more common terms for mental disability and include a rationale for my own preferences. My intent is not to demonstrate that some terms are good and others bad; rather, it is to map the social, political, and historical contexts through which various terms operate. In doing so, I follow the urging of Tanya Titchkosky, who argues that the aim of analyzing language about disability should not be to mandate particular terms but rather "to examine what our current articulations of disability are saying in the here and now" (138). The problem of naming has always preoccupied disability studies scholars, but it acquires a particular urgency when considered in the context of disabilities of the mind, for often the very terms used to name persons with mental disabilities have explicitly foreclosed our status as persons. Aristotle's famous declaration that "the function of man" requires "rational principle" gave rise to centuries of insistence that to be named mad was to lose one's personhood (1735).

I use *mental disability* to indicate a broad range of conditions and impairments that affect the mind. These can be subdivided into a number of categories: mental illnesses (madness), cognitive disabilities (mental retardation, intellectual disabilities), autism spectrum disorders (neuroatypicality), and learning disabilities (learning difficulties). But the categories blur considerably. There are important reasons to distinguish one type of mental disability from another, but there are also important reasons to consider them together, using an umbrella category. These sorts of disabilities are always and inevitably caught up with an individual's rhetorical power, what Cynthia Lewiecki-Wilson calls *rhetoricity* (see also Prendergast). She suggests the term *mental disability* to indicate the rhetorical disablement of persons with disabilities of the mind:

> Despite the varieties of and differences among mental impairments, this collective category focuses attention on the problem of gaining rhetoricity to the mentally disabled: that is, rhetoric's received tradition of emphasis on the individual rhetor who produces speech/writing, which in turn confirms the existence of a fixed, core self, imagined to be located in the mind. (157)

In other words, according to Lewiecki-Wilson, the notion that one's self—and hence one's disability—is located in one's mind unites this category, not because such a thing is inherently true but because persons with these kinds of disabilities share common experiences of disempowerment as rhetors.

Importantly, Lewiecki-Wilson's statement also acknowledges that the rhetor's self is conventionally confirmed by the rhetor's production of speech. This problem often constitutes the crux of rhetoricity for those with mental disabilities. For example, a study published by the Association of Higher Education and Disability revealed that faculty members with so-called hidden disabilities experience their impairments as being highly noticeable in arenas that require them to speak. As one faculty member pointed out in an interview, "A meeting can be a disaster for someone on the [autism] spectrum. . . . Awkwardness is presumed to be pervasive" (Avinger, Croake, and Miller 211). Further, in some cases rhetors with mental disabilities do not make use of rational discourse; this problem has led to a number of works that investigate the possibilities of facilitated communication (Lewiecki-Wilson; Erevelles). The lack of access to normative forms of speech or to conventional rational discourse is a critical reason that mental disabilities constitute what Licia Carlson has called "the philosopher's nightmare" (18). If the "good man skilled in speaking" (Quintilian 197; bk. 22, ch. 1) does not speak or does not speak well (in normative terms), what does this lack do to our comfortable notions of rhetorical agency?

My search for adequate terminology follows Lewiecki-Wilson's call for coalition politics. Although it is important to note the differences between specific experiences, in general I believe we need both local specificity and broad coalitions. Persons with impaired minds have been segregated from one another enough. I have found that efforts to find collective language often come from activist groups of people who have mental disabilities or have been diagnosed as such, while efforts to diagnose, divide, parse, and separate tend to come from clinicians. Here I explore one of the world's foremost technologies of the divide-and-disempower approach to mental disability: the *Diagnostic and Statistical Manual of Mental Disorders* (DSM), a taxonomy whose importance to the field of mental health "cannot be overstated" (Aho 245). This manual's claims to objectivity, its implication with capitalist structures such as the pharmaceutical and insurance industries, and especially its efforts to conceal the rhetorical processes of its own revision and publication help sustain the impulse to regard mental disability as something radically other to everyday life.

The DSM was first published in 1952 by the American Psychiatric Association. Its appearance was fueled by American psychiatrists serving during World War II, who advocated for outpatient treatment of servicemen and veterans. The manual has since undergone a series of revisions, each designated by a Roman numeral: DSM-II (1968), DSM-III (1980), and DSM-IV (1994). A new revision, DSM-5, is expected in 2013. Each revision includes changes to the system of classifying mental disorders, sometimes dramatic ones; one of the most often cited shifts between DSM-II and DSM-III was the removal of homosexuality as a mental disorder (although it was replaced, at the time of that specific 1973 revision, by the diagnosis of "sexual orientation disturbance"). Most analysts agree that the publication of DSM-III was a watershed event. According to the manual's authors, "DSM-III introduced a number of important methodological innovations, including explicit diagnostic criteria, a multiaxial system, and a descriptive approach that *attempted to be neutral* with respect to theories of etiology" (*Diagnostic and Statistical Manual* xxvi; emphasis added). However, critics of the manual describe this revision in strikingly different terms. According to a discourse analysis conducted by Lucille Parkinson McCarthy, a rhetorician, and Joan Page Gerring, a psychiatrist, DSM-III constitutes "a dramatic shift in psychiatry toward the biomedical model and away from competing models" (157). In other words, revisions of DSM indicate an increasing adherence to a model of mental disability as a measurable and biological phenomenon, and DSM-III was a key turning point in this process.[1]

As a result of this shift, mental disability was understood and talked about quite differently after 1980. Mitchell Wilson points out two important changes: first, the power base of psychiatry shifted, with researchers replacing clinicians as the most powerful voices in the psychiatric profession (400); second, DSM-III's claim of objectivity allowed the manual to begin to seem "natural—not made by human hands" (408). By setting itself up as objective or neutral, scientific discourse provides an argument for its stance while also insulating itself against the possibility of alternative arguments. Donna Haraway calls this strategy a "god-trick" (189), and Thomas Nagel the "view from nowhere"—that is, it claims a gaze that comes from nowhere and everywhere all at once, omniscient and unlocatable, and therefore shielded from any counter-gaze.

The criticisms mentioned here are only the tip of the iceberg. Their total must number in the hundreds, perhaps even in the thousands. One common concern is the DSM's sheer number of diagnoses for disordered states of mind once thought to be ordinary (such as shyness). As Lawrence Davis observed in 1997, the abundance of DSM diagnoses suggests that "human life is a form of mental illness" (62). Yet, although decades of work have exposed not only the rhetorical nature of psychiatry but also the dubious agendas of the rhetors who compose its key texts, most people accept psychiatric rhetoric on its own terms: as an objective, benign, and stable authority. As a result, our everyday practices reflect its biases, so that the mentally disabled subject in public and private life is repeatedly diagnosed, cured, ostracized, fetishized, or expelled.

I want to balance the gigantic (both in terms of page count and in terms of influence) DSM with another taxonomic story, this one of a term that arose from activist movements and is gaining ground among persons with all sorts of mental disabilities. The term is *neuroatypical* (the collective phenomenon is *neurodiversity*) and is used to denote all whose brains position them as being somehow different from the neurotypical run of the mill. Used as both noun and adjective, *neuroatypical* most often indicates persons on the autism spectrum but has also been used to refer to persons with mood disorders (Antonetta) and traumatic brain injuries (Vidali). In her "bipolar book" (13) *A Mind Apart*, Susanne Antonetta argues that neurodiversity acts as a positive force in human evolution, enabling alternative and creative ways of thinking, knowing, and apprehending the world.

Unlike the fine-toothed diagnoses of the DSM, *neuroatypical* is a messy term. It can be claimed by people who have no diagnostic code to write on an insurance claim form. The term arose from the autism rights movement in the late 1980s and gained popularity in the 1990s, when Autism Network International (ANI) was founded with the goal of uniting persons with autism to speak for themselves. ANI's current philosophy includes the statements "The best advocates for autistic people are autistic people themselves" and "Supports for autistic people should be aimed at helping them to compensate, navigate, and function in the world, not at changing them into non-autistic people or isolating them from the world" (*Introducing*). This philosophy stands in stark contrast to that of organizations such as Autism Speaks, which is dedicated to "curing" autism and to finding "the missing piece in the puzzle" of autistic lives (*Our Mission*), or Fighting Autism, which has a similar goal: cure and eradication.

*Neuroatypical* is a resistant term, implying an activist stance and a rebellion against the biomedical-industrial complex. Its complement is *neurotypical* (NT), which destabilizes assumptions about normal minds and can be used to transgressive effect (Brownlow). For example, the organization Aspies for Freedom has used *NT* to parody the rhetoric of cure propagated by Fighting Autism. It did so by reconstructing one of the archetypal images of Fighting Autism, the autism clock. This clock, updated in real time, claimed to show the incidence of autism among American children, along with its economic cost, which as of February 2010 was recorded at more than $9 billion. The final line on the clock image, which is backgrounded with a photograph of a plaintive child, large eyes looking upward, gave the time that would elapse until the "next diagnosis." Fighting Autism's clock image was notorious in autism rights circles, not only for its shameless use of pathetic appeals but also for its underlying assumption that autism is a disease.

In response to this image, Aspies for Freedom published a parody in 2004.[2] The parody image uses the same color scheme (gray and red), the same square shape, and the same background image of the plaintive child. The text, however, is entirely different. Aspies for Freedom's clock announces that the "U.S. NTism population estimate" is 349 million and the "annual economic cost" is over $10 trillion (*NTism*). After these deliberately hyperbolic figures comes the denouement: "Next Diagnosis / 1 every minute / & 2 to take them." In other words, Aspies for Freedom flips the script on Fighting Autism by suggesting that NTism itself is the disease and that *that* disease is what requires curing. This turning of tables both invokes the social model of disability and functions as a form of linguistic rebellion; it is common in textual works by members of the autism rights movement. *NT* is a common locus for rebellion by definition; for instance, *Uncyclopedia* has an entry for "Neurotypical Syndrome," which is also identified as "arrogant mob syndrome."

Ian Hacking argues that mental illnesses "provoke banal debates about whether they are 'real' or 'socially constructed.' We need richer tools with which to think" (1). I suggest that mental disabilities are shaped and lived through rhetorical processes including diagnosis and resistance; that they appear unpredictably and are not always legible; and that, above all, coalition is essential among people who live under the rubric of the disabled mind. We do not all need to use the same words, but we do need to know that our myriad words, our burgeoning words, our proliferation of words, can help us move further into the lives we wish to live.

## NOTES

1. Critiques of DSM-IV have followed. Marie Crowe argues that DSM-IV constructs an implicit standard of normality on the basis of four unstated criteria: productivity, unity, moderation, and rationality. In February 2010, the American Psychiatric Association published a draft of diagnostic criteria expected to appear in DSM-5 (2013), which will no doubt receive its own round of criticisms.

2. This image is no longer available on their Web site. But many parodies remain, including two pages published by Autistics.org, which maintains a page for ISNT (the Institute for the Study of the Neurologically Typical) as well as one for DSN (the Diagnostic and Statistical Manual of Normal Disorders) (Home page). The autism clock itself has been taken down.

## WORKS CITED

Aho, Kevin. "Medicalizing Mental Health: A Phenomenological Alternative." *Journal of Medical Humanities* 29 (2008): 243–59. Print.

Antonetta, Susanne. *A Mind Apart: Travels in a Neurodiverse World*. New York: Penguin, 2005. Print.

Aristotle. *The Complete Works of Aristotle*. Ed. and trans. Jonathan Barnes. Vol. 2. Princeton: Princeton UP, 1984. Print. Bollingen Ser. 71.1-2.

Avinger, Charles, Edith Croake, and Jean Kearns Miller. "Breathing Underwater in Academia: Teaching, Learning, and Working with the Challenges of Invisible Illnesses and Hidden (Dis-)Abilities." *Disabled Faculty and Staff in a Disabling Society: Multiple Identities in Higher Education.* Ed. Mary Lee Vance. Huntersville: AHEAD, 2007. 201–15. Print.

Brownlow, Charlotte. "Re-presenting Autism: The Construction of 'NT Syndrome.'" *Journal of Medical Humanities* 31 (2010): 243–55. Print.

Carlson, Licia. *The Faces of Intellectual Disability: Philosophical Reflections.* Bloomington: Indiana UP, 2010. Print.

Crowe, Marie. "Constructing Normality: A Discourse Analysis of the DSM-IV." *Journal of Psychiatric and Mental Health Nursing* 7 (2000): 69–77. Print.

Davis, Lawrence J. "The Encyclopedia of Insanity." *Harper's Magazine* Feb. 1997: 61–66. Print.

*Diagnostic and Statistical Manual of Mental Disorders: Text Revision.* 4th ed. Arlington: Amer. Psychiatric Assn., 2000. Print.

Erevelles, Nirmala. "Signs of Reason: Rivière, Facilitated Communication, and the Crisis of the Subject." *Foucault and the Government of Disability.* Ed. Shelley Tremain. Ann Arbor: U of Michigan P, 2005. 45–64. Print.

Hacking, Ian. *Mad Travelers: Reflections on the Reality of Transient Mental Illness.* Cambridge: Harvard UP, 1998. Print.

Haraway, Donna. "Situated Knowledges: The Science Question in Feminism and the Privilege of Partial Perspective." *Simians, Cyborgs, and Women: The Reinvention of Nature.* New York: Routledge, 1991. 183–201. Print.

Home page. Autistics.org, 11 Feb. 2010. Web. 7 July 2010.

*Introducing ANI.* Autism Network Intl., 26 June 2002. Web. 7 July 2010.

Lewiecki-Wilson, Cynthia. "Rethinking Rhetoric through Mental Disabilities." *Rhetoric Review* 22.2 (2003): 156–67. Print.

McCarthy, Lucille Parkinson, and Joan Page Gerring. "Revising Psychiatry's Charter Document DSM-IV." *Written Communication* 11.2 (1994): 147–92. Print.

*Mental Health.* World Health Organization, n.d. Web. 7 July 2010.

Nagel, Thomas. *The View from Nowhere.* New York: Oxford UP, 1986. Print.

*Neurotypical Syndrome.* Uncyclopedia, 2 July 2010. Web. 7 July 2010.

*The Numbers Count: Mental Disorders in America.* Natl. Inst. of Mental Health, 6 July 2010. Web. 7 July 2010.

*Our Mission.* Autism Speaks, n.d. Web. 7 July 2010.

Prendergast, Catherine. "On the Rhetorics of Mental Disability." *Towards a Rhetoric of Everyday Life: New Directions in Research on Writing, Text, and Discourse.* Ed. Martin Nystrand and John Duffy. Madison: U of Wisconsin P, 2003. 189–206. Print.

Quintilian. *The Orator's Education, Books 11–12.* Ed. and trans. Donald A. Russell. Cambridge: Harvard UP, 2001. Print.

Radden, Jennifer, ed. *The Nature of Melancholy: From Aristotle to Kristeva.* New York: Oxford UP, 2000. Print.

Titchkosky, Tanya. "Disability: A Rose by Any Other Name? 'People-First' Language in Canadian Society." *Canadian Review of Sociology and Anthropology* 38.2 (2001): 125–40. Print.

Vidali, Amy. "Rhetorical Hiccups: Disability Disclosure in Letters of Recommendation." *Rhetoric Review* 28.2 (2009): 185–204. Print.

Wilson, Mitchell. "DSM-III and the Transformation of American Psychiatry: A History." *American Journal of Psychiatry* 150.3 (1993): 399–410. Print.

# Addressing Deafness:
# From Hearing Loss to Deaf Gain

KRISTEN HARMON

*Whatever the cause, it is certainly the case that adult deaf-mutes are some-times hampered by the instinctive prejudices of hearing persons with whom they desire to have business or social relations. Many persons have the idea they are dangerous, morose, ill-tempered, et cetera. . . . [A deaf-mute] is sometimes looked upon as a sort of monstrosity, to be stared at and avoided. . . . In fact fallacies concerning the deaf and dumb are so common as to touch us all and to suggest the advisability of seriously examining the fundamen-tal ideas we hold concerning them.*

—Alexander Graham Bell, 1884

"I just read that 'deaf mute' is an offensive term," writes one poster to the Internet discussion forum *Answerbag*. "I did not know this until now, and I have no idea what the non-offensive term would be, do you?" Answers fol-low, ranging from an observation that the term *deaf-mute* is widely used in newspaper accounts to a diatribe against "pussy-footing around" with "care-fully worded names" to, finally, the authoritative-sounding suggestion, "In modern use, deaf mute has acquired negative connotations. It is advisable to avoid it in favor of other terms such as profoundly deaf." "Thanks, that was a great answer! :)," responds the original poster, who then presumably uses this term to the chagrin of many deaf people this person will encounter.

*Deaf-mute*, like *deaf and dumb*, calls up images of raggedy, squinty-eyed boys and men, sooty from the Victorian era, while *profoundly deaf*, at least

---

The author is professor of English at Gallaudet University.

 PROFESSION

for me—also deaf and mostly profoundly so—calls up the image of a woebegone child wearing body-style hearing aids dripping with cords, an artifact of the 1960s and 1970s. Dusty relics these particular terms may be, but the persistence of the problem with naming, describing, and self-identification has implications for both sides of the "hearing line": What do I call you? What do I call myself? Who—and what—are we in relation to each other?[1] Extraction of quantifying urges (How much do you really hear?) and the shifting imbalances of the hearing-deaf frame of reference prove difficult for the ostensibly collaborative processes inherent in usage and bias-free language. How can a deaf person simply not be deaf? Do the modifying adjectives *mildly* or *partially*—as opposed to *profoundly*—ameliorate, pacify, the requirements of a hearing bias?

Given the wide-ranging connotations of terms related to deafness and deaf people, what is an enterprising writer, like the original poster to *Answerbag*, to do? The Modern Language Association advises, "Careful writers do not use language that implies unsubstantiated or irrelevant generalizations about such personal qualities as age, birth or family status, disability, economic class, ethnicity, political or religious beliefs, race, sex, or sexual orientation" (*MLA Style Manual* 82). Internet searches on suggestions for bias-free language related to deafness provide a range of mostly people-first answers: a *hearing-impaired* or *hearing-disabled person, a person with deafness, a person who can't speak or hear, a late-deafened person, a speech-handicapped person*, and so on.

This carousel of nomenclature circles up and down and around fundamental ideas regarding sensory integration and the physical body: deaf is deaf and as a substantiated generalization based on where one fits in a spectrum of sensory difference is always defined in relation to hearing, a much more powerful partner in that binary. To use one descriptive term over another is to sanction a particular ideology, with the end result that hearing status is often used in print as shorthand for an imaginary personal and social biography. Don't we all know what a profoundly deaf person's life must be like?

The nature of this bias, intended and unintended, has been well described in print with the discussion of phonocentrism (Bauman, "Listening"; Nelson) and audism (Humphries). Audism is that "system of advantage based on hearing ability" whereby "the privilege allotted to hearing people can be made visible and thus recognized" (Bauman, "Audism" 241). Further, many widely used abstractions, even some perceived to be bias-free, are complicated or deconstructed by renaming efforts made by deaf people themselves and by intracommunity reclamation of stigmatized language.

Contemporary efforts at renaming are meant to avoid impairment language and also to make key distinctions, because deaf people are not an undifferentiated mass. Importantly, usage of these terms affirms the centrality of language, signed or spoken, in a deaf person's life in ways that terms like *profoundly deaf* cannot. What is at stake is the prerogative for describing and claiming which language and social grouping is most important for a particular deaf individual. There are exceptions to each category named below and overlap between categories, but many if not most deaf people describe themselves in relation to signed or spoken language communities.

Primary affiliations to sign language–based communities are described through such constructions as *Deaf*, to describe users of American Sign Language who are also members of the Deaf-World, a sociolinguistic community;[2] *hard of hearing*, to describe a range of behaviors related to speech, sign language, and the use of hearing technology; and *oral deaf*, to describe those who have not learned sign language or who choose not to, relying primarily on lipreading, speech, and other communication technologies. These terms are perhaps less descriptive than they used to be as the post–Deaf President Now movement of 1988 and the post–Americans with Disabilities Act generation comes of age.[3]

Recently, *d/Deaf*, a somewhat unsatisfactory coinage, has been used as an inclusive term describing all deaf individuals—yet also recognizing the significant social and linguistic differences among deaf people—and as a description of the spectrum of identification with Deaf communities. The term is based on sign language fluency and other factors. Finally, there's the simple *deaf*, which is often used in print to refer to oral deaf people or to the fact of sensory difference. It is largely descriptive of social, political, and biological categories and processes and distinct from the jarring emphasis on the flattening and aggregating technicalities of hearing loss, as seen in *profoundly deaf*.

In answer to those who would focus, with obsessive shortsightedness, on the sheer profundity of loss, some Deaf activists are advocating for the reclamation of the term DEAF-MUTE or MUTE-DEAF.[4] As the Deaf activist and ASL poet Ella Mae Lentz noted on a video log (and this is a loose transliteration of a section of her argument):

> I've always preached to people never to use the phrase "deaf mute" . . . but in the last one or two years, I've been analyzing Deafhood . . . we need to look again at that phrase. . . . The sign DEAF, if you examine what it means, it means no hearing, no speech, that hearing and speech are put aside. We've been signing DEAF-MUTE, but spelling out only D-E-A-F [not mute]. When confronted with the reversal of a term, op-

pressors are made powerless; they can't use the word to hurt anymore.
. . . DEAF-MUTES are the reason why ASL has continued to be strong;
without DEAF-MUTES, ASL would either diminish or disappear.[5]

She concludes the video log by noting that this reclamation is an intracommunity concern; *deaf-mute* is not to be used by those who reiterate
the pejorative elements.

Lentz and others (Bahan) who have raised the possibility of DEAF-
MUTE as a reclaimed term emphasize signed language as a key adaptation to a deaf-mute and thus visually-oriented state of being; speech is put
aside as a diminished or irrelevant technology. To reclaim DEAF-MUTE
is to refute medicopedagogy and the valorization of speech at all costs. To
claim DEAF-MUTE is also to assert a unique sensory, linguistic, physiological identity—and a particular history—as a "people of the eye."[6]

The notion of mute is complex but ultimately revealing. Some Deaf
and hard-of-hearing people do speak but also identify primarily with
the signing, Deaf, community. Some who also speak choose not to use
their voices in various social situations but especially in fraught hearing-
deaf situations, when it is imperative that communication be unbroken.
(An airline gate change, announced only through auditory means, and a
difficult-to-lip-read, mustachioed, and harried desk clerk come to mind.)
Armed with pen and paper, a deaf-mute presence ensures, ironically, access in a way that a deaf-speaking presence does not consistently provide
("But you talk! Why do you want me to write down everything I'm saying?). After all, for many d/Deaf people, speech functions largely as a
one-way technology; return communication is not consistent and cannot
always be relied on without additional means and strategies.

When d/Deaf persons do not choose to use a clear, intelligible, speaking voice in order to get the access they demand for participation in the
(hearing) public sphere, the ways in which hearing and speech are imper-
fect bases for essentializing descriptive identity categories are revealed.
Deafness and, for that matter, muteness are conditional and contextual.
After all, a hearing and nonsigning person becomes effectively deaf and
mute in a Deaf gathering; the space is filled with American Sign Language, expressive faces, hands, bodies, linguistic motion. In this context,
the term DEAF-MUTE or MUTE-DEAF resists the clinical and stigmatized weight of socially reductive suffixes (like -*ness*) and medicalized
terms (like *mute*). Viewed through a visual modality, *profound deafness* is
diminished, made over into a common physiological factor, one that has
significant implications for the development of a visually oriented mind
and state of being in the world (see Corina and Singleton).

In a related effort to dismantle the pathologizing binaries enclosing a Deaf person in a hearing world, some scholars have expressed dissatisfaction with both the word and sign for deaf. In casual conversation and in print (see Obasi), students and scholars have tried to conceive of a term that would place the emphasis on visuality and shared language rather than on hearing or speaking status. They have proposed, as alternative terms for Deaf people, *signing people*, *people of the eye*, and ASL-PERSON (or, in English, "ASLians" or "ASL-ers"). The construct ASL-PERSON goes beyond disability as the "reception and construction of that difference" (Davis 50), in that ability is no longer the contested site; language use and access are. To some, this suggestion might feel like yet another semantic exercise about perception and self-identification, but beyond breath and water there is little more that is fundamental to being human than communication.

The original poster to *Answerbag* and others like the poster are now awkwardly navigating terminology in this context. Intra- and intercommunity usage is always in flux. In addition to the current discussion, the primary affiliations in relation to and fundamental ideas about d/Deaf communities will continue to change as the post–Deaf President Now and post-ADA generation comes of age and redefines the virtual and physical social spaces for deaf and Deaf people. Furthermore, affiliation is made all the more complex with other primary identifications not mentioned here: those related to gender, sexuality, race, ethnicity, disability, and so on.

In the meantime, the Gallaudet scholars Dirksen Bauman and Joseph Murray have proposed the construct *Deaf gain* as the opposing pair to *hearing loss*; in addition to upsetting the usual assumptions contained in the notion of loss, this phrase is used to describe the "advantages . . . of biodiversity" that Deaf people have—namely, "increased spatial cognition, speed of generating mental images, peripheral vision, and tactile acuity" ("Deaf Gain"). The Visual Language, Visual Learning Center ($VL^2$), a National Science Foundation–funded Science of Learning Center on the campus of Gallaudet University, is researching some of those physiological and neurological changes. Clearly, we have moved beyond *profoundly deaf* into considering the ways in which languages, communities, and individuals come into contact; we are now living beyond the suffix, in postdeafness.

## NOTES

This work was supported in part by the National Science Foundation Science of Learning Center: Visual Language and Visual Learning—funding grant #SBE-0541953 to $VL^2$ at Gallaudet University.

1. The "hearing line," for Christopher Krentz, is "a conscious echo of W. E. B. DuBois's 'color line'" and as such is the "invisible boundary separating deaf and hearing people . . . [where] the meanings of deafness and its conceptual opposite, 'hearingness,' [are] at least as unstable as other identity categories" (2).

2. According to Lane, Bahan, and Hoffmeister, "When we refer to the DEAF-WORLD in the U.S., we are concerned with a group (an estimated million people) possessing a unique language and culture. . . . Deaf people in the U.S. use the sign DEAF-WORLD to refer to those relationships among themselves, to the social network they have set up, and not to any notion of geographical location" (ix, 5).

3. The Deaf President Now movement took place on the campus of Gallaudet University. After a brief student-and-alumni protest, a deaf president was installed at the world's only institution of higher education for deaf people.

4. The use of all capital letters indicates that this term is a gloss of a sign in American Sign Language.

5. In signing DEAF, the signer places a finger on the ear and then on the mouth, or vice versa. Lentz makes parallels with the GLBT community's reclamation of *queer* and *dyke*. Paddy Ladd, a British Deaf studies scholar, developed the term *Deafhood* to "begin the process of defining the existential state of Deaf 'being in the world.' . . . Deafhood is not seen as a finite state but as a process by which Deaf individuals come to actualise their Deaf identity" (xviii).

6. In 1910, George Veditz, president of the National Association of the Deaf, argued that "deaf people could never abandon sign language: 'they are facing not a theory but a condition, for they are first, last, and all time *the* people of the eye'" (qtd. in Baynton 10).

## WORKS CITED

Bahan, Ben. "Developing the Deaf Nation." Deaf Nation Symposium. U of Central Lancashire, 9–11 July 1997. Address.

Baynton, Douglas. *Forbidden Signs: American Culture and the Campaign against Sign Language*. Chicago: U of Chicago P, 1996. Print.

Bauman, Dirksen. "Audism: Exploring the Metaphysics of Oppression." *Journal of Deaf Studies and Deaf Education* 9.2 (2004): 239–46. Print.

———. "Listening to Phonocentrism with Deaf Eyes: Derrida's Mute Philosophy of (Sign) Language." *Essays in Philosophy* 9.1 (2008): n. pag. 12 Jan. 2009. Web. 7 July 2010.

Bell, Alexander Graham. *Memoirs upon the Formation of a Deaf Variety of the Human Race*. Washington: GPO, 1884. Print.

Corina, David, and Jenny Singleton. "Developmental Social Cognitive Neuroscience: Insights from Deafness." *Child Development* 80.4 (2009): 952–67. Print.

Davis, Lennard. *Bending Over Backwards: Disability, Dismodernism, and Other Difficult Positions*. New York: New York UP, 2002. Print.

"Deaf Gain Concept Introduced." *On the Green* 38.7 (2009): n. pag. Web. 7 July 2010.

Humphries, Tom. "The Making of a Word: Audism." 1975. TS.

"I just read. . . ." *Answerbag*. 21 Aug. 2007. Web. 8 July 2010. <http://www.answerbag.com/q_view/378952>.

Krentz, Christopher. *Writing Deafness: The Hearing Line in Nineteenth-Century American Literature*. Chapel Hill: U of North Carolina P, 2007. Print.

Ladd, Paddy. *Understanding Deaf Culture: In Search of Deafhood*. Clevedon: Multilingual Matters, 2003. Print.

Lane, Harlan, Benjamin Bahan, and Robert Hoffmeister. *Journey into the Deaf World*. San Diego: DawnSign, 1996. Print.

Lentz, Ella Mae. "Reclaiming 'Deaf-Mute.'" *Ella's Flashlight: A Deaf-Mute's Search for Deafhood Enlightenment*. Lentz, 21 Feb. 2007. Web. 10 Jan. 2009. Blog.

*MLA Style Manual and Guide to Scholarly Publishing*. 3rd ed. New York: MLA, 2008. Print.

Nelson, Jennifer. "Textual Bodies, Bodily Texts." *Signing the Body Poetic: Essays on American Sign Language Literature*. Ed. H-Dirksen L. Bauman, Nelson, and Heidi M. Rose. Berkeley: U of California P, 2006. 118–29. Print.

Obasi, Chijioke. "Seeing the Deaf in 'Deafness.'" *Journal of Deaf Studies and Deaf Education* 13.4 (2008): 455–65. Print.

# The Financial Landscape
## of Higher Education:
## Mapping a Rough Road Ahead

LINDA RAY PRATT

The lingering national fiscal crisis enters year 3 with the beginning of academic year 2010–11. Institutions are feeling the stress of the deepest budget cuts to American colleges and universities since the post–World War II boom, and few have found their way out of budget difficulties that began in 2008. To make matters worse, forty-three states are again reducing their support for higher education (Johnson, Oliff, and Williams). The expansion of faculties, research grants, and growing state budgets that led to the development of the multicampus megauniversities has stalled. The pressure of growing student enrollment that drove this development has not abated, however, and institutions faced with declining state funds are shifting the costs to students, sometimes through tuition increases over 10%. Even with substantial tuition increases in some states, higher education institutions face a third—and most likely a fourth—year of no raises, furloughs, larger classes, reduced travel, and a host of other restrictive measures.

Budget cuts are hardly new to higher education, but the size and the conditions behind this fiscal crisis are different. The budget shortfalls in FY03 and FY04, for example, were the low point of a recession that deepened sharply after 9/11 shocked an economy that had been slipping into recession since March 2001. In 2003–04 many public colleges and universities had a zero increase in their state budget allotments, and a few had actual cuts. In that context, a 5% cut was a terrible thing. At its lowest

*The author is executive vice president and provost of the University of Nebraska system. A version of this article appeared in the* ADFL Bulletin *41.1 (2009).*

points, the budget shortfall in the states was $75 billion in 2003 and $80 billion in 2004. In contrast, the shortfall in state budgets for 2009 is likely to be $106 billion, and the projected shortfall for 2010 is $145 billion. Predicting 2011 is risky, but those who study these trends estimate that it could reach $180 billion (Lav and McNichol). The persistent unemployment figures will undermine state revenues despite the trend toward recovery in the stock market. A September 2009 report from Moody's Investors Service examines a variety of factors and concludes that the harshest days for higher education could still be ahead (Carew). In some states, that will clearly be the case.

Many of our institutions had budget cuts over 10% for 2009–10, and some had to make midyear cuts in 2008–09. According to data from the Center on Budget and Policy Priorities, public colleges and universities in at least thirty states received cuts in their budgets in 2009 (Johnson, Oliff, and Koulish). Some cuts were as high as 26%. In all but a few states, public pressure or legislated restrictions have suppressed tuition hikes that would be large enough to compensate for the cuts. Those public institutions, such as the University of California, that have significantly increased tuition or fees have limited access for many students, which may have long-term consequences for their state support.

Many of the institutions facing the most severe cuts are already in their third year of reductions. In FY09 thirteen states had midyear shortfalls of more than 10%.[1]Arizona topped the list with 15.9%, followed closely by Illinois, Massachusetts, North Carolina, and California. Of the states that initially projected a budget gap in FY10 against the FY09 general fund, California took the lead with 33.5%, followed by Nevada with 31.7%; Arizona with 29.8%; New York with 29.0%; and Illinois, Connecticut, Florida, Washington, Wisconsin, Louisiana, North Carolina, and Vermont with gaps of 20% or more. (See Lav and McNichol for charts of midyear FY09 budget gaps and projected FY10 budget gaps for each state.)

Stimulus money and reserve funds in many states were able to reduce the size of these gaps by almost half. According to Scott D. Pattison, executive director of the National Association of State Budget Officers, the flow of stimulus money staved off paralysis in many states (qtd. in Goodnough). About 40% of the deficits in state budgets have been covered by the 2009 American Recovery and Reinvestment Act (ARRA) Fiscal Stabilization Fund (Lav and McNichol). This money was primarily targeted for education, and even in states that put little of it in higher education, ARRA assistance to the state budget in other areas freed up funds that could then be redirected to higher education. Without the nearly $140 billion over two years from the ARRA stimulus package, state deficits in the last eighteen months would have been much higher, but the stimulus money must be disbursed by September 2011. Many states and public institutions of education are facing the "cliff effect"—the loss of millions of dollars in stimulus funds from state support or federal research grants.

The budget for the University of California system dwarfs that of most other institutions, but if we scale the numbers to fit their budgets, the system's situation is instructive of what happened to many states. In a 17 June 2009 letter, President Mark G. Yudof laid out the options to meet a net state funding shortfall for FY09 and FY10 of $570.8 million, the still uncovered part of a total University of California shortfall of nearly $800 million. The memo described three options to reduce salaries for all staff and faculty members by 8%, a measure that would add $195 million in savings toward the deficit. In 2009 the California system still had about $350 million to cut, and Yudof's memo says, "The remainder of the projected cuts will fall to the campuses, and likely will affect course availability, class size, student services, and other aspects of the educational program." Not all faculty members accepted the budget plan, and many participated in protests against it. The state's budget troubles are still in turmoil, and students in fall 2010 will have a 32% increase in their costs and a reduction in enrollments by 2,300 (Johnson, Oliff, and Williams).

In 2009–10 Arizona State eliminated over 550 staff positions and 200 faculty associate positions, consolidating several schools and departments and furloughing most employees for ten to fifteen days. The state of Arizona now has more than $3 billion in deficits, and Arizona State, Northern Arizona State, and the University of Arizona are increasing tuition between 16% and 20% (ABC News). The University of Florida eliminated 150 faculty and staff positions in 2009–10 and increased tuition by 15%. A budget cut of 26% to the University of Washington resulted in eliminating positions despite a 14% increase in tuition (Johnson, Oliff, and Koulish). These large public institutions are the ones we hear the most about, and their situation gives us some indication of the stress higher education as a whole is feeling. The kinds of cuts we read about at the big universities typically extend to all the public institutions in a state, often in similar proportions.[2] In some states, community colleges have been spared deep cuts, but community colleges in general face significant increases in enrollment in the fall without the possibility of an increase of funds to help them meet it.

I have focused on the public schools because, first, 75% of the 18 million students in the United States are in them and, second, their budget data are usually accessible to the public. The scenarios in private colleges and universities revolve around loss of endowment income, the impact of debt on credit ratings, maintaining enrollment, and tuition or scholarship stability (Beja). Most endowment funds declined between 25% and 40% in 2008 and suffered an 18.7% loss overall in 2009 (Lavelle). There was clear improvement in financial markets by the end of 2009, but the markets have been unstable and erratic so far in 2010. The Dow and S&P averages have risen but are still significantly below where they were at the high point in October 2007 (Lauricella). The degree of cuts to the privates depends on how much of their budget relies on endowment and how much is covered by tuition. A survey released in August 2009 reported that as many as two-thirds of private colleges are freezing salaries and over half are cutting salaries.[3] Many face an immediate cash-flow problem. Even universities with huge endowments, such as Harvard and Stanford, are making significant cuts. Generally, smaller institutions fared better than larger ones, but not always. Greensboro College in North Carolina had a 40% decline in its endowment income and a drop in enrollment. In April 2009, it ran short of money to complete the fiscal year and imposed a 20% pay cut, canceled sabbaticals, and suspended many benefits (June). A few small colleges, such as Dana College in Nebraska, have gone under or been purchased by for-profit institutions. Sustaining enrollment is critical to private colleges financed more by tuition than by endowment, but some students are migrating to the publics for the lower tuition.

Although higher education has had a bumpy ride in the past twenty years, it was unprepared for a fiscal crisis of this magnitude. The crisis felt sudden, yet the omens have been on the horizon for almost a decade, both in the inflated national financial markets and in the expansion of higher education on permanent budgets that ran close to the bone. The collapse of Enron in 2001 and then of Arthur Andersen, the accounting giant associated with Enron, was in retrospect a forerunner of what happened in the summer and fall of 2008. Enron's rise in the 1980s and 1990s relied on marketing, fraudulent accounting, and fraudulently inflated stock prices. Andersen's once reputable accounting practices were compromised by the desire to please clients who wanted to cut corners to make big profits and by Andersen's own interest in growing their client list.[4] The greed and arrogance of Enron and Andersen were one with the practices of an entire financial structure that came crashing down in the collapse of Bear Stearns, Lehman Brothers, and AIG. Banks and other businesses that built on bad credit and risky expansion of expenditures, not to mention individual citizens whose personal lifestyle reflected similar practices, have experienced their own versions of financial collapse.

Colleges and universities expanded with the general economy. The growth of federal funds from the National Institutes of Health, the National Science Foundation, and the Department of Defense doubled and tripled the federal research investment in some universities. Research funding in the high research universities runs from $100 million to over $800 million a year. The University of Michigan reached $876 million in 2008, according to the 2009 annual report to the Board of Regents (Swanson and Jones). Most of these federal grants return 45% to 48% of the money to the institution in indirect costs. For every million in federal grants, the campus distributes about half that amount back to the administration, college, department, and faculty investigator, depending on the institution's formula.

As the dollars grew for science research, so did the space, maintenance costs, and demands on faculty time. Concurrently, we've had a steady decline in the percent of state budgets going to higher education, but most public institutions continued to fund core programs and faculty salaries with state funds. To meet the growing research and teaching demands, the course load shifted from tenured faculty members to temporary faculty members, who could be hired for less money and without a long-term budget commitment. Research faculty members were hired off the tenure track and paid from federal grants. The need to expand facilities was assisted by the generosity of donors, who pay for buildings but not for maintenance and operations. The increase of non-tenure-track faculty members may have been a barometer of fiscal stress in institutions that continued to grow even as funding tightened and the public grew more impatient with rising college costs. Our institutions kept the enterprise afloat with revenue growth in the four major sources of income that support virtually all our colleges and universities: tuition and fee income, state support, endowment income, and federal research grants. Three of the four—tuition and fees, endowment, state support—experienced deep stress in the last fiscal year. The fourth factor, federal research grants, has exploded in size, thanks to the ARRA, but these funds will disappear in 2011. The ARRA research money was intended as a bridge for institutions that needed time to make cuts to the permanent budget. It is not yet clear how well higher education will handle the drop-off when the funds expire.

Although there have been some signs of recovery in the economy, they have not yet translated into lowering unemployment. With unemployment at about 10% nationally and higher in some areas (Oregon is at 16%), with personal income taxes down 26% for the first quarter of 2009, and with heavy losses still accumulating in finances, dry goods, manufacturing, and tourism (Prah), few forecasters expect that the next fiscal year will recover to the level of two years ago and that the effects of the recession will end by 2011. The end of the recession does not mean, however, that everything goes back to where it was before the crisis hit. It means only a resuming of growth, and we should temper our expectations. Too much of the wealth of the lost economy was based on fraud, bad credit, and inflated value in unregulated markets. A recovered economy will be leaner than the one that collapsed. We need to be thinking about what the post-free-fall economy will look like and about how higher education must shape its future to fit it.

Given what happened in FY10 and continues in FY11, the reshaping of higher education budgets will affect the stability of the tenure system, academic freedom, the size of the faculty, salary levels, class size, course load, the number of academic degree programs, research, enrollments, new building, and campus facilities. Institutions are restructuring some departments and colleges; some may even merge smaller campuses. The constraints of academic budgets allow for little flexibility without cutting personnel and programs. Between 70% and 80% of a campus's permanent budget is typically in personnel.

If cuts are to be managed, it is crucial to understand costs. Faculty members frequently point to the increase in the number of top administrators and their salaries, but the area of real personnel increase has been in managerial and support staff. This group of employees nearly doubled since 1987, but instructional jobs rose only by about 50% (Brainard, Fain, and Masterson). Faculty salaries have not been the major driver of increased costs that most people assume. Jane V. Wellman, who is the best scholar of higher education budgets, has shown that new revenues from tuition increases essentially all went to nonclassroom costs (Wellman et al.). Parents and students who complain about increased tuition would no doubt be even more upset to realize that those increases did not go into academic program budgets. Staff cuts have been heavier than faculty cuts in many places, and most institutions are trying not to cut their tenure-track faculty.

Our institutions have not had much time for long-range planning for reduced budgets, and they have little appetite to do such planning. The window of time the ARRA money afforded us to reorder priorities to accommodate new budgets is closing. What can we expect, and what can we affect? We can expect a significant stall of real salary growth. One hopes that a year or two from now, most institutions will no longer be cutting payroll, but salaries are likely to level out for at least the next three years. Hiring was frozen at many institutions in 2009–10, and little hiring is likely to be done in 2010–11. Enrollments are still going up in most public institutions, but the size of the faculty is not. Many faculty members are teaching more students, whether by increased course assignment or larger class size. For English composition and language instruction, larger classes will challenge the current teaching methodologies, which are designed for classes of eighteen to twenty-two students. Pressure to change how we teach is likely to cause academic freedom problems.

The most vulnerable academic areas will be programs that have few majors or few student credit hours in the core curriculum. English departments are typically among the largest departments in an institution, but many modern language departments are already struggling to sustain enrollment in anything but Spanish and French. Historically, tenured faculty members in French and German were the core of most modern language departments, and how to make equitable teaching assignments for faculty members in languages that no longer have healthy enrollments is a familiar problem to every chair. Also at risk in many departments will be the efforts to teach Chinese, Arabic, and Hindi, three languages of emerging global importance but for which enrollments are still small. To use their faculty efficiently, many institutions have imposed enrollment minimums per section and degree minimums per program. All but a few institutions must give priority to undergraduate education or face erosion of their tuition base. President Obama's goal that 55% of Americans attain a college degree will require a 42% growth in college enrollments. Our institutions will be hungry for this enrollment but have few resources to accommodate it. Greater efficiency in the use of faculty members and greater concentration in undergraduate degrees both seem inevitable.

Faculty members in English and modern languages will need to take a cold-eyed look beyond this fiscal year. The best chance of getting through the next three years with work that preserves jobs and offers professional fulfillment is creative management of the change. The first thing to do is understand what is really happening to the budget of one's institution and what its sources of funds are. That knowledge will enable departments to assess the scope of the trouble and plan accordingly. English departments that include the required composition program have the advantage of student credit-hour production but the vulnerability of the largest number of non-tenure-track faculty members. Terminations of part-time and temporary faculty members can mean major changes in a department that has heavily relied on their assistance to teach the composition program. Departments that may be swamped by first-year composition requirements may want to implement a strong writing-across-the-curriculum plan if they do not already have one. A core general education requirement should be considered the business of the units that require it, not just the department that has historically taught it.

Programs that are campus priorities will be protected, and collateral programs that address those priorities will have a better chance of holding on to their funding. Tenured faculty members are a department's most valuable asset, and they must be protected if the program is to have a future. Leadership that looks to increase productivity in ways that help sustain the budget, such as improving student credit hours per full-time equivalent instructor (SCH/FTE), will come out better than leadership that cannot come to terms with a new fiscal reality. Departments that can connect their interests with those of other programs will gain strength in numbers and program support. For example, a department's interest in languages may be aligned with the burst of commitment to global studies and study-abroad programs. If a school has a program in international business, a modern language department might provide business students with a deeper understanding of the languages and customs of the international world. Curricular interests in interdisciplinary areas may lead to fruitful connections to faculty members in history, political science, English, art history, and international studies. Russian professors faced with declining enrollments may find work in programs in Eastern European studies or modern European history.

For some departments, distance education offers possibilities of expanding enrollment and sustaining degrees. If faculty losses threaten a program's integrity, perhaps departments can collaborate, each to preserve its own program. Faculty members who actively recruit students from high schools with language fairs, campus visits, and calls to students may be able to increase interest in language study and bolster enrollments. Service learning can be a bridge to the community. It attracts students and builds goodwill. It is good to have friends when one is on the chopping block. A department might involve itself in K–12 education, one of the few areas that most states must make a budget priority. Many programs are already doing these and other things. The point is that chairs should think as creatively as possible to strengthen their departments' value and sustainability in the institution.

Even in a fiscal crisis there are opportunities, and it is important for morale and our future to find ways to move forward in the midst of retrenchment. In open, inclusive, and transparent processes, departments should articulate their priorities and develop a strategy to keep what they most need and go after what they most want. Chairs have a special responsibility to think hard about what can be done and to take leadership in helping others see and understand the possibilities. Never underestimate what a difference good leadership can make or how the practice of transparency and inclusion can mitigate bitterness and anger. Overcoming a difficult challenge is the source of our satisfaction, and departments will look to their chair to help them through the next few years. Programs, careers, lives will be changed before we get through this austere landscape, and how we get through it will revise our understanding of an academic career.

## NOTES

1. All but four states—Alabama, Michigan, New York, and Texas—begin their fiscal year on 1 July (Goodnough).

2. Western Washington University in Bellingham, for example, has a $6 million cut, resulting in the elimination of 164 positions, increased class size, and reductions in maintenance, according to President Bruce Shepard (qtd. in Millage). Florida State University announced a three-year plan that would cut $56 million and lay off up to 200 faculty and staff members ("New FSU Budget").

3. The survey, done by Yaffee and Company, was based on 259 responses from private colleges in 39 states (Fain).

4. Numerous accounts of the fall of Enron and Arthur Andersen are available online. For a selection of the extended coverage by *Time* in 2002, see *Behind the Enron Scandal*. Of particular interest are the essays by Kadlec; Pellegrini.

## WORKS CITED

ABC News. "Arizona Universities Vote to Raise Tuition." *ABC News on Campus*. ABC News, 11 Mar. 2010. Web. 9 Aug. 2010.

*Behind the Enron Scandal. Time.* Time, n.d. Web. 16 Oct. 2009.

Beja, Marc. "Moody's Warns of 'Sharp Deterioration' in College Finances." *Chronicle of Higher Education*. Chronicle of Higher Educ., 8 June 2009. Web. 15 Oct. 2009.

Brainard, Jeffrey, Paul Fain, and Kathryn Masterson. "Support-Staff Jobs Double in Twenty Years, Outpacing Enrollment." *Chronicle of Higher Education*. Chronicle of Higher Educ., 24 Apr. 2009. Web. 15 Oct. 2009.

Carew, Emma L. "Recession Eases, but Worst Effects May Still Be Ahead for Colleges, Moody's Report Says." *Chronicle of Higher Education*. Chronicle of Higher Educ., 16 June 2009. Web. 15 Oct. 2009.

Fain, Paul. "Private Colleges Freeze Salaries and Slash Benefits, Survey Finds." *Chronicle of Higher Education*. Chronicle of Higher Educ., 17 Aug. 2009. Web. 15 Oct. 2009.

Goodnough, Abby. "States Turning to Last Resorts in Budget Crisis." *New York Times*. New York Times, 22 June 2009. Web. 15 Oct. 2009.

Johnson, Nicholas, Phil Oliff, and Jeremy Koulish. "An Update on State Budget Cuts." *Center on Budget and Policy Priorities*. Center on Budget and Policy Priorities, 13 May 2009. Web. 15 Oct. 2009.

Johnson, Nicholas, Phil Oliff, and Erica Williams. "An Update on State Budget Cuts." *Center on Budget and Policy Priorities*. Center on Budget and Policy Priorities, 4 Aug. 2010. Web. 9 Aug. 2010.

June, Audrey Williams. "Sharing the Pain: Cutting Faculty Salaries across the Board." *Chronicle of Higher Education*. Chronicle of Higher Educ., 26 June 2009. Web. 15 Oct. 2009.

Kadlec, Daniel. "Enron: Who's Accountable?" *Time*. Time, 13 Jan. 2002. Web. 15 Oct. 2009.

Lauricella, Tom. "Is This Bull Cyclical or Secular?" *Wall Street Journal* 15 June 2009: C1. Print.

Lav, Iris J., and Elizabeth McNichol. "State Budget Troubles Worsen." *Center on Budget and Policy Priorities*. Center on Budget and Policy Priorities, 18 May 2009. Web. 15 Oct. 2009.

Lavelle, Louis. "University Endowments: Worst Year since Great Depression." *Bloomberg Businessweek*. Bloomberg, 28 Jan. 2010. Web. 9 Aug. 2010.

Millage, Kira. "WWU Adopts Budget with Staff Cuts, Tuition Increase." *Bellingham Herald*. Bellingham Herald, 12 June 2009. Web. 15 Oct. 2009.

"New FSU Budget Calls for Elimination of Two Hundred Jobs." *Jacksonville Observer*. Jacksonville Observer, 14 June 2009. Web. 15 Oct. 2009.

Pellegrini, Frank. "Andersen: The Whistle Not Blown." *Time*. Time, 17 Jan. 2002. Web. 15 Oct. 2009.

Prah, Pamela M. "Reports: State Income Levels Plunge." *Stateline.org*. Pew Charitable Trusts, 19 June 2009. Web. 15 Oct. 2009.

Swanson, Kyle, and Mallory Jones. "'U' Posts Strong Research Funding Numbers." *Michigan Daily*. Michigan Daily, 22 Jan. 2009. Web. 15 Oct. 2009.

Wellman, Jane V., et al. *Trends in College Spending: Where Does the Money Come From? Where Does It Go?* Washington: Delta Cost Project, 2009. Print.

Yudof, Mark G. Letter to the University of California community. *Budget News and Information*. Univ. of California, Riverside, 17 June 2009. Web. 15 Oct. 2009.

# Literary History and the Curriculum: How, What, and Why

## JENNIFER SUMMIT

The undergraduate literature major, as the MLA *Report to the Teagle Foundation* reminds us, can and should reflect the vitality of the discipline. But by the same logic, the major's weaknesses, as we or our students experience them, emerge from and render visible some of the discipline's unresolved conflicts. One of these conflicts centers on literary history, a topic that drifted from critical attention decades ago but has survived in undergraduate literary curricula, where it now poses a serious problem. The MLA report diagnoses a worrying aimlessness in the current pedagogy of literary history. If there is to be a solution, it will emerge from a new English major that rewrites the historical paradigms that undergird the undergraduate curriculum. This essay describes one such model in the hope of reopening, along with the MLA report, the question of how and why we teach literary history.

Among the aims of the undergraduate major, the MLA report states, is to foster a range of literacies, including what it calls "historical literacy." This is a useful and interesting term: useful because it underscores the humanities' traditional focus on "the value of considering the past," interesting because it situates the study of the past in an array of reading and writing practices that form the central pursuits of the major. By reterming literary history "historical literacy," the report suggests not only an archive of cultural memory that provides background and context but also a

*The author is professor of English and chair of the Department of English at Stanford University, where she is also Eleanor Loring Ritch University Fellow in Undergraduate Education. A version of this article appeared in the* ADE Bulletin *149 (2010).*

dynamic praxis in its own right, manifested in students' enhanced analytic and interpretive skills: knowing literary history, the report asserts, makes us better and more adept readers and thinkers. It thus makes an appeal to the pragmatic value of students' studies. It asserts further that historical literacy advances a more abstract but no less vital goal of personal development: meaningful engagement with the literary past broadens readers' perspectives "beyond our insular selves" (4). Literary history, reconceived as historical literacy, thus offers at once knowledge, skill, and ethos. This represents a significant advance over past thinking about literary history and the curricula that continue to reflect it. But it also begs an important question: How does historical literacy differ from the literary history that structured the traditional curriculum, and how is this difference registered in the objects, methods, and curricula of the new English major?

Many of the questions that the MLA report raises about the teaching of literary history dovetail with issues that Stanford's English department, which I currently chair, grappled with over the academic year 2008–09, when we undertook a major revision of our major. If our rejection of the old major was driven by a sense of the outdatedness of its literary-historical paradigms, the experience of crafting a new major taught us that any curricular reform must begin with the ideas about literary history, implicit or explicit, enshrined at the major's core.

## LITERARY HISTORY AS PROBLEM

The current state of literary history and its pedagogy is best described as transitional: moving away from the certainties of a canonical past, the English major is still structured historically, even if it remains unclear what historical vision or objects that structure manifests. The MLA report reflects—and perhaps to some degree shares in the uncertainties of—this transitional moment, starting with the very language it uses to frame the problem of what it calls the major's "knowledge base." The aim of the English major "should be . . . to acquaint students with representative cultural examples through a designated body of works" and "engage them with . . . cultural traditions" (5); yet "literary studies have properly freed themselves from a knowledge base" grounded in "a fixed, standard set of canonical or representative works" (9).

So the English major should teach "representative examples" and "cultural traditions" through "a designated body of works," yet these contrast with the "canonical or representative works" from which "literary studies have properly freed themselves," raising the question, How are the designated body of works, representative examples, and cultural traditions of the new English major different from the fixed and standard canon of the past? What differentiates the representative cultural examples that we will teach from the canonical or representative works of the canonical past? What, in other words, do these new representative works represent?

## The View from Stanford

My department became convinced of the need to revise its curriculum after surveying our majors and recent graduates, followed by a series of focus groups. These told us that students were very happy with the individual classes they took, most of which we offer as small, intense seminars whose sharp focus is honed by the time constraints of the quarter system. At the same time, our majors and graduates felt that the major as an aggregate lacked coherence. Again and again, students asked us plaintively for a big picture that would supply connections between and across their classes: they confirmed what many of us have long perceived and lamented, that they lack a basic grid of historical knowledge that could give broader perspective and unity to their individual classes. Repeatedly, they told us that they felt the absence of an arc in which their classes could fit together; and in the focus groups, they passionately expressed their collective wish for a historical core or survey class that could provide the background and connections that they lacked.

Colleagues with a long tenure in the department were not surprised to hear that students lacked historical knowledge; they were astonished, however, that the same students now wanted a core, given that the department had rejected its long-standing core as outdated some forty years ago. Like many English departments, ours had a core sequence that surveyed the development of English literature from the Renaissance to the nineteenth century, with separate requirements in Chaucer, Shakespeare, and the English language. A version of this sequence formed the core of the English major in the university's catalog of 1906, when the major was defined around three axes: a "history of English Literature from the beginning to 1798," a language requirement (reflected in the fact that ours was then the Department of English Literature and Rhetoric), and courses in the major canonical authors: "Chaucer, Shakespeare, and Milton (or Wordsworth or Spenser)" (*Announcement* 97). This trinitarian structure of requirements—language, history, and canonical authors—held steady until 1967, when it was dropped in favor of distribution requirements across six broadly defined areas: language, medieval, Renaissance, neoclassic, Romantic and modern, and American (the first time that an American requirement was introduced [*Courses*]).

By replacing the historical core with area requirements, Stanford was slightly ahead of the national trend: in 1985, seventy percent of English departments still required a historical survey; in 1989, it was fifty percent (Laurence 1; Lawrence 13). In place of the survey came area requirements like Stanford's, which are now widespread. Yet, as Gerald Graff observes, the distribution of English department faculties and courses along a chronological array of period specializations still reflects an ideal of historical coverage, however outdated many faculty members find it (6); and the distribution continues to maintain the ideal that drove the old core. The difference is that area requirements disperse responsibility for that ideal over the department as a whole instead of concentrating it in a single survey course or sequence.

Stanford's catalog from 1970 explains the English department's new distribution requirements, while holding fast to the coverage ideal:

> The English Department recognizes that the interests of its majors are extremely various: for this reason the stated formal requirements are minimal. At the same time the Department strongly recommends that all English majors take courses with broad historical perspectives on language and literature . . . , and also more concentrated courses on the great major figures, notably courses in Chaucer, Milton, and Shakespeare.

And it stresses:

> No one of these courses is mandatory, but those covering the background and the evolution of English and American literature, or focusing on the greatest writers, constitute the best preparation . . . of all students seriously interested in the study of English and American literature.   (*Courses* 270)

This statement reflects a paradigm shift in thinking about literary history and its curricular manifestations: while allowing that students come to the study of English with "extremely various" interests, it insists that those who are "seriously interested" in the discipline should still elect to follow a traditional curriculum—even when not compelled to by requirements—in a comprehensive model of literary history and the canonical authors.

Both approaches fell into question in the decades that followed. Stanford's debates over the traditional Western Civilization requirement made the university an easy target of the culture wars of the 1980s and challenged the implicit canon that had anchored the English major requirement. Also in steady decline was the developmental metanarrative of literary history inherited from nineteenth-century philologists, for whom the history of literary works illustrated, as Hans Robert Jauss put it in 1981, "the idea of national individuality on its way to itself" (3). Here it's worth pointing out that literary history and the canon were two distinct entities, both conceptually and pedagogically, though today we sometimes use them interchangeably. My department maintained a sequence of courses called Masterpieces of English Literature (and Masterpieces of American Literature) for nonmajors that was distinct from the required historical survey for majors. But until the abolishment of the historical core, majors also had to take separate courses in single authors, which dominated the curriculum. In other words, the survey represented background and evolution; the single author courses provided culmination. Together, they produced a topography that incorporated the mountains of Chaucer, Shakespeare, and Milton and the valleys of Lydgate and Fulke Greville.

With the switch from the core to area requirements, the canonical authors were absorbed into their background, while the evolutionary model that had informed the core survey was distributed laterally across the periods. Professionally, this switch reflected the decline of generalists and the ascent of specialists, in a fraught dynamic that Graff charts across the first half of the twentieth century. The triumph of the specialist resulted in the much-remarked explosion of research in the subdisciplinary fields that made the old goal of coverage no longer tenable. It also created a situation where no individual could claim to possess the comprehensive view implied by the survey class and projected as the aim of the English major, thus compelling departments to hire evenly across the subfields to maintain the illusion of a common knowledge base that specialization had forced them to abandon.

It is easy to see how departments—Stanford's included—could reach a point that Patricia Schroeder describes in 1993, when "the ostensibly 'objective' goal of coverage has been replaced by consciously directed sampling" (38). It's also easy to see how students—like Stanford's—could find themselves not liberated by such a tasting menu but longing for the historical scaffolding that could bring their disparate classes—however vibrant, challenging, and popular—into a coherent whole.

## Toward a Coherence of Aims rather than Objects

The MLA report asserts, "The requirements for a major should amount to more than a list of courses" (*Report* 5), and calls for "a coherent program of study" that follows "an integrative, synergetic model" (3) and guides students through the acquisition of the English major's distinct knowledge base and skills. These are compelling goals, to be sure; yet at Stanford we were forced to confront the fact that our students were asking for something that we no longer believed in: the arc of literary history no longer holds sway as a dominant mode. If the concept of a developmental metanarrative had long fallen by the wayside—its illness diagnosed by Jauss and its death pronounced by Foucault—today literary history occupies the status of a vexing, but unresolved, question. Indeed, the most provocative recent works on the subject have framed themselves not as vision statements but, literally, as questions. David Simpson asks, "Is literary history the history of everything?"; Mario J. Valdés asks, "Is literary history history?"; and David Perkins asks, in a work whose title says it all, "Is literary history possible?"

On the level of curriculum, our discipline's response to its own unease with literary history has been to erode the period requirements into ever-broader categories, which no longer claim the coherence of the grand narratives that undergirded the historical survey class or the checklist of historical areas from medieval to modern. Thus many departments, Stanford's included, gradually reduced the historical requirement to "two courses before 1750" (or 1660, 1798, 1800, or 1830, as other departments variously define the watershed between literary-historical past and present). As a result, students are administered the literary past in homeopathic doses: they must take two classes before a date that stands for modernity, but these are now unlikely to bear much relation to each other, let alone to those that follow. Meanwhile, we have collapsed the vista into the close-up: if the old English major balanced the study of masterpieces with the topographic survey, the new English major has done away with the justification both for the specific focus (i.e., the distinctness of the masterpiece) and for the big picture (which provided background to or illustrated the evolution of the masterpiece).

Yet if we've abandoned the traditional rationale for literary history and its curricular forms, we haven't abandoned literary history: every course in any period implies a literary-historical model, however submerged. In the temporal arc of our quarters or semesters, we habitually trace miniature lines of development, whether these follow the contours of an author's career or the unfolding of a literary movement, period, genre, or idea. And we routinely posit the principle of historical change in the very language we use to talk about our subject (e.g., "modernity," "print culture," "the postcolonial"), which implies temporal markers before which our subject did not exist and from which our subject emerged into historical distinctness. The real challenge of producing a coherent major on the level of its historical requirements lies in reintroducing the vista, bringing together our various microhistories, and showing students how they join up with or conflict with one another, what stories they tell about how and why a given literary work—and literature itself—matters on a large scale.

## Toward a New Curriculum of Literary History

At Stanford, the necessary first step in rethinking our approach to literary history was to reconsider not just what we teach but why we teach it in the first place. We wanted students' literary-historical training to be multilayered. We hoped to offer students a basic scaffolding of historical terms and concepts; we wanted them to come away with a sense of which historical boundaries and generic markers define the period and literature of the Reformation, the Restoration, Romanticism, modernism; and we wanted them to come away with a sense of how these terms followed from one another that would allow them to perceive the *longue durée* of literary conventions. In so doing, we shared some of the aims that informed the traditional English major survey.

But beyond the goal of historical knowledge, we wanted students to learn to think historically, by which we meant something similar to what the MLA report calls "historical literacy." Thinking historically begins by bringing the past into active and meaningful dialogue with the present. It means not only discovering continuities between the present and past (no matter how remotely or proximately defined) but also unsettling the fixities, and exposing the contingency, of the present moment, since experiencing what one of my colleagues called "the strangeness of the past" also has the power to estrange the present. As Fredric Jameson observes, "the vocation of historical thinking . . . is surely to bring us up short against the radical difference of other societies and of their lived experience, and against the radical historicity of everything we may be tempted to think of as permanent" (367). This point dovetails with the MLA report's ethical vision of historical literacy, its ability to move us "beyond our insular selves." Above all, we wanted to excite students' curiosity about the past, as neither an antiquarian object nor a monument to be revered (to adapt Nietzsche's terms [67]) but as the building material of the present, subject to rearrangement, displacement, loss, and recovery.

How do we design a curriculum that achieves these aims? From the beginning, we decided to do away with the checklist approach to historical area requirements, whether in the old, comprehensive form or in the newer, homeopathic version (two courses before 1750); instead, we sought new models for teaching the big picture. This search led to the question, What is literary history for, and what is literary history the history of? By defining our goal as a balance of knowledge and skill—that is, to give students a broad perspective of history as well as the ability to think historically—we opted against instituting a core that represented a single historical narrative. We did not want a literary history that simply presented background or traced evolution. We were drawn instead to models of literary history organized around both the threads of continuity across time and the breaks that create discontinuities in time, as these threads and breaks are registered in and through literary works.

We created a three-quarter sequence aimed at delivering broad, synthetic perspectives and organized around literary-historical throughlines and paradigm shifts over the broad sweep of thirty weeks, with the collaborative participation of many faculty members from many fields. In so doing, we strongly agree with the Teagle report's call for seeing the major as "a collaborative educational project." Where the report's authors offer team teaching as a way of enlivening pedagogy, we see it as a necessary disciplinary bridge across the historical isolation of the fields. The collaborative and team production of this new sequence is essential to its character and differentiates it from the old survey or core, in which the major periods were defined as sequential yet autonomous.

What defines a work as representative is determined each year by the team that is teaching the course and by the throughlines the team elects to pursue. For example, if we bring in a postcolonial specialist to teach the spring sequence and a specialist in Victorian sexuality to teach the winter, the fall course might develop sections on medieval and early modern exploration and colonialism, gender and desire. Conversely, a sequence that begins in the fall with a medievalist's teaching works on cognition and imagination may continue in the winter and spring with Blake and Virginia Woolf. The works chosen will thus be representative but not fixed. The lesson is that they become historically meaningful not simply because they existed in the past but also because they form part of a longer story that tells us how literary-historical change happens and how it registers in the horizon of expectations by which individual texts become legible at particular moments. But literary works also reverse the horizon of expectations that they enter—and this reversal allows Jauss to observe that "the specific achievement of literature in social existence is to be sought exactly where literature is not absorbed into the function of a *representational* art" but assumes a "*socially formative* function" (45). Literary history, so conceived and taught, is not an inventory of masterpieces or a succession of periods as embodied in typical works; it's a dynamic process that we enact anew every time we bring texts into relation with one another. It's this dynamic and relational process that we wanted to open to our students in our new historical core.

The lack of a unifying arc that our students experience was diagnosed twenty years ago by Graff as a disciplinary atomization, beginning with the division of fields. Field specialization, he points out, isn't a problem itself—indeed, it's the most efficient way to organize a complex body of knowledge; the problem is its by-product, historical isolation, by which we lose sight of the disciplinary forest for the trees of the subfields (8). If the discipline thereby loses its rationale, so do the fields themselves. When we become too immersed in fields, we lose sight of the temporal markers, and the horizons, that define them.

There are many ways to teach literary history—and perhaps even more ways to teach historical literacy. At Stanford, we worked to find an approach that would serve the needs of our students and our own vision for the discipline. No doubt there are approaches that could serve other needs and visions better. But we learned that the revision and revitalization of the English major begin with literary history and its big questions: what it is, what it is for, and why it remains necessary—as we believe it is—to the enterprise of academic literary study.

## NOTE

I would like to acknowledge the vision and collaborative efforts of the colleagues responsible for the curriculum revision I describe in this essay, namely, Franco Moretti, the department's curriculum director, and the members of its curriculum working group in 2008–09: John Bender, Michele Elam, Nicholas Jenkins, and Blakey Vermeule.

## WORKS CITED

*Announcement of Courses, 1906–07.* Stanford U, n.d. Web. 2 Dec. 2009. Stanford U Libs. Bulletin Archive.

*Courses and Degrees, 1969–70. Stanford University Bulletin* 21.1. Stanford U, n.d. Web. 2 Dec. 2009. Stanford U Libs. Bulletin Archive.

Graff, Gerald. *Professing Literature: An Institutional History.* Chicago: U of Chicago P, 1987. Print.

Jameson, Fredric. "From Criticism to History." *New Literary History* 12 (1981): 367–75. Print.

Jauss, Hans Robert. *Toward an Aesthetic of Reception.* Trans. Timothy Bahti. Minneapolis: U of Minnesota P, 1982. Print. Theory and History of Lit.

Laurence, David. "From the Editor." *ADE Bulletin* 95 (1990): 1–3. MLA, n.d. Web. 2 Dec. 2009.

Lawrence, Karen. "Curriculosclerosis; or, Hardening of the Categories." *ADE Bulletin* 90 (1988): 13–17. MLA, n.d. Web. 2 Dec. 2009.

Nietzsche, Friedrich. "On the Uses and Disadvantages of History for Life." *Untimely Meditations.* Trans. R. J. Hollingdale. Cambridge: Cambridge UP, 1983. 57–124. Print.

Perkins, David. *Is Literary History Possible?* Baltimore: Johns Hopkins UP, 1992. Print.

*Report to the Teagle Foundation on the Undergraduate Major in Language and Literature. Modern Language Association.* MLA, Feb. 2009. Web. 2 Dec. 2009.

Schroeder, Patricia R. "Covering the Waterfront versus Taking the Plunge: Curriculum Revision in a Liberal Arts College." *ADE Bulletin* 104 (1993): 36–39. MLA, n.d. Web. 2 Dec. 2009.

Simpson, David. "Is Literary History the History of Everything? The Case for 'Antiquarian' History." *SubStance* 28 (1999): 5–16. Print.

Valdés, Mario J. "Rethinking the History of Literary History." *Rethinking Literary History: A Dialogue on Theory*. Ed. Linda Hutcheon and Valdés. Oxford: Oxford UP, 2002. 63–115. Print.

# Shakespeare in Slow Motion

## MARJORIE GARBER

The last several decades have seen a sustained interest on the part of literary scholars in the contexts of Shakespeare's plays, from political, social, religious, and cultural history to biography. Studies of the court, of the "middling sort," of women in early modern England, of witchcraft, of race and exoticism, of travel, of economics, of philosophy and theories of personhood and power, of affect and emotion in the period—all these have come increasingly to occupy the attention of scholars. Textual studies have often focused on the history of the book and the book trade, as well as on questions of editing, bibliography, authenticity, and textual variants. Stage history and the history of productions, film, and adaptation offer another kind of context through the permutations of material culture.

My objective in "Shakespeare in Slow Motion" is to slow down the move to context, if not reverse it altogether, by redirecting attention to the language of the plays, scene by scene, act by act, moment by moment, word by word. Let "Shakespeare" be the designation we give to the author of the plays published under his name. Let us not speculate on his personal or professional motives, his inner thoughts, his relationships with his wife or children, his cultural aspirations, his finances, his religion, or his attitude toward the reigning monarch. Let us discuss not "the opinions or creed of the being whom we sometimes oddly call 'Shakespeare the man,'" to quote A. C. Bradley, writing skeptically about such matters a little more than a hundred years ago (6), but rather the text of the play and what it tells us.

The author is William R. Kenan, Jr., Professor of English and of Visual and Enviromental Studies at Harvard University.

My title, "Shakespeare in Slow Motion," is drawn from a 1959 essay called "Reading in Slow Motion," by Reuben Brower, but its energy comes in part from the description offered by one of Brower's teaching assistants, who was struck by the "critical, even subversive, power of literary instruction" that could emerge from a rigorous process of close reading. Here is an account of the process, as recalled more than twenty years later by the literary theorist Paul de Man:

> Students, as they began to write on the writings of others, were not to say anything that was not derived from the text they were considering. They were not to make any statements that they could not support by a specific use of language that actually occurred in the text. They were asked, in other words, to begin by reading texts closely as texts and not to move at once into the general context of human experience or history. Much more humbly or modestly, they were to start out from the bafflement that such singular turns of tone, phrase, and figure were bound to produce in readers attentive enough to notice them and honest enough not to hide their non-understanding behind the screen of received ideas that often passes, in literary instruction, for humanistic knowledge. This very simple rule, surprisingly enough, had far-reaching didactic consequences. I have never known a course by which students were so transformed.        (23)

The passage hints at the radical nature of close reading, achieved through the analytic rigor of attention to the philological or rhetorical devices of language. The results of this pedagogical decision were startling, de Man reported:

> Mere reading, it turns out, prior to any theory, is able to transform critical discourse in a manner that would appear deeply subversive to those who think of the teaching of literature as a substitute for the teaching of theology, ethics, psychology, or intellectual history. Close reading accomplishes this often in spite of itself because it cannot fail to respond to structures of language which it is the more or less secret aim of literary teaching to keep hidden.        (24)

This statement is tendentious but also suggestive. What does it mean to close read Shakespeare in the twenty-first century, after the most recent period of attention to historical, cultural, and religious context? To explore this question in the classroom, I decided to spend each meeting time on a single act of a play, assigning no literary or historical criticism. This exercise of focusing on "the way meaning is conveyed rather than on the meaning itself" is harder than it may seem (de Man 23), perhaps paradoxically more difficult for Shakespeare scholars than for beginning students. I anticipated that our discussions would generate theories of reading and of language as well as theories of Shakespearean meaning, that Shakespeare in slow motion, like a frame-by-frame analysis, would offer some unpredictable and counterintuitive insights. Participants were not expected to forget what they knew about "Shakespeare" or his time, but they were invited to put pressure on the language before presuming any sense of its meaning and to expect to be surprised as they returned to the text of the play.

I have taught Shakespeare in Slow Motion both as an English department seminar that brought together college freshmen, English majors, and graduate students in English, comparative literature, and law and as a faculty seminar on literary studies hosted by the National Humanities Center in Research Triangle Park, North Carolina (NHC). The participants on this second occasion were assistant professors of English, whose own professional training took place during the years when historicism was the unstated but assumed basis of much though not all academic literary study. The ground rules were simple. In each case we read slowly, one act of a play per session. For the NHC faculty seminar, I purposely did not specify in advance the play to be read—indeed, I didn't select it until shortly before the group was scheduled to meet. A few weeks before our session, the participants received a packet containing the Brower and de Man essays and some readings on slow motion and visuality; the play text was sent to them, under separate cover, a day or two before we convened as a group. Instead of studying the play in advance, they were asked to think about slow motion as a theoretical practice. My suggestion to the participants in these seminars, whether they were published scholars or first-time readers of the plays, was to read until they were halted by something contrary to their expectation—something "wrong," something that stopped them in their tracks, something they did not already "know" from their cultural consciousness of what Shakespeare had said, written, intended, or meant in the play.

Brower's essay used the phrase "slow motion" as a metaphor. The phrase appears in his title and is explicated once ("a method that might be described as 'slow motion,' by slowing down the process of reading to observe what is happening, in order to attend very closely to the words, their uses, and their meanings"), but elsewhere it is shortened to "slow reading," both in the text ("why a course in slow reading?," "the family reading circle, where books were read aloud and slowly, has all but disappeared," and "let me now attempt to describe Literature X, a course in slow reading") and in a footnote of acknowledgment ("my colleagues [at Harvard and at Amherst] will best know how much I owe to their ingenuity and their cheerful support in making experiments in slow reading") (4, 5, 9, 3n). But for all its literary references, justifying and amplifying the process of "slow reading," there is nowhere a reference to film, photography, visual art, dance, or performance. The motion of "slow motion" in Brower's essay is simply that of the eyes on the page, of the voice reading aloud, and of the contemplative mind. What would happen if the idea of "slow motion" were taken more literally, or more historically, or more precisely, to accord with developments in the visual field?

## "Unconscious Optics"

Slow motion, "the technique of filming a scene at a faster speed than normal so that when it is projected the action will appear to be slowed down" ("Slow"), was invented in 1904 by August Musger, an Austrian physicist and priest. Musger's experiment in cinematic time, space, and vision was preceded by the work of the French scientist and chronophotographer Étienne-Jules Marey and the English photographer Eadweard Muybridge. Muybridge's studies on animal and human locomotion began in the 1870s; one of his most famous early experiments was designed to prove former California governor Leland Stanford's belief that a galloping horse had all four feet off the ground at once, a phenomenon known as "unsupported transit." What seemed to some impossible, the stereoscopic camera, taking pictures every one-thousandth of a second, demonstrated was true. In 1879, Muybridge invented a device called a zoopraxiscope, which projected images on rotating glass disks to produce the impression of motion, and at the World's Columbian Exposition in Chicago in 1893 this early version of a movie projector showed motion pictures to a paying public.[1]

At the same time that these advances in photography and optics were taking place, a parallel revolution was developing in the analysis of mental images and spoken language. Sigmund Freud's *Interpretation of Dreams* was published in November 1899, but the book bore the date 1900, ushering in the new century. The following year Freud published *The Psychopathology of Everyday Life*, one of his most popular books, in which he demonstrated that the same unconscious activities that shaped the logic of dreams—displacement, condensation, overdetermination, and compromise formations—were also at work in commonplace daily events like forgetting, slips of the tongue (and slips of the pen), misreadings, screen memories, and the belief in chance or fate. Freud's examples included some from Shakespeare: Portia's slip of the tongue in *Merchant of Venice* 3.2 ("One half of me is yours, the other half yours,— / Mine own I would say, but if mine, then, yours, / And so all yours") (Freud 97–98), a similar slip in *Richard II* 2.2 (100), and a fatal coincidence of names in *Julius Caesar* 3.3 (117–18). Suddenly everyone, not just neurotics, were found to make these "mistakes": the unconscious, like a camera, saw more than the waking or conscious mind, or the unaided eye, could ever see.

The connection between these two developments, slow-motion photography and unconscious mental processes, was noted by Walter Benjamin in his essay "The Work of Art in the Age of Mechanical Reproduction," first published in 1936. The immediate analogy that came to his mind was between film and psychoanalysis:

> The film has enriched our field of perception with methods that can be illustrated by those of Freudian theory. Fifty years ago, a slip of the tongue passed more or less unnoticed. Only exceptionally may such a slip have revealed dimensions of depth in a conversation which had seemed to be taking its course on the surface. Since *The Psychopathology of Everyday Life* things have changed. This book isolated and made analyzable things which heretofore floated along unnoticed in the broad stream of perception. For the entire spectrum of optical, and now also acoustical, perception the film has brought about a similar deepening of apperception. (235)

Benjamin was particularly taken with the close-up, which appeared to expand space, and with slow motion, which appeared to extend movement. He wrote:

> Slow motion not only presents familiar qualities of movement but reveals in them entirely unknown ones, "which, far from looking like retarded rapid movements, give the effect of singularly gliding, floating, supernatural motions." Evidently a different nature opens itself to the camera than opens to the naked eye—if only because an unconsciously penetrated space is substituted for a space consciously explored by man. Even if one has a general knowledge of the way people walk, one knows nothing of a person's posture during the fractional second of a stride. (235)[2]

"The fractional second of a stride" recalls Muybridge's studies of the male and female figures in motion. The internal quotation about the "gliding, floating, supernatural motions" is taken from Rudolf Arnheim's *Film as Art*, where the phenomenon had led Arnheim to suggest, "Slow motion should be a wonderful medium for showing visions and ghosts" (111). Noting these effects, Benjamin concluded, in a phrase that became foundational for our discussions in Shakespeare in Slow Motion, "The camera introduces us to unconscious optics as does psychoanalysis to unconscious impulses" (237). "Unconscious optics"—trying to see what the eye has missed—underscored the importance of reading not only slowly but also against the grain of expectation.

To the avant-garde filmmaker Maya Deren slow motion offered a similar confluence of the visual and the affective:

> My own attention has been especially captured by the explorations of slow-motion photography. Slow-motion is the microscope of time. . . .

> [It] can be brought to the most casual activities to reveal in them a tex-
> ture of emotional and psychological complexes. For example, the course
> of a conversation is normally characterized by indecisions, defiances,
> hesitations, distractions, anxieties, and other emotional undertones. In
> reality these are so fugitive as to be invisible. But the explorations by
> slow-motion photography, the agony of its analysis, reveals, in such an
> ostensibly casual situation, a profound human complex.          (47)

Deren's list of these latent conversational performances is both an
index of ordinary psychopathologies and a lexicon for actors (an actor
playing Macbeth or Hamlet, for example, would presumably deploy all
these in performing the role). Deren's attention to slow motion was not
principally metaphoric, however: as a filmmaker, film theorist, poet, and
choreographer, Deren saw its specific visual potential:

> A running leap has, with slight variations, a given tempo; slow-motion
> photography creates of it a reality which is totally unnatural. But a use of
> slow-motion in reference to a movement which can, in parts, be even more
> creative . . . one creates a movement in one tempo which has the qualities
> of a movement of another tempo, and it is the dynamics of the relationship
> between these qualities which creates a certain special effectiveness.  (48)

As with Benjamin's citation of the stride, Deren's initial reference
point, the running leap, seems to tie her imagination of slow motion to
photographic sequences like those of Muybridge. The formal analogy she
drew was between film and poetry—or, rather, between the practice of
filmmaking and the practice of writing poetry: "Just as the verbal logics
of a poem are composed of the relationships established through syntax,
assonance, rhyme, and other such verbal methods, so in film there are
processes of filmic relationships which derive from the instrument and
the elements of its manipulations" (48).

It was precisely a set of logics like these—dramatic, visual, verbal, even
specifically Shakespearean—that I thought reading Shakespeare in slow
motion would permit participants to derive and explore.

## "A Seeing Which Is a Reading"

The logic of slow-motion photography and film, like the logic of the
dream, can sometimes seem alogical or counterintuitive. For Shakespeare
such incertitude was not merely an occasional effect but also a fundamental technique. "This dream is all amiss interpreted," says the conspirator
Decius Brutus, brushing aside the prophetic dream of Caesar's murder
dreamt by Calpurnia and substituting his own, plausible reinterpretation:

both come true (*JC* 2.2.83). Malvolio finds a letter thrown in his path and interprets it as a love missive sent to him by his employer, the lady Olivia. Macbeth compels the witches to speak to him, though they warn that he should "seek to know no more" (*Mac.* 4.1.103): inevitably what he takes from them is a fatally partial message, the dangerous and slippery echo of his own desire. Errors in reading are not only semiotic and syntactic but also visual and observational: Iago shows Othello a tableau in which Desdemona seems to flirt with Cassio; Claudio watches while his beloved and virginal Hero seems to be engaged in dalliance with another man. Here the logic is that of the mistake or sometimes of the double take, a term that developed in early-twentieth-century film and theater practice.[3]

To say that these misreadings are evidence of character flaws (Othello's self-doubt, Claudio's lack of sexual experience, Malvolio's vanity) is necessary but not sufficient: what is being performed here is not only character but also language, and in many cases the spectator or listener makes, at least briefly, the same mistake. If King Lear were immediately to reward Cordelia for her plain speaking, not only would there be no play, there would also be no role for language. In *The Merchant of Venice*, the choice of three caskets would have no dramatic value if the first chooser chose the right casket. The bad choosers here can be retrofitted with character flaws and psychic blindnesses that keep them from seeing right, but the logic that animates their choices comes as well from other kinds of agency. The impetus could, for example, be generic (the fairy tale), narratological (the play requires its own continuation), affective (the audience, like the audience of a thriller or a horror film, desires a negative outcome), or gendered (the woman's choice is inscribed by her father). Reading Shakespeare in slow motion resists the idea of determination by character and motive unless these elements can be descried in a particular linguistic formation. Puzzles and loose ends remain as puzzles and loose ends, instead of being neatly tied up. (Lady Macbeth's "I have given suck" [1.7.54] produced a famous set of exchanges on this topic, as has, more recently, Viola's abandoned plan—or Shakespeare's textual false start—to appear as a eunuch in Orsino's court [*TN* 1.2.55–56].) Character and motive, in fact, are revealed or produced as critical fantasies—which is not at all the same as saying that they do not exist.

But when the text is read in slow motion in a legal context, to determine guilt or innocence, to impute character and motive, such fantasies, and such existences, may become determinative. Slowing down a film or video can exhibit not only unconscious optics but also unconscious (or even conscious) politics. Judith Butler's essay on the Rodney King case and the use of videotape in court to exonerate the arresting officers of the charge of police brutality brought this issue vividly to mind. The event took place in Los Angeles, 1991; Butler's essay was published in 1993. It is instructive to quote from her analysis:

> The video shows a man being brutally beaten, repeatedly, and without visible resistance; and so the question is, How could this video be used as evidence that the body being beaten was *itself* the source of danger? . . . How was this feat of interpretation achieved?
> That it was achieved is not the consequence of ignoring the video, but, rather, of reproducing the video within a racially saturated field of visibility. If racism pervades white perception, structuring what can and cannot appear within the horizon of white perception, then to what extent does it interpret in advance "visual evidence"? (15–16)
>
> From these two interpretations emerges . . . a context within the visual field, a crisis in the certainty of what is visible. . . . (16)
>
> The defense attorneys broke the video down into "stills," freezing the frame, so that the gesture, the raised hand, is torn from its temporal place in the visual narrative. The video is not only violently decontextualized, but violently recontextualized; it is played without a simultaneous sound track which, had it existed, would have been littered with racial and sexual slurs against Rodney King. In the place of reading the testimony alongside the video, the defense attorneys offered the frozen frame, the magnification of the raised hand as the hyperbolic figure of racial threat, interpreted again and again as a gesture foreshadowing violence, a gesture about to be violent, the first sign of violence. . . . (20)
>
> This is a seeing which is a reading. (16)

This last phrase, like Benjamin's "unconscious optics," came to represent for the Shakespeare seminars both the opportunity and the necessity posed by reading in slow motion. The video required, Butler asserts, an aggressive counterreading, one that "the prosecutors failed to perform." Instead of that counterreading, there interposed a set of terms from literary and narrative analysis, foremost among them "intention." By what Butler calls "a transposition and fabrication of dangerous intention" (21), it was King, the unarmed black man, not the police officers armed with Tasers and batons, who was said to pose a threat that had to be subdued by force. The essay's insistence on the activity of reading (the essay was first published in a collection called *Reading Rodney King / Reading Urban Uprising*) brought deconstructive logic together with psychoanalysis, describing the use and abuse of videotape in court as "a form of white paranoia which projects the intention to injure that it itself enacts" (20–21).

Some seminar participants, struck by the forcefulness of this argument, wondered whether it put in question the value of reading in slow motion.

Wasn't it true that by slowing down the videotape and breaking it into freeze frames, the defense attorneys secured acquittal for their guilty clients? Couldn't one make the visual text, and the play text, say anything one wanted it to say, by such acts of decontextualization? The answer, it seemed to me, was not an answer but, again, an examination of the process. Like the prophecies of the witches in *Macbeth*, the videotape was a medium: although it was sutured to interpretation, no single interpretation could sustain or encompass all its latent and manifest "meanings." The point was not that reading in slow motion would disclose the singular truth but that many readings are not readings at all but prior identifications with meanings already there, a literary practice that projects an intention to mean. Whether such readings were historicist (based on a historical referent or cause) or generic (based on expectations of what a tragedy or a comedy was or should do) or characterological (making claims about personality and psychology and motive), or indeed whether they developed out of the sheer weight and preexistence of so much prior commentary on Shakespeare, each had a narrative to offer. Small details that seemed to interrupt or contradict the narrative could be, and often were, ignored or set aside.

## "I . . . SLOW . . . IT . . . DOWN, AND THEN SOMETIMES ISPEEDITUP."

The Rodney King video was an instance from life transformed into techne, "art" or "craft," for purposes forensic and political. But video art and live theater have also made use of slow motion in recent years to expose and critique what we think we see. Such art practices query issues of mimesis and representation, on the one hand, and determinate meaning, on the other.

A good example is the work of Bill Viola, an artist whose use of ultraslow-motion video has become a signature of his work. In a series called The Passions, Viola allows the viewer to linger in the moment of seeing, exposing a gap or disruption just at the point where the extra time would seem to offer certainty. For pieces like *The Quintet of the Astonished* (2000) and *Observance* (2003), he gave detailed instructions to the actors. For *Quintet*, each actor was assigned a different emotion and a point on which to fix his gaze; they were then free to invent gestures and expressions; no actor knew the instruction given to another or the emotion assigned to another. In *Observance*, the actors respond to an unseen object with a series of powerful expressions of grief and loss.[4] Most of the works in Viola's Passions series were shot on 35mm at a very high speed, then slowed down and transferred to video. John Walsh, a curator, describes the effect:

> In *The Passions* the familiar and the unfamiliar are tightly bound to-
> gether. Slow motion is thoroughly familiar from movies and sports
> replays and MTV, but not as a means to observe the movements of peo-
> ple's faces and speculate on their feelings. . . . We know the ordinary-
> looking people on the screen to be actors, and we know their emotions
> are feigned, or at least produced at will; yet their appeal is apt to be
> stronger than we imagine possible. . . . Viola's pieces, in short, are
> charged with the peculiar energy of consistent contradiction.      (61)[5]

This "peculiar energy of consistent contradiction" aptly characterizes the reading experience of Shakespeare in slow motion, especially when, as became essential, participants abandoned what they thought they knew from previous readings of the text and focused on the present: the indi- vidual utterance, word, or gesture in front of them.

We might compare this effect of slow motion in video and installation art to the work of the avant-garde stage director Robert Wilson. Wilson's theater is famously concerned with time and space, stretching out moments and movements so that the plays become palpably visual as well as verbal. As a director, he suggests that actors should themselves avoid too much in- terpretation, leaving the ambiguity and richness to the audience—precisely what is often said that directors and actors, unlike literary scholars, cannot or should not do. "There's so much going on in a line of Shakespeare," he has said, "that if the actor colors the voice too much, the audience loses too many other colors."[6] Wilson sets aside questions of naturalism, real- ism, and psychology in favor of openness, the "emptying out" of meaning, and the pleasures that come with *not* understanding a play. As he told the critic Mel Gussow in an interview, "Often I take much more tiiiiime than one would normally take to do something. I . . . slow . . . it . . . down, and then sometimes Ispeeditup" (Gussow). The performative language here, as transcribed by Gussow, offers a compact model for what it might mean to understand reading in slow motion in a literal, and also a theatrical, way.

What would happen if that process were directly explored in the per- formance of Shakespeare's plays? A good example from contemporary theater practice occurred in Rupert Goold's 2007–08 production of *Mac- beth*, with Patrick Stewart in the title role. The banquet scene in which Macbeth sees Banquo's ghost was staged twice, once before the intermis- sion, once after.[7] In one version the audience sees events through Mac- beth's eyes, with the ghost of Banquo an intrusive and terrifying presence. In the second version, visualized from the point of view of the guests, Macbeth's terror is inexplicable, since no ghost appears. In the withering phrase of his wife, "When all's done, / You look but on a stool" (3.4.66– 67). In another staging of the same play in 2009, the British company

Punchdrunk converted a forty-four-room school building outside Boston into an immersive theater space, through which audience members were invited to wander at will, choosing what they watched and where they went. In this production, entitled *Sleep No More*, two particular moments made explicit use of slow motion as a stage device. In the banquet scene, here performed in silence and in extreme slow motion, actors seated at a long table raised above floor level ate, drank, flirted, and whispered, moving their arms and bodies in big, sweeping gestures, while at the head of the table Macbeth, glimpsing the ghost, tried to hide his dismay. By contrast, a scene in which Macbeth encounters the witches was illuminated by strobe lights, generating a jerky, flickering sense of hyperreality, both slow and fast at once, freeze-frame modulating to frantic energy, as the witches stripped, danced, grew goat heads and horns. Whether read as a drug trip, a fantasy, or an encounter with the supernatural, the visual effect of slow motion here induced a disorienting sense of nightmare.

## "Mere Reading"

Neither Reuben Brower nor Paul de Man could have predicted the twenty-first century's profound shift toward the visual that has come with the spread of the Internet, digitization, cell phone cameras, and video culture. Slo-mo, as it is now called, is used today as much in sports and motion technology as it is in cinematic or installation art. (Sports technology now makes use of high-definition cameras that allow judges to "see" what cannot be seen by the naked eye, changing the outcomes of races that are decided by a fraction of a second and making visible formerly invisible distinctions.) But Brower's idea of "reading in slow motion" and de Man's assessment of "mere reading" as an activity with the capacity to be "deeply subversive" seem as perceptive and as necessary now as they did then. De Man wrote, in a highly characteristic sentence, "Close reading accomplishes this often in spite of itself because it cannot fail to respond to structures of language which it is the more or less secret aim of literary teaching to keep hidden." Participants in the seminar were quick to see that the rhetoric of this sentence ("in spite of itself . . . it cannot fail to respond," "the more or less secret aim . . . to keep hidden") itself performs the signature double take of slow motion, staging its function as mirror image, counterlogic, and internal resistance.

Initially developed as a technological advance with intriguing implications for the world of film, creatively deployed at mid-century by a literary scholar as a figure for a certain kind of close textual reading, slow motion today describes a practice of inventive artists, a popular mode for re-viewing key moments in sports, and a revelatory and potentially still deeply subversive mode of teaching. Whether it will have what de Man aptly called "far-reaching didactic consequences," as he said of Brower's course, will depend on the rigor of the next generation of teachers, readers, artists, and performers—and on their commitment to remain open to consternation, contradiction, resistance, and surprise.

## NOTES

1. An artist, not a scientist, Muybridge did not hesitate to manipulate his materials to produce the visual effect of an unbroken photographic sequence. "When a phase of the movement was missing—perhaps a camera failed or a negative broke or was fogged—Muybridge assembled the negatives that remained, gave them internal consistency, and renumbered them to appear consecutively in the print. At times he even went so far as to compile a sequence whose individual elements came from separate picture-taking sessions" (Braun 238). In this practice he differed from his French counterpart, Marey, whose work would come to influence cardiology, aviation, and anatomy, as well as early cinema. Marey's animal studies were produced with a chronophotographic gun that allowed him to show several phases of movement in the same photograph. His own celebrated experiment, demonstrating that a cat always lands on its feet, offered visual evidence to disprove Newton's law that once an object is in motion only an external force can change the direction of that motion. (Marey's longtime collaborator, Georges Demeny, split off from him in the 1890s to pursue a wider application of the technology; in 1892, Demeny invented a simple projector called a phonoscope and began to produce short films. Both Marey and Muybridge died in 1904, the year that Musger patented his design for a slow-motion device.)

2. The internal quotation here is from Rudolf Arnheim's *Film als Kunst* (Berlin, 1932); see Benjamin's note (138). In the English translation of Arnheim, the phrase reads as follows: "Slow motion has hardly been applied at all yet to artistic purposes, although it should be very useful. It might, for instance, serve to slow down natural movements grotesquely; but it can also create new movements, which do not appear as the retarding of natural movements but have a curious gliding, floating character of their own. Slow motion should be a wonderful medium for showing visions and ghosts" (110–11). This dreamlike capacity of slow motion in cinema was utilized, to strong effect, by filmmakers like Sergei Eisenstein and Dziga Vertov.

3. *OED* cites as early instances "what Hollywood has perfected as the 'double take'" (1941) and "a double take worthy of Oliver Hardy" (1957), while "take" as a term from cinematography ("a continuous section of film photographed at one time; an instance of such filming") dates from 1922.

4. Although this piece is sometimes associated with the events of 11 September 2001, both the object of the actors' gaze and the emotions they display are fictional, which does not at all mean that they are not real.

5. Walsh notes that slow motion is also a key device for some of Viola's contemporaries, like the Scottish artist Douglas Gordon and the Dutch artist Aernout Mik (60).

6. "I'm an artist, not a philosopher. I don't make meanings. I make art. The responsibility of an artist is not to say what something means, but to ask, 'What does it

mean?' The only reason to do a play is because you don't understand it. The moment you think you understand a work of art, it's dead for you. The last moment in any play must be a question. What happened? What was said? What is this? A play doesn't conclude. It should stay open-ended. The last word must be a beginning, a door opening, not closing. A play is not a lecture in a classroom. I don't dictate meaning to the viewer. Theatre that imposes an interpretation is aesthetic fascism. By emptying out the meaning of a sentence, the text becomes full of meaning—or meanings. Actors, however, are trained to interpret; they feel it's their responsibility to color the text and the situation for the audience. So they reduce the possibilities of meaning. But in my theatre, the audience puts it all together, and each person puts it together differently. And each night the play is different. The audience makes the meaning. I once told an actor to read the text as if he didn't understand language. There's so much going on in a line of Shakespeare, that if the actor colors the voice too much, the audience loses too many other colors" (Robert Wilson qtd. in Holmberg 61–62).

7. The Goold production opened at the Chichester Festival Theatre in the summer of 2007, then moved to sold-out engagements in London and New York.

## WORKS CITED

Arnheim, Rudolf. *Film as Art*. Berkeley: U of California P, 1957. Print.

Benjamin, Walter. "The Work of Art in the Age of Mechanical Reproduction." *Illuminations*. Trans. Harry Zohn. Ed. Hannah Arendt. New York: Schocken, 1968. 217–52. Print.

Bradley, A. C. *Shakespearean Tragedy*. London: Macmillian, 1924. Print.

Braun, Marta. *Picturing Time: The Work of Etienne-Jules Marey, 1830–1904*. Chicago: U of Chicago P, 1992. Print.

Brower, Reuben A. "Reading in Slow Motion." *In Defense of Reading*. Ed. Brower and Richard Poirier. New York: Dutton, 1962. 3–21. Print.

Butler, Judith. "Endangered/Endangering: Schematic Racism and White Paranoia." *Reading Rodney King / Reading Urban Uprising*. Ed. Robert Gooding-Williams. New York: Routledge, 1993. 15–22. Print.

de Man, Paul. "The Return to Philology." *The Resistance to Theory*. Minneapolis: U of Minnesota P, 1986. 21–26. Print.

Deren, Maya. *An Anagram of Ideas on Art, Form, and Film*. Yonkers: Alicat Book Shop, 1946. Print.

"Double-take." *The Oxford English Dictionary*. 2nd ed. 1989. Print.

Freud, Sigmund. *The Psychopathology of Everyday Life*. 1901. Ed. James Strachey. London: Hogarth, 1960. 1–279. Print. Vol. 6 of *The Standard Edition of the Complete Psychological Works of Sigmund Freud*.

Gussow, Mel. "At Home With: Robert Wilson." *New York Times* 6 Jan. 1994: C1+. Print.

Holmberg, Arthur. *The Theatre of Robert Wilson*. Cambridge: Cambridge UP, 1996. Print.

Shakespeare, William. *Julius Caesar*. Ed. David Daniell. London: Methuen Drama, 1998. Print. Arden Shakespeare.

———. *Macbeth*. Ed. Kenneth Muir. London: Methuen Drama, 1951. Print. Arden Shakespeare.

————. *The Merchant of Venice*. Ed. John Russell Brown. London: Methuen Drama, 1955. Print. Arden Shakespeare.

————. *Twelfth Night*. Ed. J. M. Lothian. London: Methuen Drama, 1975. Print. Arden Shakespeare.

"Slow." Def. 14a (i). *The Oxford English Dictionary*. 2nd ed. 1989. Print.

"Take." *The Oxford English Dictionary*. 2nd ed. 1989. Print.

Walsh, John. "Emotions in Extreme Time: Bill Viola's Passions Project." *Bill Viola: The Passions*. By Bill Viola. Ed. Walsh. Los Angeles: Getty Museum, 2003. 25–64. Print.

# The Value of the History of the English Language Course for the Twenty-First Century

## TARA WILLIAMS

The "Report to the Teagle Foundation on the Undergraduate Major in Language and Literature" concludes by advocating that "all students who major in our departments should know English and at least one other language" (MLA 297). The primary intent of this proposal is to support foreign language requirements, but the first point also raises a serious issue. What does it mean to know English as a language, and how can we address that outcome through our curricula? I suggest that a course on the history of the English language (HEL) offers an effective solution. Although no one course can address the shortcomings or encapsulate the strengths of a curriculum in a diverse discipline, HEL offers promise as not merely a component but a cornerstone of the twenty-first-century literature curriculum that the Teagle report envisions.

HEL has been around almost as long as the modern discipline of English; in fact, it may seem like a relic left over from the earliest, philological phase of the discipline.[1] In the 1893 *PMLA*, Francis A. March argued for the value of the history of the language in the curriculum:

> Anglo-Saxon study, delightful and important in itself to specialists, seems also to be necessary for a solid and learned support to the study of Modern English in college. The early professors had no recondite learning applicable to English, and did not know what to do with classes in it. They can now make English as hard as Greek. (27)

*The author is assistant professor of English at Oregon State University.*

Philology allowed the discipline to claim a new kind of academic rigor, and a specialized knowledge of the nature and history of English was the foundation for that claim. Literature, instead of being the focus, served to illustrate usage, and a technical knowledge of the language, in turn, provided the key for interpreting any text. H. C. G. Brandt advocated this approach in the mid-1880s, exhorting, "Let 'English' mean as it should and as it is bound to mean more and more, the historical scientific study of the language, Beowulf and Chaucer" (61). As philological approaches gave way to literary studies, HEL persisted, but the material that had been the heart of the discipline in its earlier incarnation became condensed into a single course.

While HEL has endured in one form or another for over a century, its position in the discipline and its connection to the core purposes and values of the discipline have become progressively more tenuous. English studies continues to transform, and changes such as the rise of cultural and historicist approaches and the decline of linguistics threaten to push HEL from artifact to memory. Once widely required, HEL is now taught less frequently; once representative of the discipline as a whole, it now fails to correspond exactly to any specialty in the discipline; once fundamental to the curriculum, it is now marginal or absent in many departments.[2] The claims for rigor and objectivity have become a reputation for dryness and difficulty. As Jo Tyler explains, "Courses on the history of the English language are commonly acronymed *HEL*, and for many students 'hell' could well describe the netherworld experience they might expect upon entering the course" (464).

But HEL has not remained unchanged while the discipline evolved around it; both the subject itself and the approaches to and resources for teaching it have continued to expand and develop in innovative directions.[3] I took advantage of those developments recently when reviving the HEL course after it had gone untaught for fifteen years at Oregon State University. On the basis of my experience teaching it and the feedback of the students who took it, I contend that HEL is becoming more rather than less relevant to the discipline of English as we imagine it now, that HEL offers benefits that no other course does or can, and that we can leverage new resources—traditional as well as multimedia—and pedagogical techniques to reimagine HEL in a way that maximizes those benefits and recognizes the valuable contributions it can make to the curriculum and discipline. I present my argument in these deliberately provocative terms to counter the checkered past and precarious present position of HEL.

## The Value of HEL

In the current disciplinary context, HEL offers three valuable benefits that would otherwise be absent from the curriculum or, at best, supplied in a piecemeal fashion by other courses. First, it provides a sense of the historical span of literature in English and a forum for exploring the intricate relation between history and literature. Second, it makes students aware not only that the language has changed over time but also that it continues to do so. Finally, HEL enables students to build historically informed interpretations of texts from any period. While I focus below on how these benefits contribute to a literature curriculum, HEL also suggests how we might bridge gaps that often exist among the subdisciplines of English (literature, rhetoric, and creative writing) and between how we practice literary studies as a scholarly discipline and how we teach literature classes.

The foundational benefit that HEL offers is a fuller understanding of history and culture and their complex connections to literature in English; in other words, it helps students develop the "historical and comparative perspectives" that the Teagle report identified as indispensable to a college education (288). Most HEL courses are arranged chronologically, but those that are not nonetheless cover a historical duration greater than any other course and do so more consciously and in more depth. In addition, HEL foregrounds the relation between history and literature as an object of study to a degree that few, if any, other literature courses have the time or potential to replicate. Individual courses may elaborate on the context of a particular text, period, or genre, or on the connections between history and literature within such limits, but it is difficult for students to piece together that information and gain an understanding that covers the Anglo-Saxon scops to the American postmodernists, with every stage in between. Even introductory theory courses cannot examine the relation between literature and history in as much detail as HEL and with such a range of examples. And even literature survey courses cannot offer the same experience of the historical arc that HEL does. While it focuses on the English-language literary tradition above others, HEL more than any other literature course gives students an expansive and detailed framework in which to position a given text.

Traditionally, literature has been subdivided by period and nationality, but many English departments now emphasize its transnational character or rely on a more fluid view of periodization. The ability to connect and evaluate texts not only in but also across historical periods is a growing desideratum in literary studies; it aids students who will draw on a generalist background when going on to teach at any level, and it is a focus of cutting-edge scholarship in venues like the recently founded *Postmedieval*, an academic journal that "aims to bring the medieval and modern into productive critical relation" (*Journal Prospectus*). In any English department, the framework that HEL imparts can help students both locate texts in a historical moment—a process that requires knowledge of events and trends and of the challenges of apprehending the past from any temporal distance—and develop a stronger understanding of textual relation across apparent geographic and temporal boundaries. When students are able to imagine the scope of English literature, they can situate a text in relation to the cultural milieu but can also recognize the influences that connect Geoffrey Chaucer to Caryl Churchill as well as William Shakespeare, for instance, or juxtapose mid-twentieth-century texts in English from all over the world.

When students can approach texts in this way, they are better equipped to understand the contingent and historically specific nature of language itself; this benefit is the second that HEL provides. Students recognize that literature has a historical and cultural context, but relatively few realize that the same is true of language. HEL brings language into the cultural history where most students have already begun to locate literary texts (however provisionally). When this realization occurs, a critical shift in perspective follows: instead of looking from the twenty-first century backward—which suggests that language grows more foreign as it gets more distant—students can place themselves in an ongoing dynamic of linguistic evolution, understanding the present moment not as a telos but as one more moment in a continuing process of change. The Teagle report describes the key role of linguistic knowledge in the interpretive process: "As readers become cognizant of the complexities of the linguistic system—its codes, structures, and articulations—they become mindful of language and of languages as evolving, changing historical artifacts and institutions, intricately bound up with the cultures expressed through them" (289). This kind of awareness is also valuable in the undergraduate curriculum more broadly.[4]

The first benefit I identified for HEL involved relatively objective observations about the information the course covers, but this second benefit involves claims about how student perceptions change. To substantiate these claims, I draw directly on student feedback from the HEL course I taught in spring 2009. Because the course had not recently been offered, the students had virtually no experience with the subject and could not develop expectations based on institutional history or peer experience. They completed the feedback forms at the end of the term, and their responses confirm that one of the most significant effects of the course was the realization that English is always evolving, not only in the past but also in the present moment. The first part of the form asked students to complete the sentence, "This course taught me that the English language is. . . ." Over two-thirds of the responses mentioned the dynamic or "ever-changing" nature of English. "Before this course I assumed that the English language was static, fixed, and would always be the way it is today," one student observed. Similarly, another wrote, "I never realized the fluidity of the English language." Still another called English "a shapeshifting beast."[5] While its long history might make HEL appear old-fashioned or conservative, the course is—as these comments suggest—quite radical. It not only gives students the necessary historical and linguistic foundation for their reading but also makes them aware of the contingent nature of that foundation and allows them to take advantage of what Michelle Warren calls "the dualistic nature of philological analysis," which "creates and dismantles coherence, stabilizes and undermines tradition, multiplies and singularizes, wanders and roots" (286).

This new perspective leads to the third benefit of HEL: facilitating more historically informed close readings. It alerts students to the fact that definitions of words, standards of grammar, and conventions of writing have all changed over time. It introduces them to historical dictionaries, like the *Oxford English Dictionary* and the *Middle English Dictionary*, and to other resources that can help them trace such changes. Instead of producing a method for reading texts, the course equips students to work with textual evidence more knowledgeably in the context of any type of hermeneutic or theoretical study. The students' feedback forms indicated their confidence that they would do just that; as one commented, "I will not take words for granted." This attitude serves students well whether they are reading texts written last year or a thousand years ago. At a basic level, students who have taken HEL will not assume that *nice* signifies the same way in a Middle English poem that it does in a Victorian novel. At a more sophisticated level, they will be able to consider how any given word is being used in a variety of texts, how diction might be involved in and influenced by contemporary concerns or debates, and whether etymology haunts usage to some degree. Before taking this course, many of the students did not even realize that such issues existed and might shape their interpretations. "HEL really filled in a gap I was unaware of," a student admitted.[6]

HEL affects how students read texts in the present moment by connecting that moment in substantial and complex ways to the past. In helping students build these more accurate and nuanced readings, HEL also links two aspects of literary study: the historicist and cultural studies approaches that dominate critical scholarship and the emphasis on close reading that tends to characterize literature courses in which students are learning the fundamental tools of interpretation. These two aspects are never entirely separate, of course (not least because teachers are also scholars); the most persuasive historicist or theoretical interpretations depend on careful readings of the language of a text, and the strongest approaches to teaching literature require the responsible contextualization of the texts under consideration. This connection is becoming more rather than less important; as Karla Taylor recently argued, "In the historical and cultural turns in literary studies, the evidence of language will be indispensable" (112).

Literary studies, however, is only one facet of English. In an 2001–02 ADE survey, creative writing was "a close second to literature as the most popular new English concentration," and many departments had added well-received courses in professional and technical writing to their curricula (Schramm, Mitchell, Stephens, and Laurence 84). In its emphasis on language usage and change, HEL brings together elements from literature, creative writing, and rhetoric and composition and moves us toward the "fused" curriculum and comprehensive understanding of English studies as a discipline for which scholars have begun to advocate (McDonald 156; Gaillet). In its inclusion of all types of evidence—spoken as well as written, in new as well as traditional media—HEL prepares students to approach language more mindfully in any context. The benefits explored above pertain to reading texts of all kinds, and students who have taken this course, whether they are composing a critical essay, a villanelle, or a blog post, will use language more consciously and therefore more effectively.

The combination of HEL with a foreign language requirement offers additional value for literature majors, a point that is implicit in the Teagle report recommendation I cited at the beginning of this essay. Courses in these subjects expand students' experience in complementary ways: HEL supports "historical literacy," and foreign languages support "cross-cultural literacy" (MLA 288), but HEL and foreign language requirements are even more closely intertwined. The ability to draw on more than English enhances students' understanding of the nature of language more generally, how it functions and how it changes. Familiarity with other languages also destabilizes the idea of English—or some form of it—as the default or standard, revealing how it is typical as well as idiosyncratic and how languages influence and are influenced by one another in complex ways. This kind of awareness, along with the other benefits of HEL, makes students into better writers, readers, and even citizens. It also challenges us to become better teachers.

## The Pedagogy of HEL

Although it is one of our oldest courses, HEL paradoxically presents excellent opportunities for pedagogical experimentation and innovation. As a result of its own history, HEL is more like a language class than a literature one in many ways—so much so that it is sometimes taught within departments of or by specialists in linguistics rather than English—and demands a correspondingly different pedagogy. The textbook is not an anthology or a literary work but a secondary resource that presents technical information, often with the assistance of statistics, charts, and diagrams (which are scarce in literature courses). Although HEL requires the interpretive and analytic skills that all English courses emphasize, most undergraduates will need a great deal of preparation before they can bring those skills to bear on the subject. While HEL students absolutely engage in critical thinking, in other words, the initial goal remains comprehension rather than analysis.

The unusual nature of HEL presents both opportunities and challenges. On the one hand, the diversity of topics and the historical span covered by HEL make it well suited to some of the pedagogical strategies recommended by the Teagle report, including team teaching and interdisciplinary approaches (288). On the other hand, because HEL is unlike other literature courses and because English has moved away from philology, the connection of HEL to the discipline seems to have weakened. That connection is not always necessary; there are contexts and circumstances in which a technical, linguistic version of HEL is both desirable and feasible, given faculty expertise and student backgrounds. However, with the new resources available and with careful attention to our pedagogical strategies, it is now possible to create another version of HEL that is more integral to literary studies and more integrated with English as a discipline.

The first pedagogical element to consider is the course design, which involves choosing how much time to spend on specific periods and topics (grammar versus vocabulary, for example), where to begin (with Indo-European or Anglo-Saxon?) and end (with American English, world Englishes, English and technology, the future of English?), and how to proceed (whether chronologically or thematically, and with what emphasis on literary versus linguistic concerns). The last question is the most crucial if one seeks to devise a course that capitalizes on the benefits I have mentioned. HEL does not have to be taught chronologically, but it does need to make the diachronic development of the language apparent even as it highlights synchronic elements of language structure and change across time.[7] The connections between literary and linguistic aspects also need to be highlighted; this focus requires the instructor to weigh how much time can be spent on literary connections and which linguistic elements might have to be left out as a result (an instructor who wants to use HEL to create a framework for English studies may not be able to spend as much time on the Indo-European roots of the language, for instance).

An emphasis on literary connections will primarily take shape through the readings chosen and the assignments crafted. Recently expanded textbook options support an array of pedagogical approaches. Albert Baugh and Thomas Cable's *History of the English Language* has long been the standard text, with a few alternatives that were also heavily linguistic in their approach, but now—to cite two prominent examples—David Crystal's *Cambridge Encyclopedia of the English Language* offers a more accessible possibility that stresses current events and issues, and Seth Lerer's *Inventing English: A Portable History of the Language* traces the history of English through literary and popular culture. Of course, class lectures and discussions can expand on and add to the approaches, topics, and examples covered in the textbooks.

Such readings lay the groundwork for assignments that give students the opportunity to apply their HEL knowledge in ways that will continue to be useful in other English courses. To encourage students to begin making meaningful connections among language, text, and culture, we ask them to bring what they learn about the language in HEL to bear on texts with which they are already familiar or that have already entered the conversation about language development in the course—texts that might include anything from *Beowulf* to rap lyrics. Assignments might ask students to examine how a word evolved over time by analyzing its usage in texts from several different centuries or to perform a linguistic analysis of a passage, identifying features related to style, grammar, orthography, vocabulary, and sound. New technologies enable new research tools, such as searching for a single word or combinations of terms throughout a text or group of texts, that can support such assignments.

The traditional pedagogical elements—course design, textbooks, assignments, and so on—can be used thoughtfully to support reimagined aims for HEL. Some traditional resources, such as the textbooks, have themselves been reimagined. But HEL also has the benefit of unusual resources. There are excellent Web sites on complex topics like the great vowel shift and the history of the *Oxford English Dictionary*.[8] The peculiarities of grammar and vocabulary and how those features have evolved over time are subjects of popular interest and so are treated in the mainstream media; even Perez Hilton's celebrity gossip blog covered the decline of the hyphen in English ("End"). Contesting claims over the neologism *truthiness*, its origins, and its definition played out in the news media and in a regular feature called "The Word" on *The Colbert Report* ("Truthiness"). These resources have to be evaluated and incorporated responsibly, but they can illustrate the enduring interest in language's capacity to adapt and change and the contemporary relevance of an understanding of English's evolution.

## HEL and the Future of Literary Studies

I have argued that HEL is vital to the undergraduate curriculum as we shape it in response to the current state of the discipline, but the current state is always fleeting and often difficult to pin down. The Teagle report refers to "this exciting age whose novelty we all sense but still cannot name" (298). Because of its deep connections to the past and sedulous attention to the process of change, HEL prepares students and instructors to recognize and deal with such novelty. In fact, the "history" in its name can be misleading, since HEL also deals with the latest technologies and current trends in pronunciation and usage. One of its inherent themes is the effect of technological developments and new media, from the printing press to e-books, on language. With the perspective that HEL grants, we can recognize continuities and similarities even in the most apparently radical challenges to English literature and language. As David Crystal pointed out in *Txtng: The Gr8 Db8*, for example, texting participates in a long history of abbreviation that dates back at least to medieval scribes and encompasses purposes both academic and playful. HEL's perspective on the past also allows us a vantage point into the future.

That HEL is an unusual course may be the secret to its endurance: it offers benefits unlike those of any other literature course. Those benefits are not outside our discipline but essential to it. In the late nineteenth century, the study of the history of English offered a set of technical skills and added a sense of rigor. Those advantages are now less esteemed, but HEL imparts other skills and provides other benefits. One value remains constant, however: HEL builds a varied and rich foundation for English studies. To fulfill that purpose, it must be offered regularly, required of English majors, and vigorously promoted to students interested in improving their critical thinking and communication skills. But we cannot let our idea of HEL and its role stand still any more than the discipline does; the course needs to be reevaluated to see how it might serve students and contribute to the curriculum. Instead of dismissing it as a relic, we must approach it as a resource that, like language itself, continues to evolve.

## NOTES

I would like to thank Vicki Tolar Burton and Moira Fitzgibbons for helpful feedback on earlier versions of this essay and Rich Daniels for sharing his knowledge of the history of HEL at Oregon State University. An L. L. Stewart Faculty Development Award from OSU supported the research for this essay.

1. On the transition from philology to literary studies, see Graff and Warner, "Introduction"; Warner. Scholes traces the history of the discipline back even further.

2. It is difficult to measure HEL offerings and requirements with any precision. At my institution, such courses were required of English education majors and attracted students from various disciplines at least from the 1970s through the 1980s. In a 1984–85 survey of English departments conducted by the MLA, only survey courses and Shakespeare were required more often than HEL, which was required by 39.1%, or 243, of the responding departments (Huber and Laurence 38–40). In a similar 1991–92 survey, 39.2% of the responding departments required HEL or comparative grammar (Huber 63). A more recent ADE survey, from 2001–02, does not offer statistics on specific classes but notes the dominant curricular changes designed to attract more majors, including "the addition of topics courses, [and] the development of courses related to students' employment concerns" (Schramm, Mitchell, Stephens, and Laurence 83), which might hint at the shift away from courses like HEL that occurred at Oregon State University (and, anecdotal evidence suggests, more widely) in the mid-1990s.

3. On the evolution of HEL research, see Cable; on the evolution of HEL pedagogies, see Momma and Matto, "History."

4. Arguing in 1941 for a HEL requirement, Dorothy Bethurum pointed out this same important benefit: "The conception of language as a growing and not a static thing, which, notwithstanding all our assumptions to the contrary, students never really get until they *study* its growth—this conception is one of the most liberating and enriching ideas that can come to an undergraduate" (267).

5. There were thirty feedback forms, representing twenty-eight undergraduates and two graduate students.

6. Both this and the previous comment responded to the prompt, "In the future, what I've learned in this class will help me read or interpret medieval or early modern texts because . . . ," although the students' points might also be extended to later texts.

7. I chose to teach HEL chronologically, but for examples of other successful course designs, see Fitzgibbons; Tyler.

8. See *Great Vowel Shift* and *About*. Edwin Duncan's course page contains a wealth of resources (*History of the English Language*), and Daniel Donoghue has developed an entire online HEL workbook (*History and Structure*). For additional Web resources, see Duncan.

## WORKS CITED

*About the* Oxford English Dictionary. Oxford UP, 2009. Web. 6 July 2010.

Baugh, Albert C., and Thomas Cable. *A History of the English Language*. 5th ed. London: Routledge, 2002. Print.

Bethurum, Dorothy. "The Study of the History of the Language in the English Major." *College English* 3.3 (1941): 264–71. Print.

Brandt, H. C. G. "How Far Should Our Teaching and Text-books Have a Scientific Basis?" 1884–85. Graff and Warner, *Origins* 28–33.

Cable, Thomas. "History of the History of the English Language: How Has the Subject Been Studied?" Momma and Matto, *Companion* 11–17.

Crystal, David. *The Cambridge Encyclopedia of the English Language*. 2nd ed. Cambridge: Cambridge UP, 2003. Print.

———. *Txtng: The Gr8 Db8*. Oxford: Oxford UP, 2008. Print.

Duncan, Edwin. "Reaching Out: The Web as a Learning Tool." *Studies in Medieval and Renaissance Teaching* 15.2 (2008): 37–48. Print.

"The End of Hyphens???" *PerezHilton.com*. PerezHilton.com, 28 Sept. 2009. Web. 6 July 2010. Blog.

Fitzgibbons, Moira. "Using Gullah as a Focal Point in an HEL Course." *Studies in Medieval and Renaissance Teaching* 15.2 (2008): 55–69. Print.

Gaillet, Lynée Lewis. "A Socially Constructed View of Reading and Writing: Historical Alternatives to 'Bridging the Gap.'" Ostergaard, Ludwig, and Nugent 163–78.

Graff, Gerald, and Michael Warner. "Introduction: The Origins of Literary Studies in America." Graff and Warner, *Origins* 1–14.

———, eds. *The Origins of Literary Studies in America: A Documentary Anthology*. New York: Routledge, 1989. Print.

*The Great Vowel Shift*. English Dept., Furman U. Melinda J. Menzer, 19 Sept. 2000. Web. 6 July 2010.

*History and Structure of the English Language: English 101*. Harvard U. Daniel Donoghue, n.d. Web. 2010.

*History of the English Language*. English Dept., Towson U. Edwin Duncan, 9 Mar. 2010. Web. 6 July 2010.

Huber, Bettina J. "Undergraduate English Programs: Findings from an MLA Survey of the 1991–92 Academic Year." *ADE Bulletin* 115 (1996): 34–73. Print.

Huber, Bettina J., and David Laurence. "Report on the 1984–85 Survey of the English Sample: General Education Requirements in English and the English Major." *ADE Bulletin* 93 (1989): 20–43. Print.

*Journal Prospectus: Postmedieval: A Journal of Medieval Cultural Studies*. Palgrave Macmillan, n.d. Web. 4 July 2010.

Lerer, Seth. *Inventing English: A Portable History of the Language*. New York: Columbia UP, 2007. Print.

March, Francis A. "Recollections of Language Teaching." 1893. Graff and Warner, *Origins* 25–27.

McDonald, Marcia A. "The Purpose of the University and the Definition of English Studies: A Necessary Dialogue." Ostergaard, Ludwig, and Nugent 143–62.

MLA Teagle Foundation Working Group. "Report to the Teagle Foundation on the Undergraduate Major in Language and Literature." *Profession* (2009): 285–312. Print.

Momma, Haruko, and Michael Matto, eds. *A Companion to the History of the English Language*. Malden: Wiley, 2008. Print.

———. "History, English, Language: Studying HEL Today." Momma and Matto, *Companion* 3–10.

Ostergaard, Lori, Jeff Ludwig, and Jim Nugent, eds. *Transforming English Studies: New Voices in an Emerging Genre*. West Lafayette: Parlor, 2009. Print.

Scholes, Robert. *The Rise and Fall of English: Reconstructing English as a Discipline*. New Haven: Yale UP, 1998. Print.

Schramm, Margaret, J. Lawrence Mitchell, Delores Stephens, and David Laurence. "The Undergraduate English Major: Report of the 2001–02 ADE Ad Hoc Committee on the English Major." *ADE Bulletin* 134-35 (2003): 68–91. Print.

Taylor, Karla. "Language in Use." *Chaucer: Contemporary Approaches.* Ed. Susanna Fein and David Raybin. University Park: Pennsylvania State UP, 2009. 99–115. Print.

"Truthiness." *The Word. Colbert Report.* Comedy Partners, 17 Oct. 2005. Web. 6 July 2010.

Tyler, Jo. "Transforming a Syllabus from HEL." *Pedagogy* 5.3 (2005): 464–71. Print.

Warner, Michael. "Professionalization and the Rewards of Literature, 1875–1900." *Criticism* 27.1 (1985): 1–28. Print.

Warren, Michelle R. "Introduction: Relating Philology, Practicing Humanism." *PMLA* 125.2 (2010): 283–88. Print.

# Valuing Digital Scholarship: Exploring the Changing Realities of Intellectual Work

JAMES P. PURDY AND JOYCE R. WALKER

Because published research is a significant component of tenure-and-promotion cases, even at institutions with an explicit teaching focus, faculty members often plan their pretenure scholarly activities on the basis of their understanding of how different types of scholarly work will be valued. At the same time, new technologies have influenced tenure-and-promotion considerations, expanding not only available venues of publication but also definitions of scholarly activity and production. Because these new technologies include both new knowledge products and new approaches to knowledge construction, efforts to categorize the scholarly value of digital work have been difficult and complicated. While both faculty members using digital tools and committees charged with evaluating tenure-and-promotion cases have tried to create appropriate categories for digital scholarship, their success remains partial. Both continue to raise important questions and concerns about how to approach digital work.

The late twentieth and early twenty-first centuries have seen a range of discussions regarding the value of digital scholarship in tenure-and-promotion cases—both in the humanities in general (Andersen; Borgman) and in English studies in particular (Bernard-Donals; Carnochan; Lang, Walker, and Dorwick; Levine; Miall; Nahrwald; Janice Walker). Increasingly, these discussions have pointed to the need to account for

*James P. Purdy is assistant professor of English and director of the University Writing Center at Duquesne University. Joyce R. Walker is associate professor of English at Illinois State University.*

and value digital work. The CCCC and the MLA, for instance, both explicitly argue that digital scholarship is legitimate and should be evaluated accordingly. The CCCC advises that tenure-and-promotion committees and candidates should "account [for] technology-related work" in research, teaching, and service (*CCCC Promotion*), and in its "Report of the MLA Task Force on Evaluating Scholarship for Tenure and Promotion," the MLA asserts, "Departments and institutions should recognize the legitimacy of scholarship produced in new media, whether by individuals or in collaboration, and create procedures for evaluating these forms of scholarship" (11).

These published recommendations, as well as anecdotal accounts of attempts to follow them, have been valuable to scholars interested in exploring the potentials of digital scholarship. However, they also highlight the limitations that remain embedded in current approaches to digital scholarship. Though we are beginning to recognize the importance of digital work, discussions have tended to focus primarily on establishing digital work as equivalent to print publications to make it count instead of considering how digital scholarship might transform knowledge-making practices.

Though well-intentioned, the statements of governing institutions such as the CCCC and the MLA, which guide the decision making of tenure-and-promotion committees nationwide, can inhibit the drive toward alternative forms of scholarship, because they, perhaps unintentionally, place digital and print scholarship into narrowly constructed, oppositional genres that often privilege print and reinscribe the creative-scholarly split that has long been a problem for English studies. Cheryl E. Ball and Ryan M. Moeller point to how "many tenure guidelines . . . label research as either creative or scholarly," counting only the scholarly. In this binary, because digital texts are more visibly and consciously designed, they usually fall into the creative category; print texts fall into the scholarly category, which situates digital work outside the purview of knowledge making in the discipline. Given the inclusive intention behind the MLA and CCCC statements, this division is not what English studies wants.

This narrow binary is perhaps the most significant (and problematic) aspect of current attitudes regarding the value of digital scholarship. W. B. Carnochan, for example, reinforces a print-based affiliation in his claim that

> you can evaluate an electronic publication in the same way you evaluate anything else, except that (being old school) you may want to read it in printed form. Doctoral institutions have little experience evaluating electronic publications not because they pose a unique challenge but because they are not, or not yet, accepted currency. (198)

Carnochan is accurate that electronic work is still not widely accepted, though this situation is slowly changing, but he is less accurate that evaluating such work does not "pose a unique challenge." Not all digital publications can easily be printed out—nor should they be.

This binary relation creates a number of difficulties, both for scholars who wish to compose in and for digital spaces and for tenure-and-promotion committees who need and want to evaluate this work:

Because a binary relation always privileges one term, this positioning inherently situates either print or digital as superior. While current sentiment usually prefers print, the sentiment might eventually shift in favor of digital, which is also problematic.

Because the current binary privileges print, the perception is that good scholars (who are understandably concerned about tenure and promotion as well as the intrinsic value of their scholarship) will choose print.

To prove its merit, then, digital scholarship must establish itself as equivalent to print, using criteria developed in response to the affordances and predispositions of print genres rather than through a process that explores the potential affordances and predispositions of both digital and print texts and publication spaces.

Finally, situating print and digital publications in a binary relation focuses on the contrast of their respective materialities (i.e., one is printed out, while the other is looked at on a computer screen) instead of allowing scholars and tenure-and-promotion committees to examine and evaluate other differences and similarities that may affect the dissemination, use, and value of these texts.

The field should consider both digital and print publications in relation to larger, more systemic issues regarding the nature and value of various kinds of scholarly work: design and delivery, recentness and relevance, and authorship and accessibility.

These three areas—because they extend beyond simple materiality—provide a framework for analyzing scholarship across media and therefore define the intellectual purview of English studies as meaning making in all textual forms, not just print. A more systemic look at the affordances of digital publications can help us not only discuss ways we might reevaluate print publications but also define a more comprehensive list of the scholarly activities that we value and wish to promote.

## Design and Delivery

In this section, we consider the ways that digital scholarship affords and promotes different kinds of intellectual activities and can significantly alter perspectives regarding the design and delivery of textual information.

*Awareness and Control of Design and Delivery Choices*

Popular and academic discussions (see, resp., Jaschik; Levine) often argue that the most important selling point for a turn toward digital environments is their alteration of the form of textual delivery. While productive, such discussions tend to focus on improving the ease and minimizing the expense of bringing information to readers, thereby limiting the value of digital publications to practical aspects of delivery and framing publishing digital scholarship as a material delivery choice, not a knowledge-making practice. Other advantages, such as the promotion of nonlinear thinking, are overlooked. A more nuanced exploration of design and delivery is possible.

Opportunities for awareness and control are often unavailable in the naturalized systems of print publication, where attention to the rhetorical canon of delivery has diminished (see Crowley). For Kathleen Welch, this move is to the detriment of writing and society itself, because it "reproduces the form/content binary that drives the movement to relegate writing to skills and drills and perpetuates the status quo of racism and sexism . . . and the removal of student-written language from the larger public arena" (145). We would add that this neglect of delivery also precludes the possibility of new forms of scholarly knowledge making that might challenge this racism, sexism, and denigration of student writing.

Digital scholarship, because it requires authors to create texts that are publishable and readable online, renews the need for a consideration of delivery. As Dànielle DeVoss and James E. Porter point out, attention to how digital delivery differs from print delivery is crucial in recognizing new possibilities for textual production and distribution afforded by digital technologies—and in understanding and responding to the application of intellectual property and copyright law to online spaces. These technologies ask for "an expanded notion of delivery . . . that embraces the politics and economics of publishing" (194). Applying this expanded notion of delivery to digital scholarly journals like *Computers and Composition Online*, *Kairos*, and *Vectors* can help us better understand what it means to deliver and archive scholarship in a single venue. Practicing this expanded notion of delivery may better prepare us to recognize not only the unique forms of production and distribution afforded by digital texts but also the forms of production and distribution embedded in print texts.

We do not argue that digital publication spaces are the only locations where examination of the ramifications of design and delivery choices can occur; such considerations (e.g., about page layout and image inclusion) are also part of the decision making in which scholars engage as they publish in print venues. For example, Steve Westbrook explains how he was unable to include a desired visual image, a student's parody of a Maybelline advertisement, because the copyright holders would not grant him permission (458). Anne Wysocki's "Impossibly Distinct," an argument about the centrality of visual images in textual arguments, had to be reprinted because of mistakes with image reproduction in the initial printing (Hawisher and Selfe). Design and delivery clearly matter in print, particularly when texts explicitly engage topics related to visual design.

Despite authorial consideration of design and delivery in print, the visibility of their choices in digital environments encourages us to alter our approach to these choices in both digital and print locations. Scholars can make more informed decisions about designing print publications by attending to the design of digital ones (e.g., see LaSpina 109). Explorations of digital publications, then, can highlight an author's ability (and responsibility) to control the design and delivery options available for disseminating scholarly information. As Stephen Bernhardt, Karen Schriver, Wysocki ("Impossibly Distinct" and "Multiple Media"), and others have reminded us, the visual design of a text shapes readers' interactions with it and therefore participates in the communication of its ideas. When we do not control textual design, we lose an opportunity to influence readers' engagement with our scholarship. Conversely, when we attempt to better understand and control publication choices, we can see more clearly that they are based on a range of influences and possibilities for arranging, organizing, and structuring information as well as for facilitating a reader's comprehension and use of a text.

Design is part of all scholarly production and should be considered by those who make tenure-and-promotion decisions. The design of our online article "Digital Breadcrumbs" mimics the design of *Google* and is part of our argument that scholars often use digital resources, including popular search engines like *Google*, in nonprescribed ways for academic research-writing tasks. In presenting this article as part of our tenure-and-promotion materials, we face decisions about how best to showcase the scholarly content of the article and to highlight the ways the visual and structural design are crucial to our knowledge making. That focus on design is often necessary in the composition of certain types of digital publication highlights an opportunity: tenure-and-promotion committees might include design and delivery choices as part of the range of scholarly activities that can be considered. Instead of making a binary comparison of print and digital compositions or relying on a hierarchical catalog of publication venues based on print sources, committees might examine how a scholar uses a range of venues, tailoring them to particular kinds of work. Different publications require different scholarly activities to achieve certain rhetorical effects or to reach certain audiences.

*Use of Multiple Modes*

The use of multiple modes for the delivery of scholarly information is perhaps the most visible way in which digital publication venues can alter our understanding of how we present information. Digital venues allow authors to integrate word, sound, image, and video in new ways (Hull and Nelson; Johnson-Eilola; Selfe; Wysocki, "Multiple Media"). They thereby open the door for conversations about the relation between multiple modes of communication and the scholarly value and legitimacy of these modes. Because print publications often do not (and sometimes cannot) offer alternative modal choices, we have learned to see the paragraph-based print text as containing the highest order of logical coherence and, ultimately, knowledge making. However, when we consider alternative modes, we must also reconsider the methods through which they produce knowledge.

We can no longer evaluate both print and digital publications only according to criteria developed for print-based communications. For example, the MIT Libraries podcast series on scholarly publishing and copyright offers both podcasts and video articles on issues related to scholarly publication. These webtexts are specifically designed for faculty members and students at the Massachusetts Institute of Technology but are available to any interested reader (*Podcasts*). By using sound and video, the authors have altered not only the audience for their texts but also the ways that an audience might be reached and make use of the information. The shift to audio and video may seem relatively simple, but these alternative modes affect when, how, and in what ways users will receive and interact with the information on the site. In considering the value of such texts, one cannot stop at mode of production or genre. A podcast in this series should be evaluated in a framework of the rhetorical situation: How broad or specific is its content? Were articles solicited or submitted? How were they reviewed? How have they contributed to disciplinary knowledge? When assessed in such a rich framework, a text can escape the print-digital binary and be valued more accurately for the work it does to make or share knowledge and for the appropriateness of the author's choices for the needs of content and audience.

*Rhetorically Rich Composition Practices*

Digital publication processes can raise awareness of the relation between textual form and content. New media technologies allow us to split form and content in composing (Ball and Moeller; Perkel; Stroupe). In turn, digital work asks us to think of textual design as a communicative practice—a notion new to many writers who have been conditioned to ignore or dismiss design. Web 2.0 digital spaces, like social networking sites, wikis, and blogs, that allow for dynamic and collaborative content construction) facilitates the coconstruction of meaning and social space. *Second Life*, for example, is a collaboratively authored digital world used for everything from games to language learning to academic conferences. Its multiple users design the space of interaction, creating visual landscapes and personal avatars, as in Katherine Ellison's *Island 18*, where students re-create streets and buildings in and clothe avatars in attire appropriate for eighteenth-century London, and Bryan Carter's *Virtual Harlem*, where students work to rebuild virtually 1920s Harlem. Such digital spaces expand what it means to compose.

Digital compositions are, in fact, providing us with exigency: to compose in many types of digital environments (e.g., webtexts, blogs, wikis, Web sites, databases), authors must develop a more complex rhetorical understanding of the nature of each composition. Interestingly, at the same time as some scholars have begun to examine the nature of multimodal composition using digital tools, other scholars in cultural-historic activity theory and actor-network theory have been working to develop theoretical frameworks for understanding and mapping rhetorical activity in complex ways (Latour; Prior and Bazerman; Prior et al.; Russell). That scholars and teachers are increasingly engaging in the study and production of messy texts provides an important opportunity for us to move beyond narrow, print-based nonrecursive conceptions of publication for tenure and promotion. Explorations of more complex rhetorical mapping could significantly enrich our evaluation of scholarly work in English studies.

We would like to see the evaluation of scholarly work in English studies expanded to include not only the design and delivery for a particular textual production but also the entire range of choices made by authors for the development, production, dissemination, and reception of their ideas in various digital and nondigital venues. Such an evaluation would require a more flexible approach by tenure-and-promotion committees to the kinds of activities considered and a more comprehensive approach by faculty members to the compilation of tenure-and-promotion documents. Instead of limiting ourselves to discussions of the rigorousness of the peer-review process of a particular journal (whether digital or print), we might begin to ask about the relations among ideas and publication venues, design and delivery of content, and reader interactions and the dissemination of scholarly ideas.

## Communication of Complex Ideas

While print scholarship has frequently been considered the venue in which complex ideas are best disseminated, privileging this method for producing knowledge fails to take into account the fact that digital scholarship can also allow for the communication of complex ideas through alternative modes interconnectivity, nonlinear relations, and various kinds of author-reader interactions. As Mike Rose points out, complex processes and thoughts can be difficult to communicate in print texts because they lend themselves to presenting chronological, step-based relations between static elements ("Sophisticated Ineffective Books" and "Speculations"). Web 2.0 environments provide the opportunity for nonprint publication (video, audio, image) and more interactive exploration and development of complex ideas. In some cases, digital scholarship may provide a better location for a more speculative, associational kind of knowledge making (Joyce Walker), as in Wysocki's "A Bookling Monument," which suggests, through an interactive textual body interface, that how we see texts shapes how we see (our) bodies—and vice versa.

To take full advantage of these opportunities, we must move away from a perspective on scholarly activity that regards this kind of knowledge making as less than rather than different from a scholarly article published in a print journal. A wiki or blog that allows faculty members to compile and share resources related to their specialty has clear value as a teaching tool and community resource, but its scholarly value can be harder to assess. Gwen Tarbox's blog on children's literature, *Book Candy*, illustrates that combining resources for colleagues and students with knowledge production is indeed possible. Evaluating such a text, though, requires an exploration of not only the site but also the associated conversation in which an author endeavors to participate and its conventions and goals.

## RECENTNESS AND RELEVANCE

In this section, we discuss the recentness and relevance of various kinds of digital scholarship.

### Speed

That digital scholarship can be published quickly allows scholars to disseminate promptly the results of their research and readers to gain ready access to information for use in their classrooms or research. Conversely, print scholarship, which affords a relatively slow pace of knowledge accretion because the process of publication is more extended, allows more time for authors and editors to ensure accuracy. We draw this contrast not to establish a fast-slow binary but to emphasize that, while the speed of digital publication in scholarly journals can be important (especially for scholars publishing in fields where the state of knowledge changes rapidly), there are other, less formal scholarly venues where speed of interaction is generative. The ability to converse quickly, whether in person or across geographic distance, can stimulate and sustain knowledge making. Using Kenneth Burke's parlor conversation as our metaphor (110–11), we can envision scholarly work (e.g., participation in digital conferences, scholarly electronic discussion lists, chat spaces) that contributes to a lively, productive, ongoing conversation—where scholars at various stages in their careers and research both generate new knowledge and benefit from the insights of others. *Wikipedia* can serve this function: discussion from a range of scholars leads to new knowledge (see Bruns; Poe). Such work has long been a part of scholarly activity in the form of face-to-face conferences, but it is important to note differences created by digital spaces, such as the creation of archives of conversations that are used over time, the data mining of site archives for the production of resource materials or research, or even the production of audiovisual archives of conference proceedings that are distributed online.

## Extended and Dynamic Knowledge Production

Not only can digital scholarship be published more quickly, it can also be elaborated more fully and thus do valuable rhetorical work. With essentially no limit on length, digital texts can include more material, such as appendices, questionnaires, data sets, and interview transcripts, which allows for more critical review and replication of research studies. *Kairos* Best Webtext Award winners, for example, are nearly all much longer than a standard print journal article (Purdy and Walker, "Scholarship"). Indeed, the authors of one such award-winning webtext said they chose digital scholarship precisely because of this possibility for expanded development. Thomas Rickert and Michael Salvo assert their webtext allows for "more detailed examinations of key themes and concepts," explaining:

> The web works on a proliferation model where it costs nothing to produce more, access more, and find additional resources. . . . In creating this [webtext], then, we have done our best to make available all the resources that are stripped away during the process of creating an authoritative print-based text.

These "resources" include a glossary of definitions, extended endnotes, a list of fifty-two links to follow for additional information, five full-color images, six audio compositions, two podcasts, and a *PowerPoint* slide show.

These extended digital texts can be updated and revised over time. Mistakes can be corrected, author affiliations (which can be important for tenure and promotion) updated, and citations added. Such work, then, remains current and alive—reflecting new discoveries and perspectives and reinforcing the notions that scholarship evolves, that texts are dynamic, and that knowledge making is an ongoing process. While new editions of print books and articles can take years to be published, digital texts can be updated in days or weeks. Print texts, perhaps partly because of the slower speed of publication, tend to value knowledge produced as more permanent and less subject to (speedy) alteration. This more permanent view of knowledge creation has advantages in situations where either frequent revisions of knowledge do not need to occur or consistency over time is valued. To evaluate scholarly activity that extends across digital, face-to-face, and print venues, we need to create frameworks that allow us to consider the ongoing, recursive nature of knowledge production.

## Authorship and Accessibility

This section examines aspects of the authorship and accessibility of digital scholarship to help us think about how scholarly value, in terms of both innovation and knowledge making, may contribute to social interactions.

### Collaboration

The frequently collaborative nature of digital scholarship allows for renewed attention to the value of collaborative writing and the problems of automatically privileging single-authored publications in tenure-and-promotion decisions. The MLA task force calls for valuing "scholarship produced in new media, whether by individuals *or in collaboration*" ("Report" 11; our emphasis). Anne-Marie Pedersen and Carolyn Skinner reaffirm the vital role of collaboration in producing digital scholarship, contending, "[T]he composition of audio or video projects relies on collaborators' combined knowledge of the project's topic, its dominant modalities, the technology used for recording and editing, the medium in which the project is read or circulated, and the conventions or expectations of audiences" (39). Scholars must be proficient in multiple modalities and technologies to produce publishable digital work. For this breadth of knowledge and for greater control over design and delivery, collaboration is valuable and at times necessary. Given the rapid pace of change in digital technologies, it is difficult for any one scholar to be sufficiently conversant in all the "modalities," "technolog[ies]," "medi[a]," and "conventions" Pedersen and Skinner mention. Though authorial choices in these areas have traditionally been more limited in print, recognizing how collaboration allows for more informed decisions and production competencies can make us appreciate more its value in print as well as digital forms.

The collaboration encouraged by digital scholarship extends beyond coauthors producing texts: digital scholarship fosters more collaboration among readers, writers, and textual sources. Digital texts promote a culture of sharing as they can be circulated easily among many people—for example, through social bookmarking sites, e-mail, and discussion boards. As Ellen Cushman, Dànielle DeVoss, Jeffrey T. Grabill, Bill Hart-Davidson, and Jim Porter argue, such ease of sharing changes how we interact with and use others' texts:

> [A]udiences and writers are related to each other more interactively in time and space. Writers can easily integrate the work of others into new meanings—text, image, sound, and video—with a power and speed impossible before computer technologies[, which] may be one of the most significant impacts of computer technologies on the contexts and practices of writing.

Digital scholarship fosters not only interactivity among texts and people but also cooperation over agonism in academic endeavors—a shift consistent with theories of writing, including postprocess and feminist perspectives, that value nonadversarial approaches to knowledge production (see Breuch; Hutcheon; Mortensen and Kirsch; Moxley; Olson). The borrowing and communal engagement facilitated by digital technologies can lead to new textual forms and knowledge-making practices that enact these theoretical perspectives, so they too should be considered in the evaluation of scholarly work.

### Reader-User Interactivity

New and dynamic trajectories of composition can arise from the user interactivity that digital publications promote. Digital composition spaces encourage alternative ways for authors and readers to interact (Joyce Walker), as in electronic literature like Emily Short's "Galatea" and scholarly webtexts like Adrian Miles's "Violence of Text," where readers determine how the text unfolds. The digital nature of such texts makes them not only more usable but also reusable. It allows readers to be authors and promotes remix and assemblage, as demonstrated by Eric Faden's video "A Fair(y) Use Tale," which argues for fair use by remixing short Disney movie clips (Faden et al.). Johndan Johnson-Eilola and Stuart Selber argue that these beneficial writing practices help students "learn ways to use existing information to solve real, concrete issues" and "move from a focus on representation (what things mean) to action (how things function, and to what effect)" (378, 387). When such writing practices arise from reader-user engagement, there is greater potential for knowledge to be spread and *density of —*

used—which, after all, is the purported goal of scholarly research. Tenure-and-promotion committees judge work for its influence on the field.

The influence of print texts is traditionally measured with citation: authors provide in-text and bibliographic references. They can certainly do the same in digital scholarship, but viewing all scholarship through the lens of reader-user interactivity can help us better recognize, understand, and value other possibilities—in any medium. As Doug Eyman points out, there is a spectrum of citation possibilities in digital and print texts, including formal citation (explicit in-text and bibliographic references), informal citation (in-text mention of an author or title but no explicit citation), hyperlinks, and appropriation or quotation of part or all of a text with or without attribution (76–79). All these levels of engagement should be taken into consideration in assessing the influence of scholarship.

## Public Scholarship

Given the increasing calls in English studies to make our scholarship more public, decisions to produce and publish scholarship in ways that better reach the public should be evaluated across media. Contributors to *Profession*'s 2008 Presidential Forum, "The Humanities at Work in the World," trumpet the value of disseminating our ideas to disciplines outside English and to nonacademic audiences (e.g., Barsky 44–45; Brooks 39). Other scholars argue that extending scholarship beyond university walls is a necessary component of academic work (e.g., Cintron; Cushman). The affordances of digital technologies make it easier to export our work more widely. With the right software, readers can access many digital scholarly texts from any networked computer. They do not need to travel to a specific location, show particular credentials, or pay to subscribe to a specific journal to view these texts.

In digital environments, scholarly work can be not only brought to but also shaped by the larger public. For example, the HyperCities Project, the Clergy of the Church of England Database, and the Digital Archive of Literacy Narratives (DALN) all depend on public volunteers to contribute content and labor. The HyperCities Web site calls for people to contribute photos, maps, oral histories, and other texts that document the history of participating cities (*Getting Involved*). The Clergy database relies on volunteers from across Great Britain to compile records of clerical ordinations, appointments, and resignations between 1540 and 1835 from individual dioceses and submit them to a master database at King's College (*What Is*). The DALN asks people from varied social, cultural, and educational groups to submit print, image, video, and audio files that document their literacy development ("DALN Home"). Without public participation, these scholarly projects would not exist—or at least not be as successful. Having such an important role in these projects can make the public more connected to and invested in scholarly research endeavors, which can allow digital scholarship to have a broader influence and make the public more conscious of our work and its benefits.

The stakes of expanding the reach of our scholarship may be greater than the respect afforded English studies, however. If we believe Grabill's claim that "the work of citizenship is knowledge work" and that the skills, habits of mind, and theoretical perspectives we teach and disseminate in our scholarship are crucial to this work (2), then getting our scholarship to larger public audiences enhances and ensures the health of the citizenry of our nation. The writing and information technologies with which citizens engage are sometimes complex and always rhetorical. What scholars in English studies have to share with the public about negotiating and understanding these texts and technologies can improve the public's participation in civic activity.

## Accessibility for Research

Digital scholarship is also accessible to other scholars for research purposes. Researchers increasingly use citation managers, such as *Endnote* and *Zotero*, and social bookmarking sites, such as *del.icio.us* and *Digg*, to store and organize scholarship. With these programs, scholars can tag, annotate, and classify digital scholarship in ways that allow for easy retrieval and later use, creating a personalized record of resources and connecting to other researchers who have consulted them (Purdy). Print scholarship, unless it is digitized, cannot be stored in citation managers or social bookmarking sites. But in digital form, scholarship can be searched for key words, authors, and so on and be linked directly with other texts. Thus it can be readily found and used by others—including our students, who often turn first to online sources, which they find quickly through key word searches in *Google*. Digital work is more likely to be read and cited by younger generations conducting research.

Professional scholars also often consult digital texts for research-based writing, though they may use more sophisticated practices (e.g., employing advanced Boolean searches, searching in vetted archives). In surveying scientists about their article seeking and reading behaviors, Carol Tenopir and Donald W. King found that the "advent of digital technologies on searching and publishing . . . has had a dramatic impact on information seeking and reading patterns in science." Their study reveals that in 2005 over half the texts scientists read and over ninety percent of searches they did were from electronic sources. The digital realm serves as the primary locus of research for researchers at every level. If academics are more likely to turn to digital sources for their research, academic work published in digital spaces should be recognized for tenure and promotion.

The ability to follow hyperlinked citations in a digital article can shape future citation behavior. Not only do the science scholars whom Tenopir and King surveyed increasingly search and read digital scholarship, they increasingly cite it. Tenopir and King contend, "Following citation links in electronic journal articles may have proportionately more influence on citation behavior than reading behavior." That is, linking can increase the likelihood that a text is cited. This finding is key for scholars who want their work to be read and cited—especially given how tenure-and-promotion committees often look at citation frequency in assessing a text's success.

The affordances of digital scholarship merit attention as shaping scholarly activity. Some search engines operate on the basis of frequency of key words in a text, and page rank on search results can depend on this frequency. If scholars write with such retrieval in mind, what constitutes good academic writing changes. Writers are advised to compose titles and abstracts that contain and repeat key words. Because digital publications are often more likely than print to be read and used, academic publishing changes too. Digital availability is akin to circulation for a print journal, so scholars are well advised to publish in digital venues to maximize exposure to their work.

Further potentials for searching and data mining exist once digital scholarship is retrieved. Scholars can search in digital documents easily—for instance, to find in which section a particular quotation appears or to determine the number of times a specific word or phrase is used. Gathering this data can take considerably more time in print texts. Thus, these affordances make more feasible closer attention to both a single scholarly text and a larger corpus of scholarly texts.

Digital scholarship furthers productive research because knowledge development can be traced and reshaped more easily in digital venues. Scholars can provide a record of how they created a text, as in Robert E. Cummings and Matt Barton's *Wiki Writing*, an edited collection that was composed in a wiki. This record provides invaluable access to the development of knowledge and a site for future research. Scholars benefit from having multiple versions of their text saved for easy comparison; other researchers benefit by having a built-in repository of work to study.

The processes of knowledge making we discuss above are not unknown to the academy. They are simply less visible than the embedded values that have come to be associated with the scholarly print text. This decreased visibility is partly because a notion of single, print authorship is perhaps easier and less complicated to assess, and the more collaborative and open practices associated with digital work have, in the past, been part of face-to-face interactions and personal communications not easily archivable or sharable with others. Tenure-and-promotion guidelines are often not explicit about how this rich range of activities might be documented or assessed, and efforts to categorize activities into discrete sections for service, teaching, administration, and research often exacerbate the problem because a faculty member's scholarly activities can reach across these boundaries.

Because the category of research is often limited to narrowly defined "scholarly publications" (Boyer 16), other activities, such as those associated with digital work, which may represent significant production and dissemination of new knowledge, are considered secondary to those embodied in single-authored, print-based, textual production. Perhaps it is time we ask ourselves why. Do we wish to continue to privilege only one of the myriad opportunities now routinely available to us for creating, sharing, and contributing to the knowledge-making practices of our respective scholarly communities? Since we have long claimed to value the kinds of speculative thinking and association making that lead to new conversations and innovations, it seems limiting to place primary value on the linear, argumentative coherence that has become the province of the scholarly print essay in the American academy. As more scholars produce and value digital texts, we need ways to assess them.

The process of rethinking these values will require us to create new frameworks, like the one we begin to advance in this article, in which the nature of scholarly work is broadly defined and where the materiality of a text becomes less important than a consideration of the complex rhetorical situation in which it makes meaning for the members of a discipline. As the likelihood that more and more scholarly publication will move online combines with the knowledge that digital forums allow for and often encourage different kinds of scholarly activities, we are all faced with the challenge of evaluating texts that do not look familiar, do not do the same kind of work we are used to seeing, and do not produce the kind of information or ideas we think of as scholarly. A better, more comprehensive understanding of alternative scholarship may require us to rethink how we read a text.

One way to evaluate scholarly production that avoids a simple print-digital binary opposition is to think less about whether a text is digital or print and more about what it produces, participates in, or does. To develop a more robust, complex evaluation framework, we might ask these questions:

What kinds of knowledge or ideas does the text produce or challenge?
Who uses it? Who interacts with and changes it?
With which recognizable genre (e.g., blog, scholarly Web site, wiki) might it
 correspond?
What skills or expertise did the scholar use to produce it?
How are the media used to produce and disseminate it appropriate to the topic
 and audience?
Who has shared in this production? Can the author(s) or the community respon-
 sible for production claim expertise in the subject matter? Do those who shared
 in the production continue to use and reuse the text to produce knowledge?
Who has evaluated and assessed the ideas this production contains, and can those who
 have vetted the production claim scholarly expertise that we respect and value?

Such an approach to assessment would not look very much like the
tenure-and-promotion activities now in place at most institutions. Our
current means of evaluating scholarly activity have not caught up with our
burgeoning desire to account for nontraditional activities. These means
rarely allow us access beyond the textual artifact, whether digital or print-
based, to an exploration of the activity systems in which people interact
(with various tools, institutions, and individuals) to create texts that disseminate information, make arguments, explore ideas, and even contribute to the ways the discipline sees itself. Investing in such activities will
likely entail difficulties, but it will also enhance and expand our ability
to engage in stimulating, innovative, and valuable kinds of knowledge
production—and to reward faculty members for a more comprehensive
range of scholarly contributions to our institutions and discipline.

## WORKS CITED

Andersen, Deborah Lines, ed. *Digital Scholarship in the Tenure, Promotion, and Review
 Process.* Armonk: Sharpe, 2004. Print.
Ball, Cheryl E., and Ryan M. Moeller. "Converging the ASS[umptions] between U
 and ME; or, How New Media Can Bridge a Scholarly/Creative Split in English
 Studies." *Computers and Composition Online* (2008): n. pag. Web. 24 Mar. 2008.
Barsky, Robert F. "Safe Spaces in an Era of Gated Communities and Disproportion-
 ate Punishments." *Profession* (2008): 40–45. Print.
Bernard-Donals, Michael. "It's Not about the Book." *Profession* (2008): 172–84. Print.
Bernhardt, Stephen A. "Seeing the Text." *College Composition and Communication* 37
 (1986): 66–78. Print.
Borgman, Christine L. *Scholarship in the Digital Age: Information, Infrastructure, and
 the Internet.* Cambridge: MIT P, 2007. Print.
Boyer, Ernest L. *Scholarship Reconsidered: Priorities of the Professoriate.* Princeton: Car-
 negie Foundation for the Advancement of Teaching, 1990. Print.
Breuch, Lee-Ann M. Kastman. "Post-process 'Pedagogy': A Philosophical Exercise."
 *JAC: A Journal of Composition Theory* 22.1 (2002): 119–50. Print.

Brooks, Peter. "The Humanities as an Export Commodity." *Profession* (2008): 33–39. Print.

Bruns, Axel. *Blogs*, Wikipedia, Second Life, *and Beyond: From Production to Produsage*. New York: Lang, 2009. Print.

Burke, Kenneth. *The Philosophy of Literary Form*. Berkeley: U of California P, 1973. Print.

Carnochan, W. B. "On the Tyranny of Good Intentions: Some Notes on the MLA Task Force Report." *Profession* (2008): 194–201. Print.

*CCCC Promotion and Tenure Guidelines for Work with Technology*. NCTE, Nov. 1998. Web. 3 Dec. 2008.

Cintron, Ralph. *Angels' Town: Chero Ways, Gang Life, and Rhetorics of the Everyday*. Boston: Beacon, 1997. Print.

Crowley, Sharon. *The Methodical Memory: Invention in Current-Traditional Rhetoric*. Carbondale: Southern Illinois UP, 1990. Print.

Cummings, Robert E., and Matt Barton, eds. *Wiki Writing: Collaborative Learning in the College Classroom*. Ann Arbor: U of Michigan P, 2008. Print.

Cushman, Ellen. "The Rhetorician as an Agent of Social Change." *College Composition and Communication* 47 (1996): 7–28. Print.

Cushman, Ellen, Dànielle DeVoss, Jeff Grabill, Bill Hart-Davidson, and Jim Porter. "WIDEpaper #2: Why Teach Digital Writing?" *Writing in Digital Environments*. Michigan State U, 24 Aug. 2005. Web. 11 Dec. 2008.

"DALN Home." *Digital Archive of Literacy Narratives*. Ohio State U, n.d. Web. 21 Apr. 2009.

DeVoss, Dànielle, and James E. Porter. "Why Napster Matters to Writing: Filesharing as a New Ethic of Digital Delivery." *Computers and Composition* 23 (2006): 178–210. Print.

Eyman, Doug. "Digital Rhetoric: Ecologies and Economies of Digital Circulation." Diss. Michigan State U, 2007. Print.

Faden, Eric, et al. *A Fair(y) Use Tale*. Center for Internet and Society, Stanford Law School, 1 Mar. 2007. Web. 15 June 2007.

*Getting Involved*. HyperCities, n.d. Web. 11 Sept. 2009.

Grabill, Jeffrey T. *Writing Community Change: Designing Technologies for Citizen Action*. Cresskill: Hampton, 2007. Print.

Hawisher, Gail E., and Cynthia L. Selfe. "Erratum: 'Impossibly Distinct: On Form/Content and Word/Image in Two Pieces of Computer-Based Interactive Multimedia.'" *Computers and Composition* 18.3 (2001): 207. Print.

Hull, Glynda A., and Mark Evan Nelson. "Locating the Semiotic Power of Multimodality." *Written Communication* 22 (2005): 224–61. Print.

Hutcheon, Linda. "Creative Collaboration: Alternatives to the Adversarial Academy." *Profession* (2001): 4–6. Print.

Jaschik, Scott. "Abandoning Print, Not Peer Review." *Inside Higher Ed*. Inside Higher Ed, 28 Feb. 2008. Web. 28 Feb. 2008.

Johnson-Eilola, Johndan. *Datacloud: Toward a New Theory of Online Work*. Cresskill: Hampton, 2005. Print.

Johnson-Eilola, Johndan, and Stuart A. Selber. "Plagiarism, Originality, Assemblage." *Computers and Composition* 24 (2007): 375–403. Print.

Lang, Susan, Janice R. Walker, and Keith Dorwick, eds. *Tenure 2000*. Spec. issue of *Computers and Composition* 17 (2000): 1–115. Print.

LaSpina, James Andrew. *The Visual Turn and the Transformation of the Textbook*. Mahwah: Erlbaum, 1998. Print.

Latour, Bruno. *Reassembling the Social: An Introduction to Actor-Network Theory*. Cambridge: Oxford UP, 2005. Print.

Levine, Caroline. "Rethinking Peer Review and the Fate of the Monograph." *Profession* (2007): 100–06. Print.

Miall, David S. "The Library versus the Internet: Literary Studies under Siege?" *PMLA* 116 (2001): 1405–14. Print.

Miles, Adrian, ed. "Violence of Text: An Online Academic Publishing Exercise." *Kairos: A Journal of Rhetoric, Technology, and Pedagogy* 8.1 (2003): n. pag. Web. 26 June 2009.

Mortensen, Peter, and Gesa E. Kirsch. "On Authority in the Study of Writing." *College Composition and Communication* 44 (1993): 556–72. Print.

Moxley, Joe. "Datalogies, Writing Spaces, and the Age of Peer Production." *Computers and Composition* 25 (2008): 182–202. Print.

Nahrwald, Cindy. "Just Professing: A Call for the Valuation of Electronic Scholarship." *Kairos: A Journal for Teachers of Writing in Webbed Environments* 2.1 (1997): n. pag. Web. 11 Mar. 2008.

Olson, Gary A. "Toward a Post-process Composition: Abandoning the Rhetoric of Assertion." *Post-process Theory: Beyond the Writing Process Paradigm*. Ed. Thomas Kent. Carbondale: Southern Illinois UP, 1999. 7–15. Print.

Pedersen, Anne-Marie, and Carolyn Skinner. "Collaborating on Multimodal Projects." Selfe 39–47.

Perkel, Dan. "Copy and Paste Literacy? Literacy Practices in the Production of a MySpace Profile." *Informal Learning and Digital Media: Constructions, Contexts, Consequences*. Ed. Kirsten Drotner, Hans Siggard Jenson, and Kim Christian Schroeder. Newcastle: Cambridge Scholars, 2008. 203–24. Print.

*Podcasts and Video Tutorials on Scholarly Publishing and Copyright*. MIT Libs., Nov. 2008. Web. 3 Dec. 2008.

Poe, Marshall. "The Hive." *Atlantic Monthly* Sept. 2006: 86–94. Print.

Prior, Paul, and Charles Bazerman, eds. *What Writing Does and How It Does It: An Introduction to Analysis of Texts and Textual Practices*. Mahwah: Erlbaum, 2004. Print.

Prior, Paul, et al. "Resituating and Re-mediating the Canons: A Cultural-Historical Remapping of Rhetorical Activity (A Collaborative Webtext)." *Kairos: A Journal of Rhetoric, Technology, and Pedagogy* 11.3 (2007): n. pag. Web. 12 Feb. 2009.

Purdy, James P. "The Changing Space of Research: Web 2.0 and the Integration of Research and Writing Environments." *Computers and Composition* 27.1 (2010): 48–58. Print.

Purdy, James P., and Joyce R. Walker. "Digital Breadcrumbs: Case Studies of Online Research." *Kairos: A Journal of Rhetoric, Technology, and Pedagogy* 11.2 (2007): n. pag. Web. 28 July 2010.

——. "Scholarship on the Move: A Rhetorical Analysis of Scholarly Activity in Digital Spaces." *The New Work of Composing*. Ed. Debra Journet, Cheryl E. Ball, and Ryan Trauman. Logan: Computers and Composition Digital; Utah State UP, forthcoming.

"Report of the MLA Task Force on Evaluating Scholarship for Tenure and Promotion." *Profession* (2007): 9–71. Print.

Rickert, Thomas, and Michael Salvo. ". . . and They Had Pro Tools." *Computers and Composition Online* (2006): n. pag. Web. 2 June 2009.

Rose, Mike. "Sophisticated, Ineffective Books: The Dismantling of Process in Composition Texts." *College Composition and Communication* 32 (1981): 65–74. Print.

———. "Speculations on Process Knowledge and the Textbook's Static Page." *College Composition and Communication* 34 (1983): 208–13. Print.

Russell, David. "Activity Theory and Its Implications for Writing Instruction." *Reconceiving Writing, Rethinking Writing Instruction.* Ed. Joseph Petraglia. Mahwah: Erlbaum, 1995. 51–78. Print.

Schriver, Karen. *Dynamics in Document Design: Creating Text for Readers.* New York: Wiley, 1997. Print.

Selfe, Cynthia L., ed. *Multimodal Composition: Resources for Teachers.* Cresskill: Hampton, 2007. Print.

Short, Emily. "Galatea." *Electronic Literature Collection: Volume One.* Ed. N. Katherine Hayles, Nick Montfort, Scott Rettberg, and Stephanie Strickland. College Park: Electronic Lit. Organization, 2006. Web. 19 Feb. 2009.

Stroupe, Craig. "Hacking the Cool: The Shape of Writing Culture in the Space of New Media." *Computers and Composition* 24 (2007): 421–42. Print.

Tenopir, Carol, and Donald W. King. "Electronic Journals and Changes in Scholarly Article Seeking and Reading Patterns." *D-Lib* Nov.-Dec. 2008: n. pag. Web. 1 Dec. 2008.

Walker, Janice R. "Fanning the Flames: Tenure and Promotion and Other Role-Playing Games." *Kairos: A Journal for Teachers of Writing in Webbed Environments* 2.1 (1997): n. pag. Web. 11 Mar. 2008.

Walker, Joyce R. "Hyper-activity: Reading and Writing in Digital Spaces." *Kairos: A Journal of Rhetoric, Technology, and Pedagogy* 10.2 (2006): n. pag. Web. 28 July 2010.

Welch, Kathleen. *Electric Rhetoric: Classical Rhetoric, Oralism, and a New Literacy.* Cambridge: MIT P, 1999. Print.

Westbrook, Steve. "Visual Rhetoric in a Culture of Fear: Impediments to Multimedia Production." *College English* 68 (2006): 457–80. Print.

*What Is the Clergy of the Church of England Database Project?* King's Coll. London, 2008. Web. 11 Sept. 2009.

Wysocki, Anne Frances. "A Bookling Monument." *Kairos: A Journal of Rhetoric, Technology, and Pedagogy* 7.3 (2002): n. pag. Web. 3 June 2009.

———. "Impossibly Distinct: On Form/Content and Word/Image in Two Pieces of Computer-Based Interactive Multimedia." *Computers and Composition* 18.3 (2001): 209–34. Print.

———. "The Multiple Media of Texts: How Onscreen and Paper Texts Incorporate Words, Images, and Other Media." *What Writing Does and How It Does It: An Introduction to Analysis of Text and Textual Practice.* Ed. Charles Bazerman and Paul Prior. Mahwah: Erlbaum, 2004. 123–63. Print.

# The English Major as Social Action

## SIDONIE SMITH

In conversations with departmental colleagues and administrators, we talk of so many concerns: decreased state funding for higher education, collapse of endowments, steep budget reductions, canceled searches, increasing imbalance in the academic workforce, the vanishing job market for our doctoral students, the assault on the tenure system and academic freedom, the intensified corporatization of the university, the crisis in publishing, and the continuing devaluation of the humanities in higher education. This list is exhausting to think on. In the face of these daunting crises and transformations, our concern about the undergraduate major can seem a minor preoccupation. After all, don't our majors work pretty well? And yet, as Rahm Emanuel has so quotably opined, "You never want a serious crisis to go to waste." In one or two years, we cannot solve the problems facing higher education or the humanities, but we can revise our undergraduate concentration in that time. Our motivation may well be pragmatic: we need to keep up enrollments and concentrators as two of our key performance indicators, as they are called in the liberal arts college at Michigan. To do so, we have to attract more students, those consumers across the curriculum. But we can also approach revision as process, a collaborative enterprise that remaps what the early-twenty-first-century English concentration could be and do for our undergraduate students, our graduate students, and ourselves. And, since about seventy percent of our undergraduate concentrators and graduate students are women, ours

The author is Martha Guernsey Colby Collegiate Professor of Women's Studies and English at the University of Michigan, Ann Arbor. A version of this article appeared in the ADE Bulletin 149 (2010).

PROFESSION

too is a process of educating women for their multiple roles as readers and interpreters in the first half of the twenty-first century.

Having recently spent two years guiding the revision of our undergraduate concentration, I recognize many of the phrases, intents, cautions, anxieties, and aspirations implicit and explicit in the MLA *Report to the Teagle Foundation*. I applaud "the mandate for the future" that calls for our departments to implement an integrative major and for our concentrators to demonstrate to us knowledge of another language as part of their requirements (10–11). That said, I want to explore what for me are key issues for consideration in our conceptualization of the major today.

## THE INTEGRATIVE MAJOR

The Teagle report calls for crafting an "integrative major" (5) organized as a series of progressively advanced engagements with English language and literatures over the course of study. I would qualify this apparently unassailable goal for the undergraduate language major. Perhaps my move makes a virtue out of necessity: the practical difficulties of scheduling and course assignments and the facts of student behavior make an integrative major more an ideal than a reality, at least at large research universities serving from five hundred to over a thousand majors. Some students move through our majors purposefully, some randomly. Many are double majors struggling to complete two sets of requirements. Some come to us late. Some have significant pressures on their time—work, athletics—and thus choose a curriculum based on time of day. We can set goals, recommend prerequisites, include a modest number of requirements, and clarify our course-numbering system, but we cannot ensure that students move through the major in the way we want them to. Nor can we adequately account for the affective environment they inhabit. At Michigan, the English major was revised sometime in the 1990s, and a capstone seminar was introduced in line with views of the ideal major at the time. In our revision of the major four years ago, we eliminated the senior seminar and introduced an optional junior seminar. Faculty members found that students in the last term of their senior year were often not present to the course even if they were present in the classroom.

Moreover, our attempts at coherence are often thwarted administratively. Courses don't fill. Faculty leaves come in late. Some faculty members are recruited for service duties that take them out of the classroom. The curriculum is set almost a year ahead of time but then collapses about four weeks before the term begins. We rush to staunch the gaps, reassigning teachers and assistants even into the first week of classes.

But beyond these practical matters, I would argue that a curriculum as a coherent series of progressively advanced courses is only one way to imagine a major. I'm a creature of relatively large public universities, after all. I'm not against an agenda of coherence and integration if you can achieve it, but I see value in the synergies of thwarted planning. I think of our heterogeneous courses as scattered opportunities to generate, with students, questions of the literary, the linguistic, and the cultural from a kaleidoscopic array of angles. Even repetitions on lists of required reading can be beneficial, the layerings of interpretations and theoretical frameworks productive for students. We cannot project what will grab students or when. Like our interests, theirs are diverse, idiosyncratic, often belated. For some students the hook will be the texts to be read; for some, the larger questions of history; for some, the sound of words; for some, the genres; for some, the opportunity to think and talk in new ways; for some, a friend sitting next to them; for many, the professor.

Each course is itself a hub of intellectual interests and affective attachments. Students come to us having been regimented and age-stratified all their educational lives, and often level-stratified as well. Let's celebrate the mix of level and commitment, sophistication and naïveté, routine brilliance and hard-earned improvement. It's much of the pleasure (and the disappointment) of the class we enter each term, and much of the challenge, to meld a diverse group of students into a collaborative learning community.

The English major is always changing, even when it is not being revised. Successive generations of scholar-teachers remake long-lived courses and introduce new ones, individually or collectively. In the last decade and a half, our major changed without changing formally, as my colleagues introduced into their courses sexuality studies, hemispheric studies, global studies, archipelagic studies, transatlantic studies, comparative studies, material studies, visual studies, and most recently digital studies. Transformation is ongoing. Periodically, we bemoan the shortcomings of our major and then work to provide new guideposts that figure for students our collective vision in our local contexts and communities. So let's give them a set of goals, a few gateway courses perhaps, some requirements, and a map of the discipline as it now is configured in a particular department. And let's give them good teaching in the classroom. That is our challenge. As Derek Bok noted in *Our Underachieving Colleges*, "New courses and new knowledge regularly find their way into the curriculum, but teaching methods change very slowly" (318).

Our conversations about the major, then, might effectively become sustained conversations about student learning and teaching pedagogies that take seriously the idea of the classroom as a collaborative learning community, whether large lecture or intimate seminar, whether general education or advanced disciplinary course. In a profession where one's intellectual bona fides seem always to be on the line, we are too prone to approach teaching through our compensatory desire to show what we know. We often approach our discussions of the major as a chance to tell students what they need to know, but we could reconceptualize it as social action rather than a set of contents.[1]

Our colleague Marshall Gregory observed in a recent *Profession* piece:

> Information we can always look up, but when a thing gets absorbed, it turns into ideas and skills, and it turns into forms of socialization and cognition that shape students' intuitions and that strengthen their powers of language, imagination, judgment, and reasoning. (120)

To recognize this afterlife of our courses is to shift attention from the major as formal to the major as performative. Its performative dimension involves the enactment of disciplinary (and interdisciplinary) habits of attention, analysis, interpretation, and intensity of affect that our courses, individually and accumulatively, encourage students to observe, internalize, reproduce, hone, and revise. Approaching the major as performative social action is to facilitate the classroom as an intergenerational learning community, where everyone collaborates in setting questions, seeking answers, making claims, and producing work. In such an environment, the classroom becomes a kind of social network.

At Michigan, our recent revision of the major was modest, focused on content. There were careful articulation of the goals of the major, general agreement on the function of the gateway courses to it, introduction of optional subconcentrations to encourage some depth of knowledge with one piece of the field, minimal period requirements, and a new traditions requirement (antiquated in its terminology but dear to all of us, if left flexible in terms of its reference). We reviewed and rationalized all our courses and their numbering. We achieved something, though it was not remarkable in its details. But these issues focus on "teaching to students," a phrase borrowed from Gregory (122). What we didn't take on four years ago and what I would want my department to take on in our next revision is the major not as a thing in itself but as performative of social action.

## REAL WORK, NOT HOMEWORK

Randolph D. Pope chides us that "[w]e have transformed reading into a chore, novels into pretexts for papers, poems into subjects for an exam" (25). An overstatement certainly, but, as a salutary call to think about how we enact an English major, it captures the sense of routine in our exchanges with students around writing. A colleague of mine, Eric Rabkin, offered a pedagogy workshop to the department last winter, focusing on his concept of real work, not homework. Homework he describes as the usual kind of papers we ask students to write: formulaic, deadline-driven, inconsequential after submission. Effort, deadline, grade, discarded archive. Real work engages students in activities and writing projects that contribute to the shared classroom experience; it advances the conversation and enhances the learning environment. It has an afterlife—a phrase that continues to reverberate for me, even though I am not always sure how to reconceptualize what I ask students to do in my courses.

"Student research" has become a mantra that admissions counselors and deans invoke in addressing applicants and their parents. At Michigan, UROP (the undergraduate research opportunity program) has been a great success in foregrounding opportunities for undergraduates to work with scholars who engage them as research assistants, though less often in the humanities. This is one kind of real work outside the classroom environment.

Another aspect of our undergraduate majors that involves real work is study abroad, as the Teagle report suggests. Many of our departments offer other kinds of lived experiences of literatures and languages. In our department, the Prison Creative Arts Project takes undergraduates into nearby prisons to work with inmates on creative projects, theater productions, poetry volumes. A large number of those students are transformed in the process and continue in careers related to prison activism. Our New England Literature Program takes forty students to Maine in the late spring to study literature on location. There are many enlivening and transforming programs designed for students to take their major into the real world and gain experiential depth in their understanding of the power of the word and of the cultures of writing, reading, and interpreting.

But every course, and at all stages of the curriculum, could be directed to the real work of producing knowledge and incorporating meaningful student research. We could imagine the end point of every course as something left behind for the next generation of students: a link on the department Web site, contributions to digitized databases on which later student researchers draw. Let me cite two examples. My colleague Anne Curzan, a scholar of linguistic change and an inspired classroom teacher, asked all her hundred students in a winter 2009 grammar course to enter three of their past papers into a searchable digital database of student essays. That database, combined with historical databases, then became the archive through which students explored and theorized about grammatical formations and shifts. These students were engaged in real work, producing part of the database, developing hypotheses, searching for grammatical patterns across time, rethinking the constantly changing configurations of linguistic usage. At the June 2009 ADE Summer Seminar in Las Vegas, David Damrosch talked of the classroom as an island of wikis.[2] In one course he asks students to do the real work of teasing out transnational interfaces in national literatures for one another and then to leave for future students that archive of intersections. In such ways cohorts of majors are linked in an intellectual network.

## TRANSFORMATION, NOT DELIVERY METHOD

Many of our students sit before us with laptops or netbooks. They multitask. They log on to social networking sites. Soon they will come to campus with electronic gadgets like the new Kindles and Sony Readers that give them easy access to the Google library of 500,000 texts. These exciting, daunting, and, for some, disturbing changes require us to understand our digital environment in a new way. They compel us to engage in a sustained conversation about generational change, about the ways we and our students now study, research, write, and compose. Technological change is not just another way of delivering the English major. The digital revolution is having a profound impact on knowledge organization and production and on subjectivity itself. It is bringing with it another way of being a humanities major.

Brian Rotman argues that the "alphabetic self" of written inscription, conceptualized as a disembodied interiority that is accorded the authority of the singular, is now being displaced by a new notion of the subject, one that is distributed, networked, and plural (4). For Rotman, pervasive digitalization signals an end to the interiority and individuality we now identify, at least in the West, as defining aspects of subjectivity. There are other effects as well. Networking technologies are reorganizing desire as the desire to be in the know and, increasingly, to be locatable. In the ongoing negotiation of person and technology, the subject is becoming a networked concatenation of information. Moreover, the notion of privacy is being recast as publicity in a world of instant dispersal through code. Embodiment itself may become technologized as so many digital circuitries reroute synapses, hormones, and heartbeats. Networked and accessible as so much code, we find ourselves living in a world of increased relationality and intensified surveillance.

The digitized environments in which we live are changing how we think, feel, learn, and work. They are, as N. Katherine Hayles notes, reorganizing our very consciousness through the shift in cognitive styles from processes of deep attention (and deep reading) to processes of hyper-attention (and fragmented reading). The dynamic media environments in which young people now live and make their relationships instantiate the restless mobility of hyperattention in neural circuits of the brain. Hayles enjoins us to address this shift in our pedagogies, precisely because

> critical interpretation is not above or outside the generational shift of cognitive modes but necessarily located within it, increasingly drawn into the matrix by engaging with works that instantiate the cognitive shift in their aesthetic strategies. (197)

We thus need to think about how we stage increasingly sophisticated digital literacies. To suggest the scope of this literacy challenge, I quote from a proposal I coauthored with four other humanities chairs for our submission to Michigan's presidential interdisciplinary faculty initiative this past year:

> We're all struggling with projects in the digital humanities or digital environments. Social networking, viral marketing, data mash-ups, hypertext, collective intelligence, "googling"—the new coinages heard in conversations across the Diag and on blogs across the nation attest to the digital revolution's transformation of social identity, work, education, politics, the economy, and the most foundational interactions of everyday life. We increasingly live in and through a variety of capacious and dynamic digital environments, and this revolution has already made a host of practices, from academic research to journalism to establishing new forms of community, easier, more collaborative and more inclusive. And yet this revolution also poses serious, fundamental problems for the university, society and world affairs. How do we know what information is credible and reliable? In virtual environments with often unknown, unseen participants, how can we assess expertise? Who and what should we trust? At the same time that information has proliferated as never before, there has emerged a crisis in accountability, authority, intelligibility—indeed, in epistemology itself. As educators and as humanities scholars, we need to find solutions to the central problem confronting our students and society: Our students and the general public have not yet developed the critical literacies to negotiate these new environments for information, communication, ethical exchange, and social identities. They and we have not adequately explored the implications of digital environments for the production and dissemination of knowledge. . . . The technology will continue to develop, both inside and outside the academy; and public anxieties—about increasing surveillance, "viral sleaze," the dumbing-down of reading, the culture of confession and display, and the uneven distribution of technologies, skills, and literacies across class, race, gender and national lines—will continue to mount. On campus,

our students will continue to amass the technical skills to access various databases and navigate emergent digital landscapes; but they need to develop interpretive, discriminatory skills for assessing what they find and analyzing the effects of these technological environments on society and on their own lives. They and we will need to expand, dramatically, the notion of literacy to encompass environments joining words, images, moving images, and sound; because even if our students are technically adept, they may be much less so when it comes to negotiating these environments with the requisite sophistication they now demand.

They and we are being remade through our extension in digital environments. Their work and our work in the classroom and out are being remade.

Here too the need for intergenerational collaboration seems inescapable—in puzzling through the meanings of these profound changes, in comprehending and assessing the benefits and threats of digital environments, in mounting real-work projects, in linking work done inside the academy to that outside. This is an arena in which we can genuinely collaborate with students, learning from them. As William B. Warner and Clifford Siskin conclude, "The challenge of English departments . . . is to transform ourselves to meet the historical challenge of remediation" (105). There must be remediation of print through the new technologies that saturate our lives and transform us and our objects of study.

## The Digital Interface of the English Major

We just had an incoming freshman write the department suggesting that the creative arts departments collaborate on producing creative videos showcasing Michigan students for mounting on *YouTube*. Here's his suggestion:

> I was thinking that if you made things like these, you could get a *YouTube* channel very inexpensively, or for free, and put these videos up to get maximum exposure. You could even try to put it on the local public television station. On top of that, you could put the videos up on the school's website to showcase the talented people who go there, enhancing the image of Michigan as a creative, exciting place. If even a couple people hit it big off of them, it would greatly increase the standing of the university, as well as help to recruit more people.

Welcome to the new world of collegiate webvertisement.

But this is our world now, the Web and its social networking formats that join us with our students. Many of our campuses have courseware tools that are fast becoming compulsory or at least necessary to communicate with students and respond to their expectations of us. We need to take seriously our Web sites. As a student-faculty interface, the departmental

Web site commands ongoing attention, because it puts the English major in action on campus and off. We might well start our revision of the major with creative maps of our discipline and its interdisciplines in our individual departments. The mapping of local faculty expertise and interests would provide a visualization of the department as a hub of networked research and teaching interests that link our faculty with others across campus. A language map of the department would capture for us and for students what languages we speak, read, and need for research and how our language competencies relate to our scholarship and teaching and that of colleagues in other language departments. Another kind of map would operate as a kind of *LinkedIn* site. Here we could indicate our connections with scholars around the world, those with whom we have worked or whom we consider colleagues and collaborators, and institutions with which we have been affiliated as fellows or visitors. These multidimensional Web maps visualizing our departmental hub—much as the MLA Language Map did for the many languages spoken in the United States—would present a digital-visual sense of the capaciousness of what we do, its extension, its sets of networked relations. In this way, our Web site would present the English department as a living entity, a collaborative organism, always in flux.

The Web site can also become a place for the internal publication of the real work that students do| digital databases they have participated in creating, live streaming of their creative work, wikis that serve as encyclopedias for successive groups of students. It might also be a place where majors create their own visual or digital map of their trajectory through their studies, indicating where it took them—into the depths of language and text, across boundaries, through theoretical paradigms, to dispersed but linked global locations. Students might even be asked to provide a linked-in component of a senior portfolio that would articulate for us and for them what relationships their English major sparked, damped, or rejuvenated for them.

Finally, the departmental Web site is valuable because our majors have afterlives. They leave us to become the major in action. Current communication technologies keep us better connected with them after they leave campus. At Michigan, we already attempt this networking through a part of our departmental Web site that asks our graduates to send us a photo (if so desired) and a short statement on what they have done with their English major. We have alums from twenty-two to sixty-four on the site. And we are continuing to think about how to adapt the technology of *YouTube* and *FaceBook* to promote our vision of the English major in action.

If we reconceptualize the English major as social action in the sense that is presented here and that Gregory's phrase "teaching to students" captures, then we will need to revise far more than our sets of requirements and our course content. We will need to revise our guidelines and expectations for tenure and promotion to achieve more flexible criteria and more focus on teaching to students; our mentoring programs for tenure-track and non-tenure-track faculty members, the balance between resources dedicated to visiting scholars and to scholarly colloquia and conversations in pedagogy, the teaching component of our graduate programs, our Web site design, and our hiring priorities.

A tall order. But perhaps, in the midst of all the crises that exhaust us with their implications, we can recover for ourselves and for our majors the dynamism of the study of languages and literatures. Texts are not fixed; interpretations undo themselves; identities are relational; influence fluctuates; histories are reimagined; national boundaries persist as porous; spatial location is multiply perspectival; affiliations occasion transversals; juxtapositions illuminate; media are remediated. Our "field-imaginar[ies]," to invoke Donald Pease's phrase, are in process. As are all our majors in action.

## NOTES

1. I am adapting here Carolyn R. Miller's concept of genre as social action from her 1984 essay in the *Quarterly Journal of Speech*. As glossed by G. Thomas Couser, the concept calls us to read genre for what it does rather than what it is.

2. A version of his presentation was subsequently published in the *ADE Bulletin*.

## WORKS CITED

Bok, Derek. *Our Underachieving Colleges: A Candid Look at How Much Students Learn and Why They Should Be Learning More*. Princeton: Princeton UP, 2006. Print.

Couser, G. Thomas. "Genre Matters: Form, Force, and Filiation." *Life Writing* 2.2 (2005): 139–56. Print.

Curzan, Anne. U of Michigan, Ann Arbor. 27 Mar. 2009. Address.

Damrosch, David. "National Literatures in an Age of Globalization." *ADE Bulletin* 149 (2010): 26–37. Print.

Emanuel, Rahm. "You Never Want a Crisis to Go to Waste." 20 Nov. 2008. *My Squawk*. My Squawk, n.d. Web. 23 Oct. 2009.

Gregory, Marshall. "Do We Teach Disciplines or Do We Teach Students? What Difference Does It Make?" *Profession* (2008): 117–29. Print.

Hayles, N. Katherine. "Hyper and Deep Attention: The Generational Divide in Cognitive Modes." *Profession* (2007): 187–99. Print.

Miller, Carolyn R. "Genre as Social Action." *Quarterly Journal of Speech* 70 (1984): 151–67. Print.

Pease, Donald E. "New Americanists: Revisionist Interventions into the Canon." *Boundary 2* 17 (1990): 1–37. Print.

Pope, Randolph D. "The Major in Foreign Languages: A Four-Pronged Meditation." *ADFL Bulletin* 40.1 (2008): 24–26. Print.

Rabkin, Eric. "Real Work Is Better Than Homework." U of Michigan, Ann Arbor. 19 Nov. 2008. Address.

*Report to the Teagle Foundation on the Undergraduate Major in Language and Literature.* Modern Language Association. MLA, Feb. 2009. Web. 23 Oct. 2009.

Rotman, Brian. *Becoming beside Ourselves: The Alphabet, Ghosts, and Distributed Human Being.* Chapel Hill: Duke UP, 2008. Print.

Warner, William B., and Clifford Siskin. "Stopping Cultural Studies." *Profession* (2008): 94–107. Print.

# On Capstones, Service Learning, and Poetry

By senior year, the talented English majors at my college know just what to do when handed a poem: read it with painstaking attention to textual detail and apply technical jargon to its features. They might approach these tasks fearfully or triumphantly, depending on their mastery of the terminology; they might even subordinate these tasks to an interdisciplinary argument; however, they accept the protocol of beginning with line breaks and figurative language. Accordingly, while they enjoy the Billy Collins poem that lampoons this basic classroom practice, "Introduction to Poetry," my undergraduates still expect to read poems closely. "All they want to do," Collins laments, "is tie the poem to a chair with rope / and torture a confession out of it" (58). Some of my students have retorted with complaints about the unproductiveness of trying to interrogate Collins's own poetry. "Too simple," they grumble—the form doesn't complicate the meaning, the metaphors don't fall into interesting patterns. These student-critics vary in their tastes, but generally they most admire moderately difficult poems, pieces that they don't quite understand at first but that they have the skills to break down and analyze.[1]

My teaching reinforces this bias. Although all my poetry courses find room for works and methodologies that challenge close reading as a strategy, I evaluate students chiefly through essays that employ it. I teach and test competence in textual analysis and believe that the ability to reason carefully and persuasively through such evidence is one of the most important outcomes higher education can produce. The advanced undergraduate

*The author is professor of English at Washington and Lee University.*

PROFESSION      © *2010 by The Modern Language Association of America*      207 courses taught by my colleagues acculturate English majors to this kind of literacy, too. However, especially in the senior year, we ought also to make room for some discussion of the costs and benefits of such practices. An ideal place to do so is a capstone course. A particularly provocative and effective way of catalyzing that conversation is through service learning.

In English studies, writing teachers—primarily in the field of composition but also in creative writing—have made the most effective and extensive use of community service assignments in their academic classes.[2] The few published arguments for service learning in literary studies, however, express much more uncertainty about the value of this pedagogy.[3] The implication is that while service learning can play a positive role in entry-level courses for college students, it is less useful if the focus shifts from composition to literature. There is even less published discussion about capstone experiences in the undergraduate English major. Tracts on the future of the liberal arts do mention capstone courses; many other disciplines, especially in the social sciences, have extensive bibliographies on the subject. English professors, nevertheless, refer to these culminating experiences only in terms of their absence, when the subject is the culture wars and the resulting incoherence of contemporary English curricula.[4]

This essay broaches a conversation about the culmination of the English major by describing how service learning can address the goals of capstone courses. Senior English majors can be intensely reflective about how their education might translate into life after graduation. Most will enter professional contexts in which there is little agreement about how splendid it is to ponder the nuances of poems, plays, or narratives. What, they wonder, might be the use of literature beyond the classroom? Service learning can provide a partial answer through its very challenges to the aesthetic prejudices fostered by universities. Issues of audience and reception become far more vivid in community contexts than a classroom lecture could ever render them. Further, service learning has especially high potential to transform the study of poetry, an art that can be portable, accessible, and instrumental in creating and nurturing a sense of community. Community-based learning may not be feasible or desirable in every poetry course, but it is an immensely helpful and undervalued pedagogy for this literary genre.[5]

## CAPSTONE COURSES

As Carol Geary Schneider recounts, a "scorching" 1985 report by the Association of American Colleges and Universities inspired faculty members and administrators in many liberal arts disciplines to "create purposeful structures for the beginning, middle, and end of the major" (242, 249). English professors, it seems, were not among the inspired, although outcomes assessment has certainly pressured us lately to be more deliberate about our objectives and how we achieve them. Barbara D. Wright, for example, observes that capstones and senior projects can serve as a focus for outcomes assessment, particularly when these endeavors involve public presentations and external judges. According to Wright, such courses can "provide an opportunity for students to synthesize what they have learned in their major, and perhaps to fill in gaps," and "to apply what they have learned in some kind of project appropriate to the discipline." She also notes that they have the potential to integrate the entire college experience. Students in capstones might be encouraged to "synthesize knowledge in their major with skills and knowledge developed in their general education coursework" (579).

The English major at my highly selective liberal arts college already involved a notoriously grueling culminating experience when I arrived in 1994: for two days in late April, senior majors wrote comprehensive examinations including identifications of passages, sight readings of poems, and comparative essays that required students to draw on a stunning range of periods and literary genres. These exams did confer coherence on the major. Not only did students bond during the arduous experience, studying for weeks in small groups, but they also prepared for it by assembling at least a rudimentary sense of literary history from among otherwise disconnected courses. This looming ritual also gave advisers some clout when they suggested that majors study a wide variety of fields.

My hire was part of a demographic shift in the department, and within a few years many of its members had become skeptical about the educational value of "the comps." Turf battles over the relative importance of authors, traditions, and genres played a surprisingly small role in our conversations. The main source of dissatisfaction was the low quality of student thinking manifested in the exam essays. We knew from our classes that our majors were bright and inventive. For this rite of passage, however, most of them adhered to formulas, presenting predictable readings of pieces worked up in study groups. Why should they aim higher or take risks when they received no feedback beyond a composite grade (fail, pass, or, rarely, honors)?

In response to the mass discontent, and inspired particularly by the senior year student-faculty research courses offered by the psychology department, my colleague Suzanne Keen, then acting chair, developed an alternative. During 2003–04, she worked on the proposal in consultation with department faculty members, students, the dean, and members of the Courses and Degrees Committee. The result, implemented shortly after and now highly successful, was a two-track capstone requirement. Of our thirty to forty majors per year, a handful of ambitious, independent-minded students opt to write a two-term honors thesis under the direction of a willing faculty mentor. The rest enroll in a section of English 413: Senior Research and Writing.

Our original vision for the course emphasized collaborative research; Keen attempted to name it Senior Lab, in fact, until science professors on the Courses and Degrees Committee objected. Each teacher of 413 would devise a topic based on some aspect of his or her current research. Students would sign up by lottery for the topics that interested them most, so that seniors could follow their interests yet section sizes would remain roughly equal. While all the capstone seminars would begin with some shared readings and discussions, the relative openness of the topic and advanced level of the group would enable students to pursue idiosyncratic directions in individual research projects culminating in long papers. The class size would be limited to no more than six students to maximize the professor's ability to mentor students during the research-and-writing process.

Although we would need to offer six sections of the class each year and our other advanced offerings would thereby be somewhat curtailed, we were excited about the possibilities from the beginning. This course suggested a fresh model for meshing the enterprises of teaching and writing that informed our own professional lives. As professors with a range of interdisciplinary commitments, we hoped that it would encourage interdisciplinary exploration. The course also incorporates a writing pedagogy focused on inquiry, process, and revision, which we hoped would elicit better work from our students than the comprehensive exam did and be a more satisfying culmination of our reading-and-writing-intensive major for the students themselves.

Indeed, according to our subjective impressions, course evaluations, and senior exit surveys, the capstone has achieved all these goals. These seminars are different in some ways from what we had imagined. If any of us expected to gain well-prepared research assistants, we were certainly disappointed. We have learned to build flexible syllabi to accommodate the divergent academic histories of the students in each group. Students particularly treasure this flexibility as well as the small enrollments; the capstone is now one of the major's most popular features.

The readings for the courses may be geared around methodologies, genres, periods, or topics. Generally, however, elements of all those organizational principles inhere in the capstone courses. Since 2006–07, for example, I have annually taught a section of Senior Research and Writing focused on poetry and community. The readings shift in each iteration but always spring from nineteenth-, twentieth-, and twenty-first-century poetry in English. We also discuss history, memoir, poetic manifestos, and literary criticism pertaining to the movements and communities at hand.

As we hoped, student research is often interdisciplinary, testing and expanding the boundaries of our expertise. In my own classes, for instance, English and science double majors have examined the intersections between poetry and medicine. Future teachers have written papers on poetry in education; musicians have explored the influence of jazz on the Beats; and a dancer wrote an essay on movement in poetry performance. The result of freeing students to follow their most ambitious idea is that their investment in these writing projects is exceptionally high. Unlike the generic essays we received on the comprehensive exams, the capstone projects tend to be adventurous and are occasionally transformative for the writer.

The capstone experience not only offers an opportunity for intellectual integration but also increases the sense of community students experience in the English major.[6] Members of each small group discuss aspects of their work together at length, from brainstorming and shared sources to drafting and revision. These classmates become one significant audience for the final projects. Another audience is the group of teachers and students in concurrent capstone sections. At the end of the term, we all gather, and the students present brief descriptions of their projects. Later, an appointed second reader (the teacher of a concurrent section) assesses each essay; we use these evaluations to measure how well our students are succeeding at the objectives of the major. Thus our classes are, at least to some degree, in conversation with one another; students can glimpse both likenesses and differences among the capstone sections and feel themselves to be part of a greater enterprise.

## Service Learning in the Capstone English Course

The boundaries of this enterprise are and should be in flux. The English professors in my network, including those with deep commitments to cultural studies, remain interested in literary power for its own sake. Service learning in a literature classroom, conversely, tests the practical usefulness of art, requiring approaches to literature that can clash radically with academic discourse. Laurie Grobman, for example, reports using service learning to enrich multicultural literature courses but worries that it can paradoxically have a reductive effect. "I remain concerned," she writes, "that service learning may reinforce the insidious notion that texts by writers of color are valuable only as sociological documents, not as works of art, or that ethnic writers of imaginative literature must be authentic spokespersons for their racial group" (130). This problem exists to some extent in every interaction between literary education and community service. The goals of literary study and the goals of service learning do not necessarily match.

Integration of the intellectual content of the course with the realities of service learning is in fact the most challenging part of the capstone I teach on poetry and community. The logistics are manageable, since my college employs a service learning coordinator.[7] The placements, with rare exceptions, have suited my students' capacities, the issues at stake in the course, and the community's needs. Some students work in elementary, middle, or high schools teaching poetry units in regular classes or running poetry clubs; others visit seniors either in a senior center or in an extended care facility; one volunteered to assist the programming activities of a local arts organization; two others helped devise poetry-related programming for a botanical garden. Since this campus has a lively service culture, many of my students had already tutored in local schools or participated in community outreach in other ways. One was involved in hospice work, so she helped create a placement that involved reading poetry to patients. Another had previous experience at a nearby juvenile correction center and returned there to conduct a poetry workshop.

The chief intellectual value of the placements lies in the pressures they apply to our collective assumptions about English as a discipline and literature as an object of study. This value is evident in how students write about their experiences. At the close of each version of the course, my students submit a letter addressed to future Poetry and Community participants. These letters describe the challenges and rewards of each placement and offer advice; I circulate them to the members of every new section, and they help demystify the process and encourage successful tactics. They also reveal the gaps between the services students perform in the community and the learning they do in college classrooms. When the service requirement for my class places students in educational settings, this disjunction can be minimal and easily recuperated into a narrative of mutual transformation; when they must work with adults, it is more difficult to resolve.

Undergraduates who undertake assignments in nearby public schools seem best able to convert their own educational experience into useful outreach behaviors. Their summary letters tend to emphasize the pleasures of teaching poems to groups of young people who do not yet suspect that they might enjoy them. "A few students even commented that they didn't know poetry could be so outlandish and fun," wrote my 2007 student Aaron Fulk. "Though students may seem uninterested at first, they will love you for the energy and creativity that you bring, and will reflect it in their work," offered Sarah Kientz in 2008. The mandated Standards of Learning exams that now dominate curricula in Virginia do not test students on poetry, so the genre plays a minimal role in lesson plans. In this context, my students quickly begin to see themselves as literary missionaries, saviors of the young and poetically underprivileged. Even when their students are initially hostile, my undergraduates find placements with young people incredibly rewarding, not least because this kind of community service affirms the value of their own educational choices.[8]

My students do register some dissonance between their literary values and those of their service learning clients, even in the most congenial placements. Poetry becomes an occasion for appreciation, inspiration, and conversation at least as much as it is for intellectual analysis (although one undergraduate perceived this approach as an underestimation of her students' abilities and cannily waged a battle against the simplistic verse her supervisor had counseled her to teach). They also describe significant challenges: the logistics of working with overextended site supervisors, discipline issues, their own fears and frustrations. "So I walked into the high school with a sense of bravado and (false) self-confidence only to be stripped down to a shallow pool of worthlessness," Fulk writes, only partially joking. Galina Yudovich, placed in a juvenile correction center, tells a story of a typical "bad day" in her letter (2008):

> The week after our "Howl" workshop, I came in with my new poem in hand. Timothy didn't write his. He spent half the time slouched over, not responding . . . it was all I could do to get him to read aloud. He had come around a bit by the end of the session, but it was clear he was losing his motivation and was thoroughly exhausted and depressed from being locked up.

My students also rapidly become aware that good teaching requires hard labor subsumed into an appearance of effortlessness and play; their sudden appreciation of the work of teachers, in turn, gratifies me. The self-affirming results that can occur through undergraduate service learning placements also apply to the professor who employs the pedagogy.

The experience of service learning can be significantly more difficult when students work with adult populations. One of the most successful students was Thomas Grattan, who led a poetry writing and discussion group in a local senior center during the winter of 2007. He expressed surprise at the challenges of teaching, just as the student volunteers in public schools do:

The first few weeks of service learning were extremely precarious. I came to the first class prepared with two lesson plans: one as the primary plan and one as a back-up in case the first did not go well. Ten minutes into the class, I had used both of my plans and still had 50 minutes left. My advice is to be quick on your feet. Some of the seniors were simply against the idea of writing poetry for entertainment and enjoyment, and no amount of discussion would convince them otherwise. So, being able to engage the obstinate group members in any discussion about poetry or poems was my first goal and was accomplished simply by asking questions, any question, that would keep the group talking.

It quickly became clear to Grattan that lessons from his college classrooms would not work in the senior center. He wrote:

I used any form I could think of that would be simple and easily taught within the time constraints, meaning I kept away from the technically difficult forms like villanelle, etc. I feel like this worked out well because the group was fluid; the same people did not show up every week, so a continuous lesson plan would not have been as useful or beneficial.

Here his avoidance of difficult poetry seems conditioned mostly by the kind of group he ran, in particular its fluctuating membership.

Other undergraduates remark on the significant distance they felt from the seniors in terms of age, education, and life experience. After "fraternizing with octogenarians" at an extended care facility, Laural Hobbes wryly reflected (2008):

I didn't really know what to expect. Part of me was hoping that the people who would attend the poetry sessions were actually closet Wallace Stevens fans or perhaps had dormant passions for Robert Frost that would reawaken after my dramatic recitation of "The Road Less Traveled." This was not necessarily the case.

I soon learned that I would have to abandon my plan of discussing the nuances of poetry with the group, which fluctuated in attendance from three to nine people. The first challenge of this placement was connecting with them; the second was making poetry relevant to their life experiences. What did a 21-year-old college student from the 'burbs have in common with retirees born and raised in rural Virginia? I tried to find poems that they had most likely encountered in anthologies back in the day. ("Trees," by Joyce Kilmer, was requested.) I spent a couple of sessions reading poems (for the majority of the hour!) that I thought would interest them. The snores told me otherwise.

Hobbes did eventually find two ways of connecting. First, the participants in her discussion group enjoyed her high-energy recitations of her own favorite poems, particularly a somewhat censored rendition of Allen Ginsberg's work.

Second, poetry about memory and history appealed both to Hobbes and the group and gave them a new way of discussing poetry. Instead of focusing on literary history as one might in an undergraduate classroom, or analyzing how the poem's power is rooted in stylistic choices, Hobbes found common ground in more personal discussions of the memories a poem triggered.

Victoria Childress had similar experiences in reading to hospice patients, but the challenges were significantly more acute. She concluded in her end-of-semester letter that she felt "proud to have been involved with such a wonderful organization," but throughout the term she reported being dismayed at the suffering of the patients, worrying that she might be distressing rather than helping them (2007). She wrote:

> I had volunteered in nursing homes before, so I thought I knew what to expect with elderly people. However, my first day really took me by surprise. The hospice workers did not give me a clear idea of what to expect, and I was shocked to see how exhausted and apathetic the patients were. For the first few weeks, the patients simply stared at me blankly as I read poems. I could not tell if the patients were enjoying the reading, or if they would rather be left alone to sleep.

Childress did come to know her three patients much better: she discovered what times of day worked best and how to converse with them while remaining respectful of their suffering. Like Hobbes, she learned that some poems triggered "a humorous or poignant memory of life in Rockbridge County" and that talking through memories was enjoyable both to the patients and to her. The question of what poems one reads to a dying woman with an eighth-grade education, however, was one Childress struggled with over the term. Poems about natural cycles, written in rhymed and metered verse, pleased her patients, as long as they didn't feature the skeptical edge that sharpens so much of Frost's poetry or the syntactic difficulty of Emily Dickinson's. She quickly burned through the Longfellow and other recitation classics in our course anthology and began to pore over the nineteenth-century collections housed in the university library.

Childress's experience in particular raises significant challenges for a service learning component in an undergraduate capstone course. What readings can best help students manage these contingencies? The gap between the poetry taught in classrooms and the poetry that works in the world can seem immense, even to a specialist in recent literary periods. Recuperating the lessons of community placements back into the intellectual framework of an undergraduate English major is not fully possible. This disjunction is what makes service learning so useful—it transforms the closure of the major into a fresh set of questions and opportunities.

## POETRY AND SERVICE LEARNING

About his own work at an undergraduate business school, Bruce Herzberg writes, "There is a good deal of evidence from our program that service-learning generates a social conscience, if by that we understand a sense of the reality and immediacy of the problems of the poor and homeless along with a belief that people in a position to help out should do so" (58). Herzberg goes on to argue for a kind of service learning that fosters both critical analysis and commitment to social change. Many of the professors who assign community service in their courses do so as a means to sociopolitical ends: to inspire their students to improve the community, become better stewards of the environment, participate in civic life, and develop as leaders.[9] These objectives pertain to the character of students and prioritize the mitigation of poverty and suffering in the world—laudable aims but not primary to literary study.[10]

Poetry-related service learning, always a demanding undertaking with personal and political implications, gives my classes a new perspective on the potential audiences and purposes of this literary genre. My initial reason for assigning service learning was intellectual curiosity: What would I learn as a teacher, writer, and scholar from this pedagogical experiment? The reason I continue assigning it is also intellectual. As a poet and poetry critic, I find questions of audience to be particularly interesting and complicated. In all my classes, we discuss the implicit audiences and purposes of the texts we read and listen to. Historical context, a poem's internal cues, and a range of supplementary documents can be illuminating on this score. Service learning adds a new dimension to these issues by requiring undergraduates not only to make poems talk but also to make them work—to become the conduit for and occasion of surprising connections.[11]

As Chris Green puts it, "A single poetry does not exist in America: there are many poetries for many readerships" (155). Whom poetry is for and what its proper medium may be remain vital questions for everyone who writes, reads, and listens to twenty-first-century literature. In the capstone seminar Poetry and Community, these theoretical questions about the value of poetry become acute. Neither the children nor the adults served by local agencies associate linguistic difficulty with merit, as my undergraduate English majors so often do. I want my students, as an essential part of their education as readers and writers, to understand that the literary values they take for granted after some sixteen years of schooling are not inevitable but socially conditioned. They will become better speakers and writers if they learn how to make the case for poems they love in a wide variety of contexts. Shifting from classroom to nursing home challenges them to reason more clearly and persuasively.[12] At least as important, it forces them to consider what poetry might mean to people who are neither students nor teachers. If they keep asking and trying to answer this question after commencement, literary culture in the United States stands a chance of remaining vibrant.

Arguments abound about the extinction of a poetry-reading public in the United States. The genre (or constellation of genres, as Virginia Jackson usefully proposes [183]) has been declared dead and then resuscitated many times over. Poetry apparently needs to be saved, as does English studies more largely, according to frequent, anxious polemics. The usefulness of service learning to writing instruction—the way it cultivates student awareness of "clashing discourses" (Chaden, Graves, Jolliffe, and Vandenberg 19), for instance—is justification enough for this powerful pedagogy. Service learning may also help mediate disputes about literary study generally, particularly where poetry is concerned. Its participants can untie the poem, stop torturing it, release it from the academic detention camp (or, one might wish, invent less brutal metaphors for close reading). By finding ways to talk about poetry that they do not learn in universities, these students can also rediscover poetry as an instrument of communication and connection.

## NOTES

1. Green is especially useful on the classroom as a community in its own right with an implicit code of behavior and value (153–55, 157–59).

2. The literature on service learning in composition courses has become vast, but many useful essays are collected in the volumes edited by Deans and by Adler-Kassner, Crooks, and Watters (*Writing*). For uses of community service in the creative writing workshop, see Green; Manolis. For a general analysis of the use of service learning in higher education, see the volumes edited by Butin (*Service-Learning*) and by Jacoby et al.

3. Schutz and Gere argue that service learning works best for English departments that "emphasize the social processes of consuming and producing texts," linking the pedagogy with the ethos of cultural studies (130). Cushman suggests that service learning can save English studies, but in lamenting "the inordinate value placed on literary texts in English departments," she alienates me (207). Minter, Gere, and Keller-Cohen reenvision English studies as a field with "literacy at the center" (670). Also see Grobman.

4. The 2001–02 ADE report on the undergraduate English major recommends "strengthening curricular cohesiveness" but barely mentions culminating experiences for seniors (Schramm et al. 86, 84). Seitz is generally useful on the complications of teaching advanced undergraduate courses (58–90). See Graff on the obscure aims of English departments and "taking cover in coverage" (125–43).

5. See Himley, however, on how "direct discussion of the use and exchange value of community service" can be problematic (421); like her, I am more interested in the

disruptions it instigates. See Butin's essay on how service learning can be a "postmodern pedagogy" that fosters openness and ambiguity ("Service-Learning" 98).

6. Peter J. Collier analyzes such effects in sociology departments.

7. I owe thanks to Aubrey Shinofield, who served in that role when I devised the course and influenced its development, as well as to her coworkers and successors Sandra Hayslette, Don Dailey, and Linda Cumming.

8. Service learning can reinforce rather than overturn social hierarchies, as many theorists of this pedagogy argue. See, for example, Adler-Kassner, Crooks, and Watters, "Introduction" 8.

9. For useful definitions of service learning and discussions of its objectives, see Deans 1–3; Speck and Hoppe viii; Eyler and Giles 1–22.

10. While some argue that literary study can produce empathy and empathy produces altruism, Keen persuasively debunks this correlation, turning to neuroscientific research to demonstrate that the evidence for this is "inconclusive at best" (vii).

11. These goals parallel what Eyler and Giles describe as the intersection between cognitive and affective modes of learning in community-based instruction (9–10).

12. This aspect of my argument echoes Chaden, Graves, Jolliffe, and Vandenberg, who argue for service learning in composition classes because this pedagogy forces students to confront "clashing discourses in action" (19).

## WORKS CITED

Adler-Kassner, Linda, Robert Crooks, and Ann Watters. "Introduction to This Volume: Service-Learning and Composition at the Crossroads." Adler-Kassner, Crooks, and Watters, *Writing* 1–18.

———, eds. *Writing the Community: Concepts and Models for Service-Learning in Composition*. Washington: Amer. Assn for Higher Educ., 1997. Print.

Butin, Dan W. "Service-Learning as Postmodern Pedagogy." Butin, *Service-Learning* 89–104.

———, ed. *Service-Learning in Higher Education: Critical Issues and Directions*. New York: Palgrave-Macmillan, 2005. Print.

Chaden, Caryn, Roger Graves, David A. Jolliffe, and Peter Vandenberg. "Confronting Clashing Discourses: Writing the Space between Classroom and Community in Service-Learning Courses." *Reflections* 5.9 (2003): 19–40. Print.

Collier, Peter J. "The Effects of Completing a Capstone Course on Student Identify." *Sociology of Education* 73.4 (2000): 285–99. Print.

Collins, Billy. *The Apple That Astonished Paris*. Fayetteville: U of Arkansas P, 1996. Print.

Cushman, Ellen. "Service-Learning as the New English Studies." *Beyond English, Inc.: Curricular Reform in a Global Economy*. Ed. David B. Downing, Claude Mark Hurlbert, and Paula Mathieu. Portsmouth: Hienemann, 2002. 204–18. Print.

Deans, Thomas, ed. *Writing Partnerships: Service-Learning in Composition*. Urbana: NCTE, 2000. Print.

Eyler, Janet, and Dwight E. Giles, Jr. *Where's the Learning in Service-Learning?* San Francisco: Jossey-Bass, 1999. Print.

Gaff, Jerry G., et al., eds. *Handbook of the Undergraduate Curriculum: A Comprehensive Guide to Purposes, Structures, Practices, and Change*. San Francisco: Jossey-Bass, 1997. Print.

Graff, Gerald. *Beyond the Culture Wars: How Teaching the Conflicts Can Revitalize American Education.* New York: Norton, 1992. Print.

Green, Chris. "Materializing the Sublime Reader: Cultural Studies, Reader Response, and Community Service in the Creative Writing Workshop." *College English* 64.2 (2001): 153–74. Print.

Grobman, Laurie. "Is There a Place for Service-Learning in Literary Studies?" *Profession* (2005): 129–40. Print.

Herzberg, Bruce. "Community Service and Critical Teaching." Adler-Kassner, Crooks, and Watters, *Writing* 57–70.

Himley, Margaret. "Facing (Up to) 'The Stranger' in Community Service-Learning." *College Composition and Communication* 55.3 (2004): 416–38. Print.

Jackson, Virginia. "Who Reads Poetry?" *PMLA* 123.1 (2008): 181–87. Print.

Jacoby, Barbara, et al., eds. *Service-Learning in Higher Education: Concepts and Practices.* San Francisco: Jossey-Bass, 1996. Print.

Keen, Suzanne. *Empathy and the Novel.* New York: Oxford UP, 2007. Print.

Manolis, Argie. "Writing the Community: Service Learning in Creative Writing." *Power and Identity in the Creative Writing Classroom: The Authority Project.* Ed. Anna Leahy. Clevedon: Multilingual Matters, 2005. 141–51. Print.

Minter, Deborah Williams, Anne Ruggles Gere, and Deborah Keller-Cohen. "Learning Literacies." *College English* 57.6 (1995): 669–87. Print.

Schneider, Carol Geary. "The Arts and Science Major." Gaff et al. 235–61.

Schramm, Margaret, et al. "The Undergraduate English Major: Report of the 2001–02 ADE Ad Hoc Committee on the English Major." *ADE Bulletin* 134-35 (2003): 68–91. Print.

Schutz, Aaron, and Anne Ruggles Gere. "Service-Learning and English Studies: Rethinking 'Public' Service." *College English* 60.2 (1998): 129–49. Print.

Sietz, James E. *Motives for Metaphor: Literacy, Curriculum Reform, and the Teaching of English.* Pittsburgh: U of Pittsburgh P, 1999. Print.

Speck, Bruce W., and Sherry L. Hoppe. *Service-Learning: History, Theory, Issues.* Westport: Praeger, 2004. Print.

Wright, Barbara D. "Evaluating Learning in Individual Courses." Gaff et al. 571–90.

# Tips for Service

## KATIE HOGAN AND MICHELLE MASSÉ

A key dilemma for women thinking about academic service is that service is both a social transformation project and an unpaid labor that can disempower women and minorities. Throughout history, selfless service has been a significant source of marginalized peoples' oppression. The *Oxford English Dictionary* defines service as "work done in obedience to and for the benefit of a master" and as "serving (God) by obedience, piety, and good works" (defs. 2 and 3). This complex history is too often ignored in current discussions of service.

With that in mind, we offer the following advice on academic service in the form of questions and tips for faculty members both professorial and in administrative positions. We divide our advice into two categories, self-diagnosis and cure. "Self-diagnosis" poses provocative questions about our everyday work lives in a broad range of institutions. These queries are meant to challenge our commonplace understanding of service. "Cure" offers six tips on service, with a focus on women and minorities.

## SELF-DIAGNOSIS

What is your own work? Have you ever answered the question, How's your work going?, in terms of a committee or a course?

Can you say no to service at your school without feeling pressured or marked? Can your colleagues, particularly junior and minority faculty members, say no?

*Katie Hogan is professor of English and chair of the Women's Studies Program at Carlow University. Michelle Massé is professor of English and director of the Women's and Gender Studies Program at Louisiana State University, Baton Rouge.*

PROFESSION

Service is traditionally not counted at many schools, not only in terms of merit, tenure, and promotion but also in terms of our time. What is the length of your work week? What does your contract say about service? Does it divide work between teaching and research? Can you imagine working to contract or working a forty-hour week? Why or why not?

Have you advertised for or encouraged untenured assistant professors to direct your women's studies program? head your writing center? develop your cultural studies concentration? If so, have you supported those colleagues for promotion or tenure on the basis of outstanding service?

Have you or your department developed a rationale for the distribution of service?

How do you evaluate service in your department? For example, is there any way to distinguish in annual reports—and in annual raises—between the sometimes present member of the cookie committee and the chair of your curriculum revision committee?

Teaching is increasingly an intensive part of graduate student and junior faculty preparation. Is talking about service also a part of your mentoring and training for graduate students and junior faculty members?

Have you suggested that faculty members on your campus address service as part of exploring collective bargaining, faculty senate or school task forces, MLA or AAUP initiatives?

## Cure

Don't idealize service. It can be an exciting way to pursue social transformation on campus and beyond, and it's a gateway for moving beyond narrow (and boring) self-interest; but at the end of the day, service is work for which one should be paid and acknowledged.

Don't denigrate service. Service projects are not inferior to writing books, publishing articles in refereed journals, or speaking on a panel at a national or international conference. Service labor can often lead to deep and complex connections and friendships as well as result in stunning creative and political contributions.

Approach service as a complex category and activity. For all its supposed one-dimensional transparency, what service is and who's doing it are hard to pin down. Some academic workers see performing service as an honorable endeavor that creates goodwill and community; for others, service labor is a CV-building necessity; for others, it's a form of activist rebellion or workplace transformation; for still others, service work is exploitative and rooted in entrenched structural hierarchies. For most of us, service is all these things.

Don't confuse service with scholarship. A popular approach to grappling with the formidable challenges of the current academic workplace has been to evoke Ernest Boyer's model of scholarship as a way to redefine faculty work ("Scholarship" and *Scholarship*). One result of that approach is to call almost any service project that academics engage in "scholarship." While we need broader definitions of what counts as scholarship, not all service projects are scholarship. Redefinitions of service—and of scholarship—can inadvertently belittle the value of writing books, publishing articles, and producing creative work, endeavors that require time, solitude, respect, and—most important—institutional support.

Avoid a knee-jerk yes or no to a service request. Saying yes to every service request is unwise. Being mindful of your time and how you spend it indicates respect for yourself and your work. The Catholic theologian Thomas Merton said that the madness of our times is the tendency of earnest people to take on too many projects. This is particularly true of women and minorities, who are often socialized to put others first, even at the expense of their own physical and mental health. If possible, seek out projects that either dovetail with your own professional, political, or personal interests or intrigue you.

On the other hand, don't automatically say no to service requests. One of the most persistent stereotypes is self-absorbed, privileged professors who, holding service in contempt, believe that the work is beneath them. Not only does such a belief fuel the stereotype, it obscures how service is part of a project of intellectual dialogue, community, human rights, and freedom of thought and expression. Service can be a way to open one's world.

Keep a service log. Recording day-to-day service labor is particularly important for untenured faculty members. A log will quickly undercut the notion of service as morally superior good works carried out by the virtuous. Logs and records make visible the staggering amount of work that most academics are doing.

These tips reflect the need to understand service not as silent and unregulated labor or as an index to one's unselfishness, moral goodness, and dedication but as a nexus of fundamental issues involving education, gender, class, labor, activism, and the politics of the profession. We need to change the way we conceive of and reward service.

## WORKS CITED

Boyer, Ernest L. "The Scholarship of Engagement." *Journal of Public Outreach* 1.1 (1996): 11–20. Print.

———. *Scholarship Reconsidered: Priorities of the Professoriate*. San Francisco: Carnegie Foundation; Jossey-Bass, 1997. Print.

Merton, Thomas. "Service." Quoteland.com, n.d. Web. 28 July 2010.

"Service." *The Oxford English Dictionary*. 2nd ed. 1989. Print.

───

To the Editor:

I was surprised to see that in "Why How We Read Trumps What We Read," the distinguished Gerald Graff subscribes to the tendentious myth that in reader-centered criticism "all readings are equally valid" (72). I consider that view a myth because even in the nontextual criticism of Erin Smith, Janet Radway, or Roger Chartier some readings are better than others if they conform with the sociohistorical conditions influencing readers. Radway suggests that women prefer certain romances to others, because of their family position, occupation, education, and so on. In the textual criticism of John Frow, Steven Mailloux, or Stanley Fish, some readings are better than others if they meet the requirements of the interpretive community, reading regime, or rhetorical practices governing interpretive practices. Fish, whose admission that sometimes he overstated his position Graff considers a rejection of "the strong version" of his theory of interpretive communities (74), argued that within but not between interpretive communities there is no such relativism.

To support his repudiation of reader-response criticism, Graff defends the position that "what we say must be responsible to the text"; however, if that position means that the text somehow compels its interpretations, it is not, as he notes, consistent with his argument, which justifies reading a popular text like *Vanna Speaks* as though it were open to the "deep reading" usually reserved for classical texts. An admirable effort at opening up the canon, such a reading illustrates his belief that how we read "trumps" what we read, but the reading goes against the grain or violates what such a text usually requires. If that position means that a reading "must refer to something that is actually there in the text," the position is either trivial (in the sense that you can say anything provided you discuss the text) or it involves a plain or "naive" empiricism, what Graff terms a reading that "could be independently discovered by other readers" (72). The key term here is "independently," which means that any reader, no matter what his or her background, education, experience, or beliefs, can see that the text warrants the reading. Since the 1970s, reader-oriented critics like Wolfgang Iser and Hans Robert Jauss have argued that no text comes to readers as a blank slate in which they grasp what is plainly there; rather, readers always bring to a text expectations that the text may confirm or explode (see, for example, Jauss's influential essay "Literary History as a Challenge to Literary Theory" [3–45]). In other words, texts have histories or fall into traditions, genres, or categories that influence the reader because they generate expectations. No doubt that is why *Pride and Prejudice and Zombies* is appreciated by those who have not read *Pride and Prejudice* and probably do not wish to read it. I do not mean to suggest that reader-centered approaches are not open to criticism or that they have no faults, but surely they merit more serious treatment than the misleading myth that they treat all readings as equally valid or "ignore what is actually there in the text."

Philip Goldstein
*University of Delaware, Wilmington*

## WORKS CITED

Graff, Gerald. "Why How We Read Trumps What We Read." *Profession* (2009): 66–74. Print.

Jauss, Hans Robert. *Toward an Aesthetic of Reception*. Trans. Timothy Bahti. Minneapolis: U of Minnesota P, 1982. Print.

*Reply:*

Philip Goldstein misrepresents me as "repudiating" reader-response criticism by subscribing to the "tendentious myth" that this criticism holds that "all readings are equally valid." What I actually said was that this relativism discredits "a version of the reader-response theory," not all forms of it.

Here is the pertinent passage from my essay:

> The argument I have been making—that it is not the text we assign that determines the educational value of reading and studying it but the questions we bring to the text or the ways we think and talk about it—

> may look like a version of the reader-response theory that came into prominence several decades ago, that textual meanings are created by readers (or interpretive communities) rather than discovered in the texts as preexisting features. That is, my attempt to shift the focus in discussions of pedagogy from what our students read to how they talk about what they read seems to lead to the relativistic conclusion that readings are not answerable to anything "there" in the texts themselves, that therefore all readings are equally valid. Such relativism is indeed entailed by the theory that readings are produced by readers without being grounded in the text, but it doesn't follow from my argument. On the contrary, if the reading I have offered [of a passage from *Vanna Speaks*] is valid, it must refer to something that is actually there in the text and could be independently discovered by other readers. In other words, to argue, as I do, that no text tells us what to say about it does not mean that we can legitimately say anything at all about it, which is the relativistic implication that strong versions of reader-response theory are unable to avoid.
>
> ("Why" 71–72)

Clearly my target here, contrary to Goldstein, is not all reader-response criticism, but those "strong versions" that argue that readers create textual meanings without being answerable to any independently existing text.

Where there is no mischaracterization and Goldstein and I do legitimately disagree is on my claim that if an interpretation is valid, it "must refer to something that is actually there in the text and could be independently discovered by other readers." As I argued, without this "regulative premise of interpretation" the process of reading would make no sense (72). Goldstein seems to think I somehow contradict myself in doing a "deep reading" of *Vanna Speaks* that "violates what such a text usually requires." But I stand by my view that, if my reading is correct, what it ascribes to White's text could be found there by any competent reader of any community.

Goldstein rejects this appeal to meanings that "could be independently discovered by other readers" and suggests that interpretations need only "meet the requirements of the interpretive community, reading regime, or rhetorical practices governing interpretive practices." But an interpretation could meet all these requirements, being consistent with the norms of its interpretive community, and still be wrong.

Goldstein himself concedes as much when he argues, invoking Iser and Jauss, "that no text comes to readers as a blank slate in which they grasp what is plainly there; rather, readers always bring to a text expectations that the text may confirm or explode." In suggesting that texts can either "confirm or explode" the expectations readers bring to them, Goldstein assumes what he otherwise denies, that textual meanings exist independently of readers.

The point has recently been conceded by Stanley Fish, who goes much further than Goldstein suggests, I think, in repudiating his earlier argument that interpretive communities create textual meanings, which do not exist independently prior to interpretation. In a 2004 response to several commentators, including me ("How"), Fish concedes that in making that argument that interpretive communities create meanings, he vacillated between

> saying that the properties (of meaning, structure, imagery, and so on) we now see in the objects of our professional attention have been established by that attention [and] saying that the objects of our professional attention have no prior shape of their own independent of that debate. To say the first is to pay due respect to the possibility of error and the premise of correction. To say the second is to render notions like error and correction incoherent, and to deprive the very act of reading of its point.

Fish concludes by quoting and agreeing with my statement that "[r]eading makes no sense unless we assume that it's a matter of discovering what is there" (284).

In retracting his earlier argument that "objects of our professional attention have no prior shape of their own independent of" interpretation, Fish embraces the idea that Goldstein rejects, that of meanings that "could be independently discovered by other readers."

It turns out that there *is* a text in this class after all!

Gerald Graff
*University of Illinois, Chicago*

## WORKS CITED

Fish, Stanley. "One More Time." Olson and Worsham 265–97.

Graff, Gerald. "How I Learned to Stop Worrying and Love Stanley." Olson and Worsham 27–41.

———. "Why How We Read Trumps What We Read." *Profession* (2009): 66–74. Print.

Olson, Gary A., and Lynn Worsham, eds. *Postmodern Sophistry: Stanley Fish and the Critical Enterprise.* Albany: State U of New York P, 2004. Print.

## 2011 ADE-ADFL JOINT SUMMER SEMINAR MIDWEST

9–12 June
Northwestern University
Evanston, Illinois

---

## 2011 ADE SUMMER SEMINAR WEST

23–26 June
Stanford University
Stanford, California

---

## 2011 ADFL SUMMER SEMINAR WEST

23–26 June
Brigham Young University
Provo, Utah

University of Utah
Salt Lake City, Utah

*For more information, visit www.ade.org or
www.adfl.org or write to dsteward@mla.org*

---

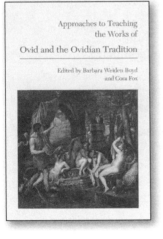